MASTERING THE COLD WAR JETS

In-depth Insights into Flying the Canberra, Harrier, Jaguar, Javelin, Phantom and Tornado

To Sheila and Wendy
Our partners of 65 years

MASTERING THE COLD WAR JETS

In-depth Insights into Flying the Canberra, Harrier, Jaguar, Javelin, Phantom and Tornado

GEORGE ROBERTSON & ALAN MUNRO

GRUB STREET • LONDON

ACKNOWLEDGEMENTS

Our thanks are due to the friends and family who have patiently proofread our drafts, corrected typos and helped to make the book more readable in places.

Sheila Robertson, Wendy Munro, James Munro, Patricia Robertson, Raphael Henry.

Published by Grub Street
4 Rainham Close
London SW11 6SS

A CIP record for this title is available from the British Library

ISBN 9781911714415

Design by Myriam Bell Design, Uk

Printed and bound by Finidr, Czechia

CONTENTS

PROLOGUE

GEORGE

When Alan and I decided to collaborate on this book, the first question was where exactly do we start? So, in the words of the song, let's start from the very beginning. In my later experience as a trainer, I always felt that those who do best in flying training are the ones who have obsessed about flying and aircraft from a very young age. What kids absorb when young conditions them in later life and gives them a head start when they begin to train for real. In my case an interest in aircraft started when I was just two years old. At that tender age as a toddler I was running around the house, slipped on some polished linoleum and broke my hip. As you can imagine, it was not easy to keep a two-year-old immobile with a leg in plaster. My two elder sisters, who were both in their late teens (I was a late baby), arranged a bunch of model aeroplanes hanging from the ceiling above my cot. I discovered that by waving my arms I could make them swing and spin and this kept me amused for hours, much to the relief of the rest of the family. That interest and obsession with aircraft remained with me ever since.

I was born to a working-class family in Dunbar, Scotland in the middle of World War II. My dad was a World War I veteran and an engineer responsible for maintaining a fleet of buses. From what I recall, he earned about £11 a week in 1950 (about £250 in today's money). My mum supplemented the family income as a seamstress and by taking boarders. We were hard up but happy. I was expected to earn as soon as I was able and started work at the age of ten as a delivery boy for a local greengrocer. As a teenager I worked during school holidays as a waiter in a local hotel, and later as a labourer on a building site. At school I was expected to do well. A work ethic was therefore hardwired into me. My two elder sisters were like surrogate mums when I was growing up. They doted on me and both called me "my wee brother" even though I towered over them from the age of 12.

I sometimes wonder if this aircraft interest is somehow genetic. My youngest grandson Raffy went through a phase of aircraft obsession at the age of four and insisted in always wearing his flying suit and my old service hat, giving smart RAF salutes to everyone. He was my co-pilot on a flight in a Piper Cherokee to Le Touquet with his mum Patricia and my wife Sheila. He did all the navigation (albeit with the help of a Garmin GPS!). For him it was a phase, and he soon moved on to other interests. For me the interest in aviation never waned.

I started building model aeroplanes at a young age and spent my pocket money on balsa wood, tissue paper, model kits and the like. I learned the basics quickly about aerodynamics, weight and balance, trim, aerofoil sections, dihedral, flying adjustments etc. If you got it wrong your prized model and big investment of pocket money would crash, so you had to learn fast. As a result, when I did eventually start flying training, I already knew the basics about how aircraft flew and made rapid progress. Others were more fortunate: if they were in the Air Cadets, they could progress through a gliding course and on to a flying scholarship. But that was not an option for me. I did well at school, becoming the school Dux and Head Boy, before going on to university.

I am often asked: "So why did you not join the RAF straight after school or apply to go to Cranwell?" The short answer is that I did not think they would take me. Back then it did not seem likely that an application to join as an officer and pilot from a young working-class Scots boy was likely to succeed, so I took the advice of teachers and applied to Edinburgh University to study chemistry for no other reason than it was my best subject at school.

When I first went to university, I was not yet 18. At the fresher's fair I discovered there was a thing called the University Air Squadron (UAS) where you could learn to fly. I immediately applied and much to my surprise was accepted. There were four people on the interview panel: the commanding officer (CO), the chief flying instructor (CFI) and two members of the Military Education Committee. I still have the report from that first interview which I obtained much later and which makes interesting reading. "A well-turned-out lad who has a keen sense of humour. Very interested in the RAF he has some sound ideas and is quite capable of presenting and defending them when challenged. He has a good academic record, is a good all-round sportsman, was head boy of his school and an organiser of activities in his youth club. A good UAS candidate."

I would also like to mention Sheila, who has been my wife and partner of 65 years, because she has contributed so much to the story of my aviation career with her steadfast support in sometimes challenging circumstances. I could not have achieved so much without her. We knew each other at school but did not hook up until I was in first year at university. We have been together ever since.

Alan and I went through training together but then our paths divided as we went on to fly different types of aircraft, however we both flew the Phantom (albeit in different roles). This book will give you a perspective on what it was like to operate the RAF's front-line jets at the height of the Cold War; what the aircraft were like to fly, their strengths and weaknesses, the tactics we employed, how we trained and how we compared with our allies. After leaving the RAF we both worked for airlines and we will go on to describe that experience, the complete change of culture from what we had been used to as fighter pilots, how we made the adjustment and what lessons we learned.

ALAN

Last year I wrote my first book, *Fast Jets on the Front Line.* It was quite light hearted and intended for all to read. My librarian cousin Angela even bought a second copy for her library. However, despite being easy to read there was some disappointment from those who wanted more technical detail. Then my publisher, John Davies, said he wanted a book that youngsters might relate to about what an RAF career meant. That's when I reached out to George to see if he would be interested in sharing. This is the result, and you have a cartesian mix of reconnaissance, attack and air defence, with a number of fast jets discussed over two very different careers.

My own background could not have been more different from George's. My dad fatally flew a Miles Master into the beach at Barmouth, north-west Wales, doing a Wings for Victory demo down the main street. Wings for Victory was the chance for an overworked qualified flying instructor (QFI) to fly over a town while good ladies with collecting tins were on the street seeking funds for a new Spitfire. In practice, it was an excuse for low-level aerobatics and beat ups of the high street. The law of unintended consequences took over, with fatal results. My mother was three months pregnant when she was widowed, so I have no idea if he even knew I was on the way.

As far as could be determined, this is what went wrong. Because a significant number of student pilots were turning the aircraft upside down on landing, the

Masters were fitted with crash switches so that once the aircraft was inverted with the gear down, the fuel automatically cut off, the generators earthed and the fire extinguishers were activated. That's what happened, as Dad performed a slow roll down Barmouth High Street. His colleagues thought that an undercarriage door had probably cracked open with the sun behind so that neither Dad nor his student, Free French NCO Sergeant Jacques Mallet, ever saw the red warning light. We will never know for sure. His best friend told me all this years later.

My mother looked after me until I was one year old, then left to seek fame and fortune in which she was very successful. My grandad was a friend of Professor Sir Henry Tizard, one of the brains behind British radar. Professor Tizard apparently got my mother the job of secretary to the Radar Commission. She flourished here under Sir Robert Watson-Watt (who I remember well), and my grieving grandparents took over my upbringing. My grandad, a Professor of Entomology, ran the Imperial College Field Station near Ascot, so it was here I was brought up in splendid isolation – and was probably spoilt.

At age seven, my mother sent me off to boarding school, where I remained until I was 18. I hated the entire institution, but like many other boys was fascinated with building and flying model aircraft kits. Then, aged 13, I was taken away from my wonderful grandparents to pass the holidays with a housekeeper in a house which my mother had bought. However, at this point I joined the RAF section of the school's Combined Cadet Force, under the leadership of an ex-National Service pilot who sported a real pilot brevet – my hero. This led to a one-week gliding course at RAF Hornchurch when I was 16, followed the next year by a 30-hour flying scholarship on the Tiger Moth. In those days that was enough for a private pilot's licence (PPL). Otherwise, I was learning to be quite anti-establishment, which probably lasted. I went on to Imperial College London to study aeronautical engineering, where I graduated in 1964 with a 2.2.

CHAPTER 1
BEGINNINGS

GEORGE

We both joined the UAS at our respective universities. In my case it was the Edinburgh UAS which operated from RAF Turnhouse, now Edinburgh Airport. Most of the larger universities had UASs and they were run like any other RAF flying training school at the time, with full-time RAF QFIs. They were seen as a good way of recruiting suitable candidates into regular service or at least of publicising the RAF amongst undergraduates who would later occupy senior positions and who would be well disposed towards the RAF. When I joined in 1959, most of the instructors still had World War II medal ribbons. Our CO was Sqn Ldr Colin Doak, who had flown Hurricanes with the Desert Air Force in World War II, and Flt Lt John Russell who had been shot down in a Sterling bomber and had spent much of the war as a prisoner of war. The CFI when I joined was Jock Urquhart, who had come from a tour on the Meteor F8. We flew the Chipmunk T10, the successor to the Tiger Moth. It was a great little training aircraft powered by a Gypsy Major engine of 140 bhp. It didn't have enough power to maintain height during aerobatics, so if you started your sequence at 4,000 ft, you would soon end up at 3,000 ft. We were given a full elementary flying training syllabus including ground training at the town HQ, normally on a Thursday evening and flying from Wednesdays to Sundays. There were additional flying training weeks in the new year and Easter plus a summer camp normally at an operational RAF base.

There were normally no restrictions on the maximum number of flying hours so you could fill your boots if you wanted, in my case at the expense of my academic studies

Edinburgh UAS with three Chipmunk T10s, flying over the Forth Bridge.

in my first year. I decided to switch courses from majoring in chemistry, which I never really enjoyed, to majoring in psychology, which I found to be much more interesting. In 1963 the RAF introduced a cadetship scheme, and if you were prepared to commit to joining the RAF on graduation, you signed on and got paid as a regular pilot officer. There was a short inauguration for the cadetship scheme which was conducted at RAF South Cerney and that is where I first met Alan. We got on well from the start and knew that we would probably meet again when we started RAF training as a regular officer after graduation. I did 220 flying hours on Chipmunks with the UAS, and this got me off to a very good start when I began flying training as a regular.

Being able to draw a pilot officer's salary in my final year was transformative, and Sheila and I decided to get married. We had to bring forward our wedding plans when we discovered she was pregnant, so in early March 1964 I found myself a married man with a child on the way. This concentrated my mind more than somewhat and it was just the incentive I needed to buckle down to some serious study before finals in June of that year. Flying took a back seat whilst I worked all hours to prepare. I think I finally got the hang of how to do serious study by understanding the syllabus, carefully reading the references and most importantly by making comprehensive revision notes. It all paid off and I graduated with a first-class honours degree in psychology.

It is worth reflecting on the RAF's attitude at the time, which was to actively discourage junior officers from getting married under the age of 25. Up to that point you were expected to devote all your time and energy to your RAF career with no distractions. A number of sanctions were applied: you did not qualify for any marriage allowance; you were not entitled to accommodation and most importantly your wife was not entitled to travel at RAF expense to join you on an overseas posting. As a result, when I got posted overseas to Malta for my first operational tour I had to go solo, leaving my pregnant wife behind. She was able to join me five months later – the day after my 25th birthday – with by then our two young children. In contrast, after the magic 25th birthday, wives were expected to take a full part in the social life of the squadron. Their opportunities for an independent career were limited by the frequent moves imposed by service life, and as you progressed in rank your wife effectively became an unpaid welfare worker in support of the squadron families. In fact, some of the more senior posts were specified as "married accompanied", in other words you needed to be married, and your wife had to be with you during that tour of duty. Divorce was very much frowned upon and could be career limiting. The modern RAF is very different from this, and looking back it is remarkable how well our wives coped under these difficult circumstances.

We have sometimes been asked "how do you recall so much detail from over 50 years ago?" You must remember that pilots keep logbooks of all their flights throughout their flying career. This is therefore a complete history of their flying, with dates, times, aircraft flown and a brief description of what the flight involved. Without our logbooks, reconstructing in detail what we did all those years ago would have been difficult or impossible.

ALAN

In the summer of 1958, I travelled out of London a long way down the District line with a friend, Chris Strachan (who sadly passed last year from Alzheimer's). We had both enrolled on a one-week cadet gliding course and on the Monday morning gathered round the gliders in one of the wartime hangars. Hornchurch then was a grass Battle of Britain airfield, since transformed into a housing estate. The gliders were a mix of T21 and T31 open cockpit two seaters. The COSIM variometer (which shows whether you are climbing or descending) was open to atmosphere through a long tube like a metal drinking straw. Inevitably everyone had a go blowing down them, to be followed by a very angry briefing on why this was a bad idea.

We started on the T21 (side-by-side) for a couple of days, where the launch height from a winch launch was typically 1,000 ft and flight duration four minutes. We then switched to the T31 (900 ft and three minutes) and finally went solo for three circuits. This earned us the B Certificate as it was then, but it was a badge; always very important to a 16-year-old. There was enough flying left over for a flight each, dealer's choice. I opted for aerobatics, which could only be done with the CO, Flt Lt Bill Verling. So, from a 900-ft release, Bill flew two very quick loops followed by a spot landing. I have heard since that Bill influenced many cadets into flying careers. From that day I wanted nothing else but to join the RAF. My mother despaired.

FAIROAKS FLYING CLUB

After the gliding, I applied for an RAF Flying Scholarship and was lucky to be awarded a 30-hour scholarship at the Fairoaks Flying Club. The aircraft flown was a DH82 Tiger Moth and weren't we lucky. We thought we had been cheated, forced to fly some ancient aircraft with no radio, no flaps, and no brakes – but looking back, it was the star prize. There was little airspace to worry about, and 30 hours was quite

Early Tiger Moth solo Fairoaks 1958.

sufficient to cover the PPL syllabus. The instructors were all ex-RAF with some ex-National Service, and in due course they all wandered off into airline jobs. We just did not appreciate what we had been given.

LONDON UNIVERSITY AIR SQUADRON

Like George, I joined the UAS in the days when flying was unlimited. It was a bit harder for us to fly since the aircraft were based 20 miles away at White Waltham. Amongst the instructors was the CFI, our own Battle of Britain pilot with a DFC, Nigel Kemp. He assumed God-like properties. Pat Courtney joined later with a history of Hurricane bombers in Burma. It was an idyllic arrangement with weekends at White Waltham and summer camps at RAF St Mawgan and RAF Tangmere, and like George, flying was all you could grab. I can see now that I was probably looking for my father.

I managed to scrounge a two-night trip to RAF Wildenrath (RAF Germany) in a Home Command Anson with two staff officers who fatally introduced me to German beer. Then, a few months later, at the traditional White Waltham September Battle of Britain cocktail party, we were watching the cars arrive at the officers' mess, when I suddenly recognised one of my RAF Germany mentors. One of his daughters got out of the car, saw me staring at her and stuck out her tongue. I went straight into the cocktail party to find her, and a couple of years later, after graduation, I married

Travel to Germany.

her. This was Wendy, and we have been together ever since. George has explained some of the problems of being married under the age of 25. After us, a number of university students arrived into the RAF already married, but at the time I think we just took the service by surprise. It wasn't easy.

George and I both joined the RAF on a cadetship scheme which involved a short induction week at RAF South Cerney. I well remember standing next to George as we took the Oath of Allegiance, so in fact we joined the RAF at the same moment in 1963.

Looking back, those formative years built not only our flying skills but also a strong camaraderie that has lasted a lifetime. The combination of rigorous training, shared challenges, and the unique pressures of service life forged deep friendships and a sense of purpose. We approached the next stages of our RAF careers with renewed confidence, ready to tackle advanced training and the responsibilities that lay ahead, drawing on the discipline and resilience that had been instilled in us from the very start.

RAF AIRCREW TRAINING

BOOT CAMP AT RAF SOUTH CERNEY

GEORGE

After graduation, we both reported to No. 1 Initial Training School at RAF South Cerney in Gloucestershire in September 1964. This was the start of our journey through the RAF pilot training system and was a traditional 'boot camp' aimed at reprogramming us from civilians into RAF officer material.

Our course consisted entirely of former UAS members and was shorter than normal in recognition that we already had some experience as officer cadets. We have all seen the films (mostly American) depicting brutal boot camp scenes of tough uncompromising drill instructors attempting to beat their charges into shape. There were some elements of this at South Cerney. The instructors were not brutal, but they did expect discipline, team spirit and hard work.

Our drill instructor was Sergeant Sparks (what a great name for a drill instructor). His job was to turn us from a bunch of casual slovenly university cadets into smart RAF officers, and he did so with gusto. Foot drill was practised on the parade ground where we learned to march in step. At the same time, our turnout, appearance and uniform were assessed. There were lectures and some tough physical training to

RAF officer training.

get us in shape. Leadership exercises were conducted at the local gravel pits where we were required, for example, to get our team safely across a 'crocodile infested' river with just a few scaffold poles and some rope. There was an escape and evasion exercise held in a Welsh forest with instruction on resistance to interrogation. At the end of about eight weeks, I left fitter than I have ever been before or since.

BASIC AND ADVANCED FLYING TRAINING

After South Cerney, our course was split: some went to RAF Syerston, while the rest (including myself and Alan) went to No. 6 Flying Training School (FTS) at RAF Acklington in Northumberland as No. 176 Course. This was the full RAF basic flying training course up to wings standard. In our case, the course was abbreviated from a year to eight months because of our previous UAS flying.

Acklington was a former World War II fighter station near the town of Amble in an attractive part of Northumberland. The station commander was a big genial Irishman whose main interest in our arrival interview was whether or not we played rugby. Those of us who were married had to find our own accommodation, of course. Sheila and I stayed in a farm cottage near Morpeth whilst Alan and Wendy stayed in Alnwick. We were 23 and had been married for a year.

We flew the Jet Provost T4, which was a robust little jet-powered training aircraft with side-by-side seating. This meant that the instructor could monitor what you were doing (and wrap you over the knuckles if necessary). The T4 was an updated version of the T3 with a more powerful Viper engine, with 2,500 lbs thrust. It could fly at up to 350 kts and climb to over 30,000 ft, but it was unpressurised, which meant that you were subject to the ambient air pressure and required to wear an oxygen mask. It was fully aerobatic, and the flight controls were manual with no power assistance, and they became heavy at the higher speeds. Its forgiving handling and sturdy construction made it an ideal basic training aircraft and I enjoyed flying it.

There was a comprehensive ground training syllabus which continued our officer training as well as our technical training. Our bible was the RAF AP129 technical training manual which we were required to know in depth. The syllabus included aircraft systems, meteorology, navigation, airmanship and the manual of Air Force law.

Our flying instructors came from a variety of backgrounds and included fighter, bomber, maritime and transport pilots. There were in addition a few so-called 'creamed off' instructors who had been selected straight after their own training courses to proceed to the Central Flying School to be trained as QFIs.

There was still a degree of suspicion of ex-UAS cadets, who were perceived (unfairly) as being rather too full of themselves. I think we proved ourselves in the final written exams when our course produced the highest marks in No. 6 FTS history! Some proof that our university training had at least taught us how to study and how to pass exams.

No. 176 University Course, George and Al back centre.

Mk4 Jet Provost.

The Jet Provost suited me well and I won both the Flying and the Aerobatics trophies at the end of the course. Alan won the navigation prize.

As a final act, as part of our course dining-out night, Alan and our course colleague Tim Gauvain wrote a panto called 'Puss in Flying Boots'. I played the part of our Irish station commander and Alan the part of Wing Commander Swart, the OC Ops and renamed King Commander Wart for the panto. This was well received and we all had a good laugh.

Our course split again after Acklington, with some going to helicopters, some to transports and the rest of us to advanced flying training on the Folland Gnat at No. 4 FTS based at RAF Valley in Anglesey, North Wales.

The Gnat T1 took over from the Vampire T11 in 1963 and represented a big step up in performance. It was a tiny little aeroplane, supersonic in a dive and highly manoeuvrable. It was originally designed as a fighter and as such is still in service with the Indian Air Force. The RAF adopted the two-seat version as their new advanced trainer, primarily as a lead-in to the Lightning fighter, which it had similar cockpit displays to. There was also a basic flight simulator where you could learn cockpit procedures and emergencies. The flying training followed the usual pattern of handling, instrument flying, (i.e. flying purely on instruments without outside reference), aerobatics, formation and low-level navigation, all designed to teach us to fly the aircraft to its limits. Low-level navigation was practised in the Welsh hills and valleys. It had a tandem cockpit, with the student sat in front of the instructor, which meant that the instructor's view forward was quite limited.

The Red Arrows flew the Gnat from when they first operated right through to 1979, when the Hawk took over as the RAF's advanced trainer. The Gnat could be unforgiving if mishandled – typical of the high-performance aircraft of that era, which demanded respectful treatment from their pilots. Just flying a visual circuit required the finals turn to be flown at 60 degrees of bank and just on the pre-stall buffet. Just before we arrived at Valley two aircraft had crashed with the death of the pilots having lost control in the finals turn.

Single officers stayed in the officers' mess at Valley. Alan and I both rented holiday cottages in the adjacent town of Trearddur Bay. Ours overlooked the Irish Sea and had lovely views but was freezing cold in the winter months.

Alan adapted better to the Gnat than most of us and he won the aerobatic trophy. The course lasted for 24 weeks and towards the end we were all asked to go to the medical centre to see if we could fit in the Lightning. Alan had already been. After checking leg length, sitting height, etc. the medical officer said to me, "I am sorry Flying Officer Robertson, but you are too tall to fit in the Lightning. In fact, you are really too tall to fly the Gnat, but it is too late to do anything about that now." Actually, the problem was more about leg length than height as I might have lost my kneecaps by impact on the instrument panel in the event of ejection. Alan and I are about the same size, so he had a similar problem. As a result, I went on to fly the Canberra and Alan to fly the Javelin, both of which had roomy cockpits. The choice of postings after advanced flying training had much to do with supply and demand, and we both felt lucky to have avoided the V Force, which none of us wanted (these were the big nuclear bombers like the Vulcan and Victor, flying initially as a co-pilot on long and boring high-level exercises). But our paths separated at that point as we followed very different but parallel careers.

Folland Gnat T1.

CHAPTER 2
OPERATIONAL CONVERSION

231 OCU – CANBERRA

GEORGE

After completing advanced flying training at RAF Valley, we went our separate ways, and for me it was to the Canberra Operational Conversion Unit (231 OCU) at RAF Bassingbourn in Cambridgeshire, a posting which suited me well. Bassingbourn had been a major USAAF base in World War II, the home of the 91st Bombardment Group, which operated B17 bombers including the famous 'Memphis Belle'. As a result, it was well equipped with extensive hangarage and infrastructure. It was also located in a pleasant part of Cambridgeshire with Cambridge within easy reach.

I rented a lovely old half-timbered house in the village, and we were very happy there. Our landlady lived next door. She was a widowed lady who had a granddaughter the same age as our daughter Patricia, and they often played together.

231 OCU had to supply crews to the many Canberra squadrons operating different variants of the aircraft. The Canberra was the RAF's first jet bomber entering service in 1952 with performance way ahead of its time. It had evolved over the years from the early marks, so the OCU concentrated on conversion to the basic aircraft type using the T4 trainer, the B2 bomber and the PR3 recce versions, in the knowledge that further type conversion would be needed when crews joined their squadrons. The OCU gave a thorough grounding in basic aircraft handling,

instrument flying, navigation, and single-engine operations, then moved on to the role-specific areas of bombing and reconnaissance. There was no training in tactics, formation flying, or self-defence, which I always felt was an omission. As a result, crews left the OCU competent enough to fly the aircraft, but still needing to learn the finer points on the job.

The first thing we had to do on arrival was crew up. Pilots and navigators were thrown together and told to sort themselves into two-man crews. It was a bit like being at your first dance where you had to find a partner and hope that the attraction was mutual. A couple of sessions in the bar usually sufficed. I crewed up with John Green, an experienced navigator who had two previous Canberra tours under his belt but was new to reconnaissance. I don't know how he must have felt ending up with a first-tour pilot; maybe I was the only one left when the music stopped. We did however develop a good working relationship and stayed as a crew for the next three years.

Navigators took great pride in the neatness and accuracy of their work and John's nav logs and maps were always immaculate. This was my first experience of working with a second crew member and we had to learn how to work together and trust each other. In the early stages of the course, I think John was reassured that I was competent in aircraft handling, could fly accurately on instruments and could cope with asymmetric handling in the event of engine failure. Likewise, I soon realised that John was very capable at navigating using dead reckoning and the rather basic nav equipment in the back of the aeroplane. For low-level navigation and for some high-level camera work he had to get out of his ejection seat and lie in the nose.

After basic conversion we moved on to role-specific training in reconnaissance using the Canberra PR3. This had a suite of high-level and low-level cameras of various focal lengths. The aim was always to capture the target area on successive frames with a 60 per cent overlap. This meant that when viewed on a light table using a stereoscope the photographic interpreters could see a three-dimensional image.

High-level photo training was normally flown at 30,000 ft or above and it involved planning a series of parallel tracks mostly over East Anglia. This involved accurate navigation to maintain the required tracks and accurate flying to ensure the wings were level when the shutter on the camera was triggered. There was a countdown to shutter activation to give some warning.

For low-level photography at 500 ft or below, an F95 camera with a four-inch focal length and a high-speed shutter would give rapid exposures in a burst to cover the target. Crews also had to give a visual report of what they had seen. All photography was debriefed by the instructors.

Towards the end of the course, we discovered that we were to be posted to 39 Squadron in Malta to fly the Canberra PR9. Although delighted with the posting, I was concerned for Sheila who was now heavily pregnant with our second child. She was already too close to her due date to fly out to Malta, even if we could have afforded the fare and accommodation. She would have to stay in Bassingbourn in our rented house with our two-year-old until the new baby arrived and until I reached the magic age of 25. That meant a wait of about five months before she could join me in Malta. It was a big ask but she coped like a trooper.

JAVELIN 228 OCU

ALAN

The Javelin was a large delta-winged all-weather fighter with some fairly advanced radar interception equipment. Its conversion was very different. Before the pilots arrived at 228 OCU, RAF Leuchars (near St Andrews, Scotland), the navigators had already done three months basic hard labour flying in the Canberra T18. There were two seats side-by-side with the student navigator sitting next to his instructor in front of an AI17 radar display. A second student occupied the jump seat waiting his turn. Usually, there was another Canberra taking turns at attacking or acting as target. All this took place well out to sea under the control of either RAF Buchan, near Aberdeen, or RAF Boulmer near Amble. I actually managed to get

No. 228 OCU RAF Leuchars.

picked up by a T18 at the end of a training sortie and never understood a word the instructor was saying. It was all about three-dimensional geometry.

However, we started the aircraft conversion by flying the Javelin T3, a dual-control version of an early model. My first solo flight was in an FAW9, including an almost vertical supersonic dive. Clothing included the pressure jerkin, which we had picked up at RAF North Luffenham, where we had practised pressure breathing with air forced down the lungs. The technique of expelling the air had to be mastered. We considered this all fair as we also received a very cool zippy battledress which was standard issue with the pressure jerkin. We had also crewed up during our days at North Luffenham not really knowing what to expect. I think we were too excited to care very much.

I explained in *Fast Jets on the Front Line* how air defence is a mental discipline. You see a blip on your radar and never forget that this blip weighs 20 tonnes. At this stage you know nothing about him but start to calculate his altitude and heading. Height is easy. You use the one in 60 rule to put yourself ideally 2,000 ft below the target. Interaction between front and back seats is critical and unambiguous. For the initial trigonometry, we have now assumed that the fighter speed (you) is M0.9 and the target is doing M0.8. We make a first assessment of the target heading and adjust our own so that we will be able to make a controlled turn in behind him. Then as the intercept progresses, we make continual refinements to our early guesses. At the same time airmanship still rules. Lookout, fuel management and weapons checks are all vital elements of a successful attack. More about this in the next chapter.

Some people never get to feel comfortable handling the target and use a complex crib of ranges and angles. Others get used quite quickly to flying the target into the best position. Once the radar has locked onto the target, much more helpful information becomes available. Personally, when I started in the Phantom back seat, I never had a problem, and years later spent a happy hour teaching an Italian Tornado GR1 pilot how to do intercepts without the benefit of locking up the target. I was surprised I could still do it. So was he.

Just for the record, in the 1950s, when our mark of Javelin, the FAW9, was specified, the threat to the United Kingdom was the Tupolev 16, the Badger, arriving at high level. The Javelin's capabilities suited this perfectly. Then, when the Badger got its tail guns, the Javelin got its Firestreak infrared missiles, while the radar received constant improvements.

So, intercepting at 40,000 ft required very steady handling, and of course the intercept might be at night or in bad weather. Medium-level attacks were considered

The Firestreak AAM (60 Squadron).

to be so easy that they were not taught. Low level was another story entirely. The aircraft's ability to accelerate and slow down made speed control straightforward, but then in the Far East we were making maximum rate turns, with 70 degrees of bank, at night at 500 ft over the Straits of Malacca in order to get in behind low-level targets. It was believed that the Indonesian C130 transports might operate at this low level.

The flight commander then takes the quarterly training schedule and breaks it down into small chunks. Crews train at each one to perfection, so that when the magic word 'scramble' happens they are ready for whatever is thrown at them. In the UK, include electronic countermeasures and ad hoc air-to-air refuelling and you have a very challenging role.

So, was it true that the Javelin lost power if the afterburner was engaged at low level? Of course it was. As the Javelin put on weight and started to fly with air-to-air missiles, more power was required, so Armstrong Siddeley designed afterburners that fitted nicely onto the back of their engines. The fuel supply was simply the unused returning low pressure fuel which increased as the aircraft climbed into thinner air. On the runway there was really none to spare, so if the afterburner was selected, fuel was taken away from the combustion chambers. The second law of thermodynamics cannot be broken, so the result was an overall power loss of about 3%. It didn't matter because there was massive surplus power, but the aircraft's detractors loved it. Typically, the afterburners were normally engaged passing around 12,000 ft and you could feel the aircraft rotate skywards. And of course, low-level afterburner was brilliant for air shows.

That was the OCU. We left with a basic competence on the aircraft, but really doing the more difficult high-level intercepts. We had little or no tactical training and just a quick look at low-level intercepts. Airmanship, however, played an important role in the training. Aircraft handling was probably all right, with an eye on the possible super stall if you got too slow, as well as the ability of the turbine casing to close onto the turbine and in some cases stop the engine. (This was called 'centreline closure', and the solution was carborundum paste around the turbine shroud). Instrument flying and formation was just about satisfactory, but nothing prepared us for the hard-nosed operational attitudes on the Far East squadrons, or the amount of training still to come to complete the full training requirements. I covered this in my first book.

On a domestic note, of course I was still under 25. As I set off on the great adventure, Wendy threw herself at the mercy of various relatives and eventually went to the MoD to attempt to get a passage. She accidently saw a charming army colonel first who saw no problem giving her a seat until he realised that she had come to the wrong office. The RAF office managed to humiliate her within minutes and she left in tears. I was debriefed on the error of our ways a short time later by a ground officer with a low opinion of aircrew. This was fairly typical. We paid £180 in the end (about £4,000 in today's money), always tricky when you have no money.

THE CANBERRA PR9

39 SQUADRON AT RAF LUQA, MALTA

GEORGE

We arrived as a crew in Malta in mid-July 1966 and started our conversion to the Canberra PR9. There is no two-pilot version of the PR9, but the squadron had their own T4 which served for handling assessments, instrument ratings, area familiarisation, and so on. Once these were out of the way, including a check flight with the CO, it was time to step into the PR9 for the first time.

It is worth giving some thought to the differences of the PR9, which was the final and most advanced variant of the Canberra to be developed.

The PR9 variant was meant to push the Canberra's height and range to the limit – flying higher than most fighters of that era. It was designed to climb to 70,000 ft, but in practice it never achieved that: it could only get up to 60,000 ft after a

The Canberra PR9.

long cruise climb and with no drop tanks. In service with 39 Squadron, it was never required to go that high, but we were equipped with pressure jerkins as well as Taylor helmets just in case. This made us look like Buck Rogers, which we thought was very cool. Our normal equipment of flying suit, helmet and oxygen mask for pressure breathing was good for up to 56,000 ft which was our normal limit. Bear in mind that commercial airliners operate in the range of 30,000 to 40,000 ft.

Short Brothers and Harland of Belfast were given the job of design, development and production of the PR9. The prototype PR9 first flew in 1958 and eventually 22 aircraft were delivered to the RAF. This was a major upgrade over the earlier marks of Canberra. The wingspan was increased and the chord (width) of the wings inside of the engine nacelles was also increased, giving a wing area of over 1,000 sq ft. Much more powerful RR Avon 206 engines were fitted, giving almost twice the thrust – 11,250 lbs of force – as the earlier B2 models. There was so much excess thrust available that we normally used just 80 per cent thrust for take-off, to lower the single engine safety speed and to save on fatigue to the tail and empennage, as full take of thrust resulted in vibration to the tailplane. The Avon 206 engine had a starter system powered with Avpin (isopropyl nitrate). This was a highly volatile monofuel which could burn without oxygen and was carried in a small tank in the inner wing leading edge. When we went on deployment, we used to carry a spare can of the stuff in the flare bay so that we could do our own turnround servicing. I doubt whether modern health and safety rules would allow this. The PR9 was also the first Canberra to be fitted with hydraulically powered ailerons and rudder.

There was also a radical change in the crew positions on the PR9 compared to earlier variants. The navigator sat within the hinged nose section in an ejection seat with an escape hatch above, which was removed via explosive bolts when ejection was initiated. He had an optical sight in front of him which he could rotate from looking down to straight ahead. There were also two small windows either side of his seat position. All the navigation and camera controls were accessible. This arrangement had really been optimised for the high-level reconnaissance role and was less suitable for low-level operations. The pilot sat above and behind the nav's position under an offset fighter-type canopy hinged at the rear. Access was via a ladder hooked to the left side. This arrangement gave an excellent all-round view for the pilot, whereas the navigator's view at low level was quite restricted. As a result, I became proficient in the use of 50k maps for the final initial point (IP) to target run, a skill which served me well in subsequent tours.

The PR9 was equipped with a suite of wet film cameras for both the high-level and low-level roles. There was a fan of F96 cameras for use when overflying areas of interest at high level. These cameras were fitted with a system of image movement compensation which moved the film to compensate for the aircraft's forward motion. More importantly there was an F96 mounted obliquely with a 48-inch lens which could take good-quality pictures from 23 miles away, thus precluding the need to overfly targets in sensitive border areas. We used this

George and John Green.

facility fairly frequently. For low-level recce there was a fan of F95 cameras capable of high-speed burst photography. We used these a lot, as our main NATO role involved low-level reconnaissance.

There was a vertical survey camera, the F52, in the rear fuselage. This was gyro stabilised and created high quality imagery for map making. We used this extensively for survey work in Aden and Oman. There was also provision for night flash photography using magnesium flares housed in the flare bay. These were ejected in rapid sequence when overflying the target at night. Peak illumination from the flare triggered the camera shutter. We used to practise night flash photography using a timed run from the lighthouse on Gozo to the island of Filfla (a big rock positioned to the west of Malta).

For navigation, our main equipment was a doppler radar system called Green Satin. This used three radar beams looking forward, aft and sideways. By comparing the Doppler shift between them, the system could compute groundspeed, true track, lateral drift and wind vector. This information was displayed on the ground position indicator (GPI). The system worked pretty well over land but was less reliable over the sea as it would receive reliable radar reflections and would unlock over a calm surface.

The PR9 had a very good autopilot, which was much appreciated on long transits. It was ahead of its time and could do a coupled approach to an instrument landing system (ILS), (in other words it would lock on to the ILS and fly the approach automatically), a system I didn't see again until operating the Boeing 737-200 many years later. It also had a high frequency (HF) radio which could provide voice comms over thousands of miles depending on atmospheric conditions. The aircraft was pretty reliable, but we did have occasional problems with fuel booster pump failures, mainly due to the waxing of cold soaked fuel during long flights at high altitude. We also had persistent problems with our main very/ultra-high frequency (V/UHF) radio, the PTR 175. But the PR9 stayed in service with the RAF for many more years. It was such a versatile aircraft that it could still do a useful job right up to its eventual retirement in 2006. With service over five decades, it was the longest serving aircraft in the RAF, having seen deployment in the Falklands, Afghanistan and Iraq. It had a number of upgrades over the years, including newer sensors and airframe strengthening. Even in its final years it proved indispensable for strategic reconnaissance.

I managed to get back to the UK one time, shortly after the birth of our second daughter. This was thanks to one of our photographic interpreters, who arranged my flight there and back to deliver some classified material as courier. Sheila and our two children travelled out to Malta the day after my 25th birthday, as overnight I officially became a married officer and entitled to the usual married benefits, which included duty travel, marriage allowance and accommodation. We moved initially into a rental flat in the small coastal town of Birzebugga on the south side of the island. After a couple of months, we were allocated a 'hiring' near St Andrews Barracks on the east side of the island. This was a traditional Malta house built with the ubiquitous honey-coloured limestone blocks and with marble floors. It had ceiling fans and was cool in the heat of summer. We were also entitled to domestic help three mornings a week. We paid for another two days, and our cleaning lady also did babysitting for us on repayment. All of a sudden, our quality of life was transformed.

RECCE OPERATIONS

39 Squadron was assigned to NATO in the low-level reconnaissance role. Our war deployment base was Eskisehir in Turkey, and our wartime responsibilities would have included the Black Sea coasts, Crimea and Ukraine. We also had national responsibilities and could be assigned to reconnaissance tasks anywhere in the Mediterranean and Middle East. Finally, we had responsibilities for aerial survey work which could take us anywhere.

Much of our time in Malta was spent on low-level recce training. For this, we had the southern half of Sicily allocated as a low-flying area, and we had a low-level route around Calabria in Italy. The Calabria route showed up the PR9's limitations in turbulent mountainous terrain, as that big wing caught every gust. We also used to fly to Libya for training, until Gadaffi arrived on the scene and banned the RAF from the area. On Fridays we usually had a squadron competition involving finding and photographing a small target, bringing back good photo coverage and also providing an accurate visual report. The results were assessed by the photographic interpreters (PIs) and photos displayed for all to see.

High-level reconnaissance was sometimes called for, and we used to deploy regularly to Bahrain for tasks around the Gulf and Oman. A regular milk run would be north to the border between Iraq and Kuwait to see what was happening there. On one occasion we spent about two weeks flying out of Bahrain down to Dhofar where we did photo runs from about 10,000 ft for the PIs to look for camel tracks in the desert (evidence of insurgents coming from Yemen). This was at a time where an insurgency was going on in that area, and the SAS were involved in war operations.

Soviet navy *Moskva.*

On another occasion, I was tasked with flying along the Syrian border east of Cyprus using the high-level oblique camera with the 48-inch focal length to peer into Syria, looking for newly built surface-to-air missile sites that might threaten aircraft movements to Cyprus.

We were also tasked with ship recce, especially after our Malta-based Shackleton squadron was withdrawn. There was much excitement when Russia's first helicopter carrier the *Moskva* appeared in the Mediterranean in September 1968. We found the ship northwest of Crete and duly photographed it from all angles, including one low-level pass using the F95 cameras. A number of its KA25 helicopters were dipping sonar in the vicinity and guns on the escorting Kashin-class destroyers were tracking us throughout. All jolly good fun!

FORWARD OPERATING BASE

At Eskisehir, we would be operating alongside the resident Turkish Air Force squadrons and the contrast in styles of operation was marked. The Turks operated American equipment, mostly RF84Fs and F100s. They had an aggressive, no-nonsense approach. Officers and especially pilots were highly regarded and their attitude to the lower ranks was dismissive. They made extensive use of conscripts who lived in an annex to the hangars with few modern conveniences. When we deployed there on exercise with the whole squadron, all our engineers below the rank of sergeant sewed on sergeant stripes so that they could make use of the sergeant's mess on the base with conditions roughly equivalent to what they had at home. It was a very autocratic regime: the Turkish Air Force had commandeered the Hilton hotel in downtown Eskisehir for the exclusive use of their officers, and that is where our aircrew lived when on deployment. We got on well with the local squadrons, who were always very welcoming and hospitable. On social evenings in the Hilton the Turkish officers would take to traditional dancing after a few glasses of Raki. We stood around and watched, and inevitably we were asked to do some English dances. Refusing to do anything would have been impolite and after some baffled discussion we decided we would do ring-a-ring-a-roses. We were given rapturous applause, especially at the we-all-fall-down ending.

ADEN DEPLOYMENT – MARCH 1967

We were tasked with two major aerial surveys during my time on the squadron. The first of these was during an operational deployment to Aden shortly before our forces were due to withdraw. There was an insurgency going on at the time and our forces were under threat from terrorist activity. IEDs and grenades were being used against personnel, and their families. We deployed with three aircraft and six crews and were accommodated in a vacated married quarter at RAF Khormaksar. This was a busy base with two resident Hunter squadrons, Argosy transports and helicopters. The insurgency was led by the National Liberation Front (NLF) who carried out urban attacks against British troops, families and local officials.

The Crater area of Aden was evacuated by British forces as a result of terrorist activity and was famously re-taken in July 1967 by Lt Col Colin Mitchell (Mad Mitch) and the Argyll and Sutherland Highlanders. The base area at Khormaksar was secure and surrounded by a chain link fence patrolled day and night. We were able to go out to a local beach at Steamer Point and were transported to and fro in a service bus where the windows had been removed and replaced with wire mesh to stop grenades being thrown in. The beach itself was lovely and protected by a shark net moored offshore. When you got close to the shark net you could see dark shapes cruising just beyond.

We did some tactical recce in the border areas looking for insurgents, but our main task during this three-month deployment was to conduct an aerial survey of the whole of what was then called the Aden Protectorate, which stretched from the border with Yemen all the way to Oman. Survey work was conducted at around 30,000 ft using the gyro-stabilised survey camera, and required precise flying and navigation, as well as clear, cloud-free weather. The idea was to complete this survey before our forces withdrew from Aden whilst we still had the opportunity. We flew parallel tracks back and forth, a bit like mowing the lawn, with a small overlap between tracks. The results were assessed by the PIs and also by a small detachment of royal engineers who worked with us. Some bits might be rejected due to cloud cover or excessive tilt and had to be done again, so there was some gap filling involved. Our sister squadron in Malta was No. 13 who also operated the PR9. They were given the task of an aerial survey of Kenya, and this was always a popular deployment, but cloud cover was always a problem especially around Kilimanjaro. They had to keep going back for gap filling every year which suited them well as nobody wanted this commitment to end.

MASIRAH DEPLOYMENT – JANUARY - FEBRUARY 1968

We went back to South Arabia in 1968, this time to the island of Masirah, to conduct an aerial survey of Oman. This was a big commitment, and we were away for two months. At the time, Masirah had no resident squadrons and was used mainly as a staging post. I remember it as a rather beautiful desert island surrounded by crystal clear water. I used the sailing club's Wayfarer dinghies a few times, but you had to be careful not to capsize as there were a lot of barracuda in the sea. There were also lots of crayfish which were harvested by the small local indigenous population. Masirah was an unaccompanied posting for the resident staff and there was not much to do,

Masirah locals.

Squadron exchange with Villafranca.

but we did head off by Land Rover to explore the rest of the island. We stopped at a local village and were warmly welcomed by the locals who insisted we join them for coffee. Their only medical assistance came from the RAF doctor on the base who ran a clinic for the locals. We gave a lift to one of the village women who needed treatment along with her husband who accompanied her.

NATO SQUADRON EXCHANGE

We had a regular squadron exchange with the Italian Air Force (IAF) Recce Wing at their Villafranca base. Villafranca is located six miles from the city of Verona and close to Lake Garda in a beautiful part of Italy. Deployments there were always popular and the resident IAF squadrons were very hospitable. They operated the Republic RF84F aircraft in the tactical-recce role. During our regular visits to Villafranca we took full advantage of our off-duty time to visit Venice, Lake Garda and Verona and on one occasion John and I went to the opera at the Verona Arena to see Cavaliera Rusticana, an unforgettable experience

PR 9 ACCIDENTS

Sadly, there were two fatal accidents with PR9s during my time in Malta, both involving our sister squadron No. 13. In both cases the aircraft inverted and crashed on the final turn of a visual approach. Exhaustive inquires could find no technical failures to explain the accidents but after much thought over the years, I think the explanation may lie in the PR9's unique control system. As mentioned earlier, the

PR9 had hydraulically powered ailerons and rudder, unlike the earlier marks which relied on traditional manual controls with trim tabs and blow-back rods. With these earlier marks the amount of control surface movement was a function of airspeed. With the PR9 you could achieve full deflection of the ailerons at any speed. When rolling out of a turn the aileron on the inside of the turn is deflected downward to lift the wing and the aileron on the other side moved in the opposite direction. At a low speed and high bank angle it would be possible to stall the wing on the inside of the turn when trying to roll out of the turn due to the large deflection of the aileron on that side. This would cause the aircraft to roll in the opposite direction to the control input which would only get worse with further aileron input. I emphasise that this is my own opinion and I could be wrong, but this explanation does at least seem plausible.

The PR9 was seen as a variation on an existing design but it was so radically different from the base line Canberra B2 that it should have been subject to a new type approval. A modern equivalent might be to compare the accidents to the Boeing 737 Max, which was based on the original type approval of the much earlier 737-200, with insufficient guidance to crews on the different handling characteristics. Boscombe Down should have been tasked with a further handling assessment of the PR9 with a subsequent revision to the release to service.

THE FORMATION TEAM

Traditionally, recce aircraft always operated as singletons 'alone, unarmed and unafraid', as there was never a need to operate in formation. There was no formation flying as part of our conversion to type and at the OCU, no advice on how best to manoeuvre for survival if intercepted by a fighter. Every year there was a Malta air defence exercise the 'Malta ADEX'. Visiting air defence squadrons, usually Lightnings from UK would take part with the resident two PR squadrons and other Canberras from Cyprus acting as targets. Our brief was to cruise in at 30,000+ ft with no self-defence manoeuvring when intercepted. It was a complete waste of time from our point of view from which we learned nothing. There was a political dimension to this as it was intended to reassure Malta that the RAF could reinforce from UK in times of trouble. I remember being bounced once by a pair of Hunters out of Gibraltar when we were returning from a weekend away. We had been socialising with the two pilots over the weekend one of whom was the legendary 'Puddy Catt' well known in Hunter circles. Fortunately, I saw them turning in behind us as we passed 15,000 ft. I stood the PR9 on its left wingtip and pulled hard forcing a fly through by the Hunters. We played around some more until the Hunters got bored and headed back to Gib. They might have got a few brief seconds of tracking time, but we gave a good account of ourselves making best use of the PR9's big wing, powerful engines and good turning performance. Fortunately, Terry O'Brian, one of our flight commanders decided that close formation flying was an important skill, and he started a four-ship formation team not least to give local flypasts for events over Malta. I flew as number four in the 'box' and was eternally grateful for this formation experience when I moved on to my next tour.

231 OCU FAREWELL TOUR

In February 1969, the CO of the Canberra OCU at Bassingbourn, Wg Cdr Cowton, decided to do a farewell tour of all Canberra bases as 231 OCU was due to close down. Two PR3s and six aircrew set off to fly via Cyprus, Masirah and Gan to Singapore, and we were required to escort them in a PR9 with our better nav equipment and HF radio. One of the PR3s was WE139, the London to New Zealand Air Race winner in 1953. This old girl performed perfectly throughout this long deployment with no unserviceability. This was to be her last flight before retirement to the RAF Museum at Hendon.

No. 231 Farewell Tour (George kneeling)

SOCIAL LIFE

The lifestyle in Malta was very pleasant. The working regime on the squadron complied with 'Mediterranean rules' in the peak summer months, with early starts and early finishes six days a week to avoid the hottest part of the day. So, from about 2 p.m. onwards we could head to the beach. There are few sandy beaches in Malta, so this meant a trip to the local lido, a rocky shore where you went straight into the water. The island was still a major military base with all three services represented. There were two active airfields at Luqa and Halfar. There were busy dockyards next to Grand Harbour which serviced the Royal Navy, a flotilla of RN submarines and a number of army barracks. The American 6th Fleet used to visit with their carriers, and we had an exchange of visits with their squadrons. I particularly remember a visit by the 'Red Rippers' VF11, a Phantom squadron embarked on the USS *Forestal.* These guys were relieved to be away from operations in Vietnam and were determined to have a ball. Three of our squadron executives managed to get rides in their Phantom F4Bs and were enormously impressed.

The Maltese people were delightful, still very proud of their reputation as the George Cross Island. They are deeply religious and every town had an impressive church, none more so than Mosta with its famous Mosta Dome. Based on the design of the Pantheon in Rome, it has one of the largest unsupported domes in the world. It famously has its own 'miracle' when the roof was pierced by a World War II bomb during mass. It fell into the congregation but failed to explode and is still celebrated to this day. Each town in Malta has its own 'festa' to celebrate the local saint and they all have spectacular fireworks displays. There was an impressive bus service using coloured buses which indicated the route radiating out from Valetta to all parts of the island. I couldn't afford a new car when I arrived on the island and instead had a beaten-up old Morris Oxford which needed constant attention. It was just as well that I am the son of a motor mechanic. The squadron had a very active social life, helped along by cheap duty-free booze. It was in many ways like the last days of the Raj where we still enjoyed colonial privilege, but that would soon change as the Maltese aspired to run their own affairs and rid themselves of British dependence.

We had visits from family and friends whilst in Malta, including a welcome catch up with Alan and Wendy who came to stay in 1968, soon after their return from Singapore.

MOVING ON

As I neared the end of my time in Malta, the boss Sandy Cobban called me in and said that he had been told to nominate pilots as non-volunteers for the Central Flying

School (CFS) course to become QFIs. He explained that I was in the frame for this. I told him that I didn't want to become a QFI at this stage in my career and that I wanted to stay in an operational role. I was aware that becoming a QFI would probably mean two tours in training command and a long time away from the front line. The boss said that he understood, but that the only way to avoid the non-volunteer posting would be for him to say that I was temperamentally unsuited to be an instructor. After some discussion he agreed to do so. This was a risky decision and could have gone very wrong, however luck was on my side and a few months later I received a posting to the Phantom, which was then just entering service with the RAF. The irony is that the second half of my flying career as a civilian was nearly all as a training captain, a role that I greatly enjoyed and for which I clearly had an aptitude. However, the decision to stay in front-line operations in the RAF was correct at the time.

MALTA TODAY

As I write this in March 2026, we have just returned from a two-week holiday in Malta, our first major visit since we lived there in the 1960s. I was amazed at the transformation of the island, which is still in progress, with tower cranes everywhere and new high-rise buildings still going up.

The old Luqa airfield still exists but is now dominated by the new 3,500-metre-long runway 33/13, completed in 1977, which serves as the main runway for the adjacent passenger terminal, now designated 'Malta International Airport'. It is served with a system of dual carriageways and underpasses to connect it with the main urban areas on the east side of the island, and as we drove by taxi towards our hotel, I did not recognise anything as so much had changed.

Malta is increasingly prosperous now, and the local economy is dominated by tourism. There are hotels everywhere and especially around the towns of Sliema and St Julians in the east and Bugibba in the north. It seems that the local Maltese do not have much appetite for working in hotels, as the majority of hotel employees seem to be immigrants from Bangladesh or the Philippines.

Malta had an unwelcome reputation for corruption in the recent past which is now apparently under control. It has become a centre for the online gambling industry because of a favourable tax regime. Malta is a member of the EU, and it is now possible to obtain a Maltese passport following a process of first becoming a resident for up to three years and then applying for citizenship and investing around £500,000 in a 'national development and social fund'. This has become a very popular route for the wealthy Chinese.

The Javelin over the Jahore Straits — 'Waking the Neighbours' by Paul Couper GAvA and by kind permission of Hansenprint.

The last Javelin flight.

The north-west side of Malta has experienced the least amount of change, especially around the ancient capital of Medina and Rabat. Valetta is as beautiful as before and is a World Heritage Site. We enjoyed our visit and will certainly go back.

JAVELIN FAREWELL

ALAN

This was my last Javelin flight (above), but the actual occasion was the disbandment of No. 64 Squadron on 10th June 1967, coincidentally Her Majesty the Queen's birthday. 64 Squadron is flying the nine-ship big arrow with the two squadron commanders leading. 60 Squadron is flying the supporting diamond; I am on the left of the diamond with my navigator, Chris Donovan. 60's T3 is in between flown by 60's QFI, who came back and did a nice little air display. 60 Squadron continued for another year, after which the airframes were flown to Seletar and either given to the new Singapore Air Force for engineer training or scrapped.

THE JET PROVOST AND THE HARRIER

CENTRAL FLYING SCHOOL

After the Javelin, for me, came CFS at RAF Little Rissington, and a conversion back onto the Jet Provost, all in order to become a qualified flying instructor (QFI). CFS in its own unique way was a kind of Jesuit college. It lived and breathed flying and all its supporting disciplines. Initially at RAF Upavon, it was one of the three pillars of the RAF established by Lord Trenchard, alongside the RAF College at Cranwell and the Technical Training School at RAF Halton. The RAF instructors were an elite who wore white flying suits to be recognised by all. CFS quickly built up an international reputation around the world, and its examiners went worldwide. That's all gone now, as privatised instructor training and standardisation is at the various flying training schools with agencies reporting into CFS headquarters at RAF Cranwell, where it apparently resides in a couple of Nissen huts.

The CFS experience was hard going, with the first half of the six-month course devoted to ground school, imitating a student's experience at an FTS. There were two Jet Provost squadrons, a Chipmunk and Varsity flight, a Gnat flight and a Meteor and Vampire display team. Instructional technique was an essential topic. One student on my entry described servicing a shotgun as his optional topic. At the end he loaded the gun, walked to a window and fired the gun out of it. Nobody minded. At the same time on the flight line, we all got used to the Jet Provost Mk3, which was reputed to turn fuel into jet noise. It was horribly underpowered, but probably just right for an ab-initio student. The flying training syllabus was pretty well what Major Smith-Barry proposed in 1916, appalled by the standard of training at the time. It was known as the 'Gosport System' and has been the basis of all hands-on training ever since. Your CFS instructor took you through a flying lesson from the syllabus, for example 'effects of control' starting with the blackboard briefing (at the time state of the art). When airborne, you taught 'Bloggs' the lesson you had been studying for a half hour, then he gave you the next lesson. 'Bloggs' was the name of the make-believe student.

Your next flight was with another course member, where you taught him your half lesson, and then he taught you his. We took this all pretty seriously. Then for the second part of the course, we moved to the Jet Provost Mk4 to cover navigation, formation, night flying and more complicated emergencies. In the meantime, some of the entry had gone to the piston flight with Chipmunks and Varsities. Some others had migrated to the Gnat flight based at RAF Kemble at the time. In the recent past there had been Hunters and Canberras, but we were encouraged to blag flights from the other units. I flew the Varsity four times, twice with an instructor and twice as P2 to a student pilot. It was years before I understood why a sleeve valve engine was different.

The Jet Provost was unquestionably the perfect basic trainer. It was rugged and viceless and would accept any number of student hard landings. It was a direct descendant of the Piston Provost. The pressurised Mk5 variant replaced the Mk3 around 1969, while the Mk4 – which had a more powerful engine than the Mk3 – continued to operate. The development ended with the BAC Strikemaster, loved by those who did a tour in Oman. The RAF economised with a smaller engine in their almost identical Mk5, which did cause some weight and balance problems.

Shortly before Christmas we were posted to our FTS. I drew RAF Linton-on-Ouse, near York, which was actually where the navy sent their pilots to be trained by a mixed group of instructors, both navy and RAF. That made instructing much more interesting as we never had to worry about student discipline. The Navy sent two General List lieutenants with each student entry so that we were left with just teaching mainly midshipmen to fly. Again, it has all gone now with the navy's pilots totally integrated into the RAF student training, both fixed wing and rotary. The jet students went on to RNAS Brawdy to fly the Hunter and in those days, it was unusual to wait for the next course, unlike the eight years inflicted on a modern-day student.

After two happy years, when I was now an A2 instructor, an instrument rating examiner (IRE) and a deputy flight commander, the Wilson Government decided to pull out of any British influence east of Suez. The RAF took a look at the number of flying schools and thus the number of instructors, and in short order the announcement was made that RAF Acklington would close, followed by RAF Syerston. We were training too many instructors, so all QFIs at about two thirds of the way through their tours were invited to suggest three choices of ground posting. Naturally I chose Naples, Cyprus and Oslo for the skiing. What a laugh. All 40 of us got ground tours inside training command, and I got the Administrative No. 3 Apprentice School at RAF Hereford for the next two years. It was the kiss of death for me; career finished in an alien ground environment. I ducked and weaved but it was no good. "That's where you're going. Be grateful."

So, two years later, when I was posted to the Lightning once again, I discussed the problem with my boss, a wing commander navigator, who advised me to get out of training command before making a fuss. That meant 30 hours in those days at the School of Refresher Flying at RAF Manby on the Lincolnshire coast on the Jet

Provost Mk4, then on to an air defence refresher at 229 OCU at RAF Chivenor near Barnstaple, confidence on the floor, but flying the Hunter. Well, the aircraft was a pure piece of magic, described by George when he did his refresher. When I saw the doctor, he agreed that I could never fly the Lightning. This was clearly a problem as the Phantom OCU had not yet re-opened. Then one day there was a Harrier parked outside 79 Squadron, and I asked the pilot what the cockpit was like. "Vast" was the answer, so I asked for Harriers, duly granted. I was moved onto the short GA course instead of starting again on the long one. The Hunter was just a wonderful aircraft to fly and one of the few where you just had to think something and the aircraft did it for you. George has gone into greater detail, and admittedly the range work of guns, bombs and rockets were a lot of fun.

NO. 233 OCU, RAF WITTERING

We moved to RAF Wittering, near Stamford, the home of the Harrier and took a married quarter. It would be a while until I could start flying so I was understudy to the ops desk and started to learn their strange language. I heard the ops officer speak to the groundcrew and ask for aircraft Delta to be put into align. He meant the Ferranti inertial nav attack system (INAS). I looked out of the window and saw that Delta was already in a line. All very confusing. Before flying started I was given a dozen hours on the Hunter with 45 Squadron, then off to RAF Tern Hill to learn how to hover a Whirlwind helicopter in preparation for the Harrier. After a quick dip in the ocean at RAF Mountbatten Sea Survival Course near Plymouth, we were ready to begin the Harrier ground school.

Harrier flying started on the T2 two-seater. Initially, vertical and conventional flying were kept apart. There were two first solos, the first with the nozzles pointing straight back. The aircraft flew like a rather soggy Hunter and of course the four-wheel fast landing was like a Formula 1 tea trolley. The nozzles could also be pointed forward five degrees for limited braking. The first vertical solo took place on a hard standing big enough for several aircraft with especially hard concrete. The aircraft was at a low weight, so that you quickly went to full power when you moved the nozzle control lever fully down. After hovering for a bit, you gently reduced power and the aircraft made its way down to the ground. The Whirlwind training had helped enormously, and it was all a great novelty.

The next stage was of course the transition to and from conventional flight. We each received a plastic whizz wheel for a small mechanical computer for calculating

First Harrier vertical solo in the hover.

the speed and nozzle angle for angling the nozzles down on take-off. This was followed by a gradual movement of the nozzles until they were pointing straight back. Transitioning to land was much more difficult, gradually adding nozzle angle as speed reduced. The head-up display became the pilot's best friend, especially the depiction of the angle of attack. Then the INAS was introduced as well as cross-country flying to simulated targets. Some aircraft still had P-type compasses with no moving map. Grass landings were introduced including a flight to RAF Newton for a landing, taxi round and take off. It was a strange feeling lining up amongst the Chipmunks. However, there was always a friendly Harrier QFI on hand to talk to. The conversion was friendly, professional and well done.

On to weapons next, and trips to the various ranges, and the limitations of the GR1 and even the GR1a with a more powerful engine became apparent. They discovered that I had no idea how to read a large-scale map. (I wondered what else I had not been taught at Chivenor.) There were two excellent 30mm Aden cannons in fuselage pods. After that there were just the four pylons of which two carried the 100-gallon fuel tanks. (There were apparently 230-gallon tanks available for transit with handling restrictions.) That left two pylons, one of which would be to carry a

Harrier grass landing, 233 OCU RAF Wittering.

practice bomb dispenser and the other a SNEB rocket pod. Much later on in the Falklands a Sidewinder AiM9L took up a pylon, leaving just one for air-to-ground weapons. That was all in the future. In the meantime, the gyro weapon-aiming sights had never worked so the test cards were used, worked by a little button for each. Someone had discovered that the tiny toothpaste tube tops on samples were just right for the buttons and these had been standard. When we got to this point in training, small switches had replaced the buttons.

The aircraft was never one that you could love like a Hunter. Handling was solid but lookout was awful, with the pilot buried in the cockpit. Fuel was always at a premium, but working a target in Devon, say, was just a possibility. The use of the nozzles for increasing turn rate was well understood, but futuristic. The nozzles were connected with something like a bicycle chain, nowhere near strong enough. Somewhere in the future these would be replaced by motor bike chains with no restrictions. Dealer's choice for the landings – short, vertical or rolling vertical – made the recovery interesting and fun. There was even an option of a 50m square metal pad or one of Wittering's many short strips. Then I was posted to 20 Squadron at RAF Wildenrath in Germany. We bought a house, rented it out, and packed our worldly possessions into the car. I was warned that 20 were a hard bunch. This certainly proved true.

NO. 20 SQUADRON RAF WILDENRATH

My first mistake was arriving with Wendy. This was not appreciated, especially when I had to leave early from the bowling night that they had put on to welcome me. 20's aircraft was the greatly improved Mk.GR3, which had a bit more capability in range. Underconfidence re-asserted itself and after that I never really felt welcome, possibly from age and background against a beginner's ability. There was a field exercise on rough strips in the Hartz Mountains as part of Wildenrath's Taceval. After a site move, I got to fly from a strip at Jagergrund. The aircraft were concealed in woodland shelters, and of course you used short take-off technique on the grass. Recovery was from an obvious initial point along a short approach, coming into the hover over a 70m mat. (RAF Gütersloh was always there as a diversion.) Road cones were placed at each 90 degrees to allow centring up as you descended. It was breathtaking fun, even though I still did not really feel accepted on the squadron. Maybe everyone was a little scared; the Harrier accident rate was worse than that of the German Air Force's F104s.

My last event was a deployment to the weapons ranges at Decimomannu in Sicily. I really felt that it was all coming together until one day I was number four in a four-aircraft range sortie in an aircraft equipped with a practice bomb carrier on one side and a SNEB rocket pod on the other. My SNEB salvo of three rockets scored a direct hit, and I was so delighted that I failed to note that the range pattern was to the right. I broke left as usual, and apparently the Italians in range control got a little overexcited. That was it. The boss grounded me, but if I'm honest, deep down, I was actually quite relieved. The aircraft was very exciting to fly, but not the role nor the squadron. After a while it was accepted that I was undertrained at Chivenor and I was at last posted to the Phantom.

The navy had from an early stage taken an interest in the Harrier as ideal for aircraft carrier work. The Sea Harrier FRS1 was produced with a pulse radar which had very limited use at low level. However, at the same time the ski jump started to be developed at RAE Bedford until the optimum rise of 15 degrees was determined. The launching aircraft would then rotate its nozzles at the start of the ski jump, just like a short field take-off, and then the pilot would gradually transition to normal flight. The Russians and Chinese have deployed fighters to their carriers, and will have discovered that without a variable nozzle the ski jump is worthless and the fighter will experience heavy payload restrictions. The combination of ski jump and vectored thrust on the Sea Harrier and later the RAF's Mk3a was simply a brilliant combination, also incorporated in the F35B. In the Falkands campaign, the navy achieved 20 kills with the Sidewinder AiM9L and gun against the Argentinians with no losses but of course relied on various forms of early warning to get the fighters in the right place at the right time.

The Sea Harrier FRS2 was an ungainly aircraft with a pulse doppler radar, ideal for low-level intercept work. The Harrier itself went on to be developed by the US Marine Corps as the AV8A. It was given a significantly more powerful engine, superb solid-state avionics, more fuel capacity and a large number of weapons stations. Externally you could see that the pilot's seat had been raised allowing excellent visibility. The RAF's GR5 copied the AV8 and at the time of the RAF giving up the Harrier, the GR9 was an excellent war machine. And of course, at the time of publication the similar AV8A Plus is still in service with the US Marine Corps. So why was the very successful Harrier suddenly taken out of service? It was said at the time that the government had to choose between the Harrier and the Tornado. In my very humble opinion, for the same reasons that the RAF was created in 1918, we had to have an ability to strike independently, which only the RAF Tornado could deliver.

CHAPTER 3
THE PHANTOM IN RAF SERVICE

GEORGE

The RAF had a number of false starts in finding a successor to the Canberras and Hunters then in service in the early 1960s. The TSR2 had been the great white hope for a new generation of strike-attack aircraft but was probably a step too far for the technology of the time. Then followed the cancellation of the Hawker P1154 project for a supersonic version of the Harrier in 1964, leaving the RAF with no viable options for the future. However, a decision had been taken to purchase the McDonnell Douglas Phantom II for the Royal Navy as a fleet defence fighter for the carriers HMS *Eagle* and *Ark Royal*, and the RAF decided to piggyback on this procurement to provide a fleet of aircraft, initially in the strike-attack role, then eventually transitioning to air defence when the Jaguar entered service.

The Phantom was, by any measure, the most outstanding aircraft of its generation. It was the first true multi-role combat aircraft, capable of just about anything from air defence to ground attack, nuclear strike, and reconnaissance. It was also deeply flawed in some ways, mostly due to compromises introduced by the Brits, who insisted on modifying a mature and stable design, thereby introducing many unintended consequences which dogged the aircraft throughout its RAF service. The Royal Navy version was to be designated the FG1 and the RAF version the FGR2. The decision to fit a reheated version of the Rolls-Royce Spey engine was necessary to allow the aircraft to operate from the smaller UK carriers. (The reheated Spey had a static thrust of 20,000 lbs compared with the 17,000 lbs of the Pratt and Whitney J79. It also caused turbine failures leading to air defence courses being cancelled).

The Phantom in RAF service.

There was also the political imperative to include as much UK content as possible in order to preserve UK jobs and foreign exchange, and there was a specific need to support Rolls-Royce, which was in the throes of the RB211 engine woes and on the brink of bankruptcy at the time. The Spey engine did have advantages in the low-level strike-attack role where it performed at its best, but at higher levels it tended to run out of puff, and this is where the pure jet J79 excelled. At low level though, the J79 produced an excessive smoke trail which was visible for miles and a dead giveaway for opposing forces. In many ways however the best version of the Phantom in UK service, especially in the air-defence role, was the F4J version. These were surplus US Navy aircraft of which 15 were bought from dry storage in the desert in 1984 and allocated to 74 Squadron.

The Spey was a bypass engine, and the wider cross section necessitated a major redesign of the Phantom fuselage and engine intake. Also, the Spey had never been fitted with a reheat before, and this installation had to be designed and developed from scratch. Although the Spey had better specific fuel consumption, this was offset by increased drag from the wider fuselage and intake cross section. Also, the redesigned fuselage meant that fatigue testing had to be done all over again at considerable cost. As a result, the RAF's F4M (FGR2) would cost twice as much as the equivalent US spec F4D, making the F4M the most expensive and heaviest of all production Phantoms with a £100 million development cost included in the bill.

Reheat light-up times were slow initially at about five seconds – an eternity when you needed extra thrust in a hurry. When the reheat did light it was sometimes accompanied by spectacular engine surges in the early versions. The time between overhauls for the engine was just 150 hours, but in the early years, the Spey failed to make even that, and frequent engine changes were the norm. Rolls-Royce for some time were unable to keep up, resulting in ever more shortages of replacement engines. For a while in 1972, the OCU had to close down so that all available replacement engines could be supplied to the front line. Eventually of course further development made the engine much more reliable and the reheat light-up times were much reduced, but this all took a while.

Much of the avionic fit was UK sourced, and the FGR2 was fitted with a Ferranti INAS. The inertial platform was married to an analogue computer, and there was no moving map display. Nevertheless, the navigation functions worked well enough, but the weapon-aiming functions never did. As a result, all air-to-ground deliveries were made using the fixed sight and a goodly amount of 'seaman's eye'. But the biggest game changer especially for the air-defence role was the inclusion of a version of the AWG-10 Pulse Doppler radar, giving the RAF for the first time a look-down/shoot-down capability. The radar had been modified by Ferranti to AN/ASWG-12 standard to integrate with the F4M systems. It was great when it worked but it had reliability issues in the early days with a minimum time between failures (MTBF) of just four hours. This meant that if we launched a four-aircraft formation, we could pretty much guarantee that one aircraft would land with an unserviceable radar. Things did improve through the life of the aircraft with successive upgrades giving improved performance and reliability.

Hydraulic problems were not uncommon, especially in the early days, and there can be few Phantom pilots who have not had to engage the rotary hydraulic arrester gear (RHAG) due to utilities hydraulic failure at some time in their career which meant we had just emergency accumulator hydraulic pressure for the wheelbrakes. To engage the RHAG, the tailhook was lowered to hook a cable stretched across the runway, a bit like landing on an aircraft carrier. These problems were greatly reduced when the original aluminium hydraulic lines were replaced with stainless steel. Nevertheless, the first hull loss to a UK Phantom was to a 6 Squadron aircraft when a hydraulic problem caused the controls to freeze on final approach. Thankfully the crew ejected without major injury.

All of the above issues meant that the Phantom was hard work for the engineers. I often used to see the night shift coming off duty grey with fatigue having spent the night getting five aircraft ready for the first wave whilst wrestling with engine changes, radar, electrical, and hydraulic problems. At the same time, spares shortages meant that a 'hangar queen' was a semi-permanent fixture, used for robbing spare parts to keep the rest of the squadron flying. By comparison, the Jaguar was conceived a generation later and designed with maintainability in mind. It was so much easier to keep serviceable and much less of a nightmare for the engineers.

But from the aircrew perspective, the Phantom, when it was behaving itself, was terrific. It was big, butch and brutish, and had the raw power that the wonderful little Jaguar could never match. A clean Phantom had close to a one-to-one thrust/weight ratio, although we, as mud movers, seldom if ever flew in that fit. Our standard peacetime configuration would include the two underwing 425-gal tanks, the Vulcan cannon on the centreline station, and a 'carrier bomb light stores' (CBLS) for the four lb practice bombs. This would give about an hour and a half at 420 kts at low level, including some burner use for higher speeds or evasion. Fully loaded, it could carry 12 x 1,000 lb bombs and eight missiles (although with that load you would need a long runway and wouldn't go very far!). Carrying 'dumb' weapons with no terminal guidance meant that much training time had to be spent on weapons ranges dropping practice bombs using the fixed sighting system in order to get reasonable results.

The SUU23 Vulcan cannon was carried on the centreline station. This was a most impressive weapon capable of firing 6,000 rounds per minute of 20mm ammunition which could either be solid ball (for practice), high explosive incendiary (HEI) or armour piercing. The gun pod weighed 780 kg and could carry 1,230 rounds of ammunition, which would give just 12 seconds of continuous fire. Even when firing in short bursts, it could take out a convoy of soft-skinned vehicles in a single pass.

In contrast with today's Typhoon, the handling characteristics were certainly not 'carefree'. In fact, the Phantom would bite hard unless treated with respect. The high wing loading and supersonic wing section meant you had to fly into heavy buffet in any hard turn, where speed would rapidly bleed off even with use of reheat. Maximum turn rate was achieved at 19.2 units angle of attack (AOA), and if that was exceeded, wing rock and departure from controlled flight would result. At high AOA, the aircraft suffered from adverse yaw, and rolling manoeuvres had to be initiated by rudder rather than aileron ("in buffet use the boot" was an easy way to remember). This was counterintuitive for those new to the type. The Phantom was not suited to close combat and turning fights, and the best tactic against low wing loading fighters was to use the aircraft's blistering acceleration to disengage by going vertical, and then, if necessary, come back in for a head-on shot with the radar-controlled Sparrow missile.

ALAN

We must not forget the Spook, a caricature of a ghostly figure that eventually appeared everywhere. He was created by a draughtsman in the St Louis factory and spread worldwide. The USAFE had an F4D at Hopsten covered in boot marks implying

Combined Spook.

that the Spook had the run out of the hangar. In the last days of the Phantom, the Greeks painted a spook all over an F4E which they brought to Fairford. The German Air Force had a more modest version. The Phantom enjoyed enormous affection.

PHANTOM GROUND ATTACK

GEORGE

Near the end of my time in Malta, I received a posting to join No. 3 Course at the recently formed Phantom Operational Conversion Unit at RAF Coningsby. This was very early days in the Phantom's RAF career. The first two courses had formed the core of 6 and 54 Squadrons also at RAF Coningsby, and No. 3 Course was to top up these first two squadrons. But first there would be a Hunter lead-in course, especially for people like me who had never done ground attack before. This was conducted at RAF Chivenor 229 OCU on No. 2 Pre Phantom Course where we were given some instruction on air-to-ground operations in the Hunter T7, flying dual-only sorties to the range with OCU instructors. I did a total of 11 sorties over the course of eight days which included strafe with the Aden cannon, 20-degree dive bombing, SNEB rocket firing and skip bombing at 50 ft. All of this was new to me and great fun, especially skip bombing which was a technique initially developed for the delivery of napalm and required a rapid descent to 50 ft, releasing the practice bomb at the last instant when the target filled the windscreen. This meant that a 'skip hit' could be achieved on just about every pass.

I also remember watching Neil Armstrong making his 'small step for man' onto the surface of the moon on the black and white TV in the officers' mess.

My only other experience of an OCU had been when converting to the Canberra at RAF Bassingbourn. The ethos at Chivenor was markedly different and much more 'gung ho'. Spirited and aggressive flying was encouraged and expected from the would-be fighter pilots on the course. You were urged to fly tactically and keep a sharp lookout even when transiting to and from the range. On one occasion my instructor took control and barrelled in behind an unsuspecting single Hunter who had not seen him coming. "That will teach him to keep a better lookout," he said.

228 OCU RAF CONINGSBY

Just a week after finishing the Pre-Phantom Course I reported to RAF Coningsby on 17 July 1969 to join No. 3 Phantom Course. The Phantom OCU was just getting into its stride, and the course was developing and changing all the time. As originally conceived it would train crews in all three disciplines; ground attack, reconnaissance and air defence, but as time went on it was realised that this was too ambitious and the course evolved into training crews primarily for ground attack. There were still elements of the other two roles involved. We had to know how to use the radar in search, pulse doppler and mapping modes and the basic elements of reconnaissance, target recognition and reporting were covered. The OCU instructor pilots came mostly from the Hunter and Lightning with a few returning from exchange tours in the USA where they had trained US crews on the Phantom. The navigator instructors came from the Javelin, Buccaneer and Canberra. There was a definite buzz around the OCU at the time as the staff were keen and enthusiastic about training new crews to fly the RAF's latest fighter/ bomber, and they brought with them the ethos and culture they were used to from their past experience.

There was a lengthy ground school, where we learned about the Phantom aircraft systems in detail. To train both pilots and navigators in the complexities of the radar there was an air intercept (AI) trainer where intercepts of varying type could be set up. The pilot controlled the aircraft flight path based on instructions from the navigator. The navigator had to control the intercept geometry using the radar display to achieve a firing solution for either the Sparrow semi-active radar missile or the Sidewinder heat-seeking missile. The radar 'B' scope mode was used which displayed target position in range and azimuth displacement and the pilot had a repeater display in the front cockpit. Interpreting the B scope display was not particularly intuitive and took a while to get used to. A typical set up would involve a head-on attack with the Sparrow missile for a '140 with re-attack'. In other words the navigator would arrange a displacement from the target's inbound track to achieve a 140-degree intercept looking to lock up and achieve Sparrow launch at about a 12-mile range, then converting to a rear attack with the Sidewinder. This required some mental gymnastics on the part of the navigator to get the intercept geometry right and the AI trainer was a great facility for teaching this. As ground-attack crews (or mud movers as we were called) there was little operational requirement, but we did need to know how to use the aircraft capabilities for self-defence so none of this was wasted time.

For ground attack, we had to learn about the conventional weapons the Phantom would use and how to deliver them with accuracy. At the time, all our weapons were 'dumb' with no form of terminal guidance so the trick was to achieve an accurate release point in space so that the ballistic trajectory of the bomb would take it to the target. Our main weapon was the 1,000 lb bomb which dated back to World War II. It could be fitted with a retard tail for low-level delivery where the tail section deployed drag fins to slow the bomb after release and allow some separation from the subsequent detonation. The ballistic tail was used for higher level deliveries where the aircraft would be well clear of the bomb's debris zone. For anti-armour attacks we were initially equipped with SNEB rocket pods of which the Phantom could carry four. Each pod could be fired in salvo to cover a big enough area to

Phantom FGR2 SNEB gun.

take out aiming errors. However, the SNEB was soon to be replaced by the BL755 cluster weapon. This was about the same size as a 1,000 lb bomb but contained minelets which would disperse over an area the size of a football pitch and were effective against both armour and personnel. The BL755 was much more tolerant of delivery errors than SNEB.

The FGR2 was fitted with the Ferranti INAS. It was based on a gyro-stabilised platform with accelerometers in all three axes which could provide velocity and position information via an analogue computer. The inertial platform also provided attitude information for the cockpit instruments and to the radar for stabilisation. When first switched on, the inertial platform had to align, sensing earth rate and this would take 12 minutes for a full align during which the aircraft could not be moved. It was possible to do a rapid align in 90 seconds if the platform had previously had a full align and the heading stored. The navigation functions of the INAS worked well and gave a good cockpit readout of groundspeed and drift, but the weapon-aiming functions never worked properly and were not used. As a result, we had to use a reversionary mode for weapon aiming using the fixed sight. The Phantom gunsight display had a reticule with an outer ring of 50 milliradians radius, and an inner segmented circle of 25 milliradians diameter and a pipper or aiming point of 2 milliradians radius. The reticule could be adjusted vertically to different angles of depression for fixed-sight weapon aiming. To set this up before flight we had to refer to various 'gizmos' or charts produced by the weapons instructors. The forecast wind for the point of delivery was plotted on the chart and the appropriate fixed sight depression read off from the 'gizmo' as well as the expected drift left or right. Most deliveries for bombs were either level (laydown) or from 10-degree dive. For a level delivery the aircraft had to be stabilised at the exact height and speed and when the target was sighted, adjusted left or right by the calculated offset to account for drift. The bomb release was pressed exactly when the pipper passed abeam the base of the target. Flying a dive attack was harder because you had to judge the flightpath so as to arrive at the correct height at bomb release.

Fixed-sight bombing was a bit of a black art and required constant practice, so a lot of training time was spent at weapons ranges. With time and practice a good crew could achieve about a 35-ft circular error probability (CEP) for ten-degree bombing attacks. Modern attack aircraft with state-of-the-art systems can achieve direct hits on every pass. That is how much accuracy has improved over 60 years. Lack of accuracy in weapon delivery was compensated by dropping multiple weapons in a stick and using high-yield weapons to achieve lethal damage even from a close miss. Collateral damage would therefore be inevitable when attacking small targets and that is no longer acceptable in today's environment. Remember this was way before the time of asymmetric warfare where an enemy would be embedded in and indistinguishable from the local civilian population. That would require a degree of precision that only smart weapons could provide years later. The FGR2 was for its time state of the art but demanded a lot from the crew.

I did however have to get up to speed quickly with battle formation. In my previous role of reconnaissance, we always operated as singletons, but mud movers always operate in tactical formations of two or four aircraft or more. This is because a large target would require more ordnance than a single aircraft could carry, and battle formation also provided the opportunity for mutual support when penetrating defended areas. The basic battle formation involved two pairs flying abeam at a spacing of about 1,000 metres, which allowed each pair to provide visual cover for the other and especially to clear their six-o-clock position for any threat. Crossover turns were required for large changes of heading where the pair on the outside would start the turn first and the two pairs would swap sides. A later development introduced the 'card' formation with the lead pair in front in wide battle and the second pair in trail about 1,500 metres behind. Any interceptor rolling in behind the first pair would then be sandwiched between the two pairs. Managing a large formation as leader was a challenge and required a lot of practice. The squadrons had their own work-up programmes for pairs and fours leaders, and it took time to get to a reasonable standard.

We did some basic air combat manoeuvring on the course and quickly learned about the Phantom's handling characteristics when flown at the limit. As mentioned before, the aircraft had a high wing loading, and best turn performance was achieved at 19.2 units angle of attack and in the buffet where speed would bleed off very quickly even when using burner. Roll control had to be initiated with rudder (in buffet use boots) which was counterintuitive at first. Modern generation fighters have 'carefree handling' where control inputs are mediated by a digital flight control computer. There was no such technology available in the Phantom and the only flight control computer was the one between the pilot's ears.

Whilst on the course we had a visit from a MacDonnell Douglas sales rep who had just visited the Israeli Air Force, which had also just received the Phantom. This was of course just two years on from the 1967 war, where the Israelis had achieved complete dominance over their Arab neighbours, so we were interested to hear about the Israeli Air Force and how they were adapting to the Phantom. He said that their culture was completely different to that of the RAF or USAF. Our selection systems still required potential recruits to have suitable officer qualities and a potential candidate could fail at that stage if there was no indication of officer potential. On the other hand, the Israeli Air Force would be happy to recruit a young blood from the streets of Tel Aviv with a black leather jacket and a motor bike provided he had the motor skills and aggression to make a fighter pilot, and they had no shortage of recruits.

The OCU staff were all senior people, and many had already been promoted to squadron leader, so the OCU felt a bit 'top heavy' and many of the original OCU staff went on to the higher ranks. I did my first three flights in the Phantom with Sqn Ldr Kip Kemball, a charming man and a very good instructor who sent me solo in the aircraft. My initial weapons trips were with (then) Flt Lt Trevor Nattrass, a dynamic little fighter pilot who had recently returned from an exchange with the USAF on the Phantom. He was a very good weaponeer and taught me a lot. We worked together later as flight commanders on the same squadron, and he eventually retired years later as an air commodore. Looking through my logbook, the OCU course was divided into a number of phases, including aircraft conversion, weapons delivery (level and dive bombing, strafe, SNEB), an air defence phase and a reconnaissance phase, so the emphasis was still multi role and had not yet adjusted to a pure ground-attack focus.

The first real public showing of the new Phantom came on 1 July 1969 when the OCU and the newly formed 6 Squadron joined forces to mount a nine-ship flypast for the investiture of the Prince of Wales at Caernarvon Castle. The flypast went well and on time in some marginal weather.

No. 3 Phantom Course had always been intended as a top up for the two existing Phantom squadrons at RAF Coningsby, 54 and 6. By the end of 1969 after a period of six months I had reached the end of the OCU and was duly posted to 54 Squadron at a point where I still had a lot to learn about the aircraft and its role.

NO. 54 SQUADRON AND AAR

I joined 54 Squadron on 5 January 1970. It was just a short walk from the OCU to 54 who shared a building with 6 Squadron. Flying started straight away with a dual check with the squadron QFI, then straight into air-to-air refuelling training as the squadron was due to deploy to RAF Akrotiri in Cyprus for its annual armament practice camp. After just three daytime air-to-air refuelling (AAR) sorties plus one at night I was declared AAR qualified and duly set off on 3 February as No. 2 to the boss, to fly direct to Akrotiri with one refuelling bracket in the South of France. The boss went in first and made contact straight away, then it was my turn and I missed the first two contacts. The pressure was now on with the end of the refuelling bracket fast approaching, but I got in on my third attempt and with much relief we carried on to RAF Akrotiri.

Air-to-air refuelling in the Phantom could be tricky. The reheated Spey engines gave it an aft centre of gravity compared to the US versions which made the aircraft sensitive in pitch. We usually refuelled from the wing hoses on the Victor K2 tanker, and the correct technique was to formate on the tanker wing and ignore the drogue once lined up about six feet back. The navigator had a good view of the drogue from the back seat and he had to talk the pilot through the final approach with calls like, "left a bit," "right a bit," "you are about one ft low," etc., meanwhile the pilot eased forward until contact was made, and continued to push the hose forward a bit to start the flow of fuel. It was all quite straightforward in smooth clear air, but in turbulence or in cloud it could get quite exciting. If the hose or the basket started to whip around in bumpy conditions, you had to concentrate hard on maintaining position whilst ignoring the gyrations of the drogue. Once things settled down you could once again advance until contact was made. In my experience over a number of years refuelling from Victors, the tanker crews were always brilliant. They could see us jousting with the basket through an optical sight. On one occasion after watching a few near misses in turbulence, some wag in the Victor said, "Would it help if we put some hair around it?"

Unlikely formation of Victor, Lightning and Phantom.

During our stay at Akrotiri we managed to get a unique picture of a combined formation with 54, 55, 56, and 57 Squadrons all together at the same time. We had a busy but productive two weeks at Akrotiri doing bombing, rocketing and strafe on the bombing range at Larnaca. That bombing range no longer exists as it was hastily converted to a major international airport after the Turkish invasion in 1974 precluded use of Nicosia airport. 54 Squadron have a 'thing' about piano smashing which dates back to their time as a Battle of Britain fighter squadron in World War II, so we had taken an old piano in the transport aircraft to Akrotiri which was duly despatched in style at the end of the detachment and the remnants burned in the car park. There was an anxious moment when we thought the fire might spread to the adjacent officers' mess, but the fire service arrived in time to stop any further silliness. We flew back to Coningsby taking 5 hrs 15 mins again using AAR.

Our next deployment was in May 1970. This was Exercise Bersatu Padu. This was to demonstrate a capability to reinforce Singapore, if necessary, after the withdrawal of UK forces in 1971. It was a big exercise involving forces from UK, Australia, New Zealand and Malaysia. 54 Squadron would deploy using AAR and four of the aircraft were tasked to deploy non-stop using AAR on a flight which would last about 14 hours. This would be the longest AAR flight to date for the UK Phantoms and additional trials were conducted to check the feasibility and ensure that the Spey engines would cope with such a long flight without topping up their oil. The lucky four crews were subjected to a 14-hour circumnavigation round the UK using AAR to confirm that a trip of this duration was feasible, not least regarding the physiological needs of the crews. The latter was satisfied by issuing 'piddle packs' to the crews which contained a compressed sponge for absorbing urine. In the event the deployment went well, and the non-stop crews established (albeit briefly) a new record for the UK-Singapore flight. I flew out in relative comfort in the back of a VC10 but had my turn on the way back with a 6 hr 50 min AAR sector from Singapore to Masirah.

NO. 54 SQUADRON
EXERCISE BERSATU PADU

Before the exercise flying started we all had to do a two-day jungle survival course at Kota Tinggi on the Malaysian peninsula. Survival in the jungle would not have been a problem (apart from biting insects and creepy crawlies) and there was plenty of food and water available. However, the primary rainforest canopy was high up and pretty solid, so getting down from a parachute descent and also being picked up by helicopter would have been a problem. Fortunately, the occasion did not arise during our time there. The main exercise entitled Exercise Granada involved us doing a number of no-notice sorties into Malaysia mostly involving forward air controllers (FAC). We had a quick liaison visit to RAAF Butterworth to say hello to an Australian detachment. We also had to get used to the local weather as Singapore usually had a heavy thunderstorm mid-afternoon resulting in a temporary flooded runway at RAF Tengah. It was all very good experience and we enjoyed the visit.

By this time the RAF Germany Phantom squadrons had started to build up, and crews were shuttled around to spread the experience. Accordingly, I received a posting to 17 Squadron at RAF Brüggen in Germany and reported there on 30 September 1970 to commence what would be a four-year stint at RAF Brüggen.

NO. 17 SQUADRON

17 Squadron had been running with the Phantom for a few months, and it already had some stellar names who would go on to much bigger things. The boss was Wing Commander Paddy Hine (later to become Air Chief Marshal Sir Patrick, CinC Strike Command), the pilot flight commander was Squadron Leader Bill Wratten (later to become Air Chief Marshal Sir William, CinC Strike Command). RAF Brüggen was still building up its Phantom force with 17 and 14 Squadrons already established.

17 Squadron Phantom.

Bill Wratten did my QFI check when I first arrived, then followed a short theatre conversion course to get new arrivals used to operations in RAF Germany.

RAF Brüggen was very much on the front line of the Cold War and together with Laarbruch and Wildenrath, formed what was known as the Clutch bases close to the Dutch border. Much further forward was RAF Gütersloh, home to a Lightning Squadron and later Harrier GR3s. At the time, Germany was divided by the Inner German Border, a 1,300-km fortified border that divided West Germany from the

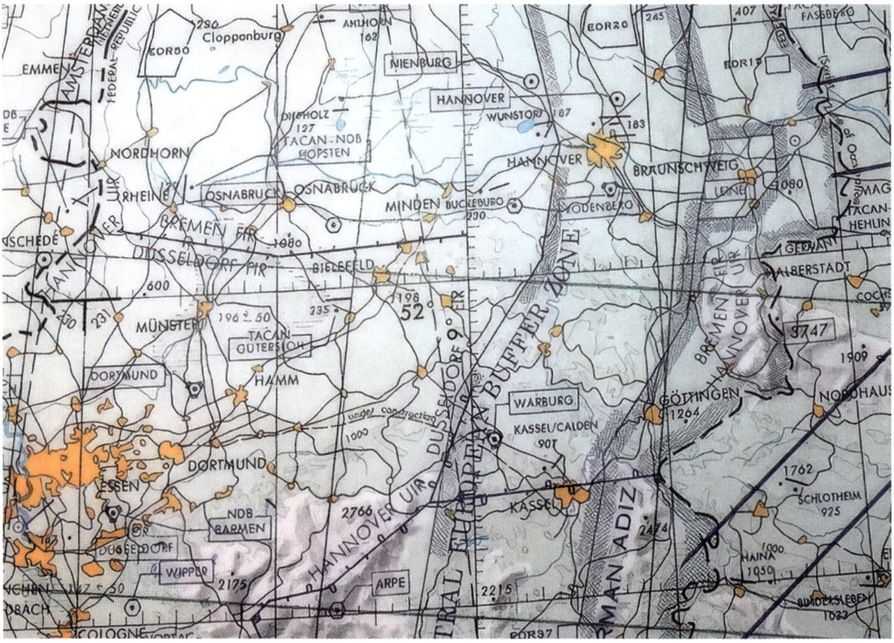

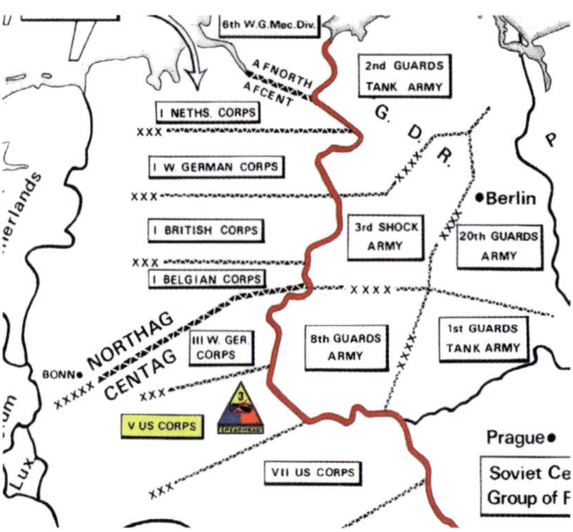

Above: Division of airspace near the Inner German Border.

Left: North Germany Military Airspace.

GDR. This line of demarcation also represented the division between NATO forces to the West, and Warsaw Pact forces to the East. We were conscious that NATO forces in this area were outnumbered three to one by the Warsaw Pact. Each NATO nation was allocated a section of the IGB, and for the Brits this roughly stretched from Hannover in the north to Gottingen in the south. Facing No. 1 British Corps was the Russian 3rd Shock Army backed up by the 20th Guards Army further east. Air operations in the German Air Defence Identification Zone (ADIZ) were prohibited and there were operational restrictions in the adjacent Buffer Zone.

The Brüggen squadrons were assigned to NATO's Second Allied Tactical Air Force (2ATAF) in the northern half of West Germany and 4ATAF in the southern half was mostly American and West German units. Low-flying training was conducted throughout NATO airspace in Germany, Netherlands and Belgium and could be flown at 250 ft AGL in specified low-flying areas. Our main weapons range was at Nordhorn, about 90 miles to the north-east. To access the low-flying areas to the north, we had first to transit to a crossing point on the Rhine under the control of 'clutch radar', which was co-located with Düsseldorf air traffic control (ATC). The North German Plain was our 'happy hunting ground' where we practised hard, finding and simulating attacks on targets and practising evasion against 'bounce' aircraft sent to test our lookout and tactics. I used to feel some sympathy for the German civilians in rural villages who had to put up with the noise of manoeuvring Phantoms in full reheat. Our usual training profile would involve a four-ship sortie with two or three simulated attacks on field targets followed by practice weapons deliveries on Nordhorn range whilst maintaining an accurate time on target at the range. It was hard work and demanding flying, especially in the often-marginal weather and poor visibility conditions in northern Europe.

THE NUCLEAR STRIKE ROLE

As aircrew we had to come to terms with our role as part of the NATO nuclear deterrent. We had to accept that if the time ever came, we would be required to deliver a tactical nuclear weapon of many times the power of the Hiroshima bomb to halt the advance of the Warsaw Pact with its overwhelming numerical superiority.

The Brüggen squadrons were assigned to NATO in the conventional attack and nuclear-strike roles. In the strike role, we were equipped with an American tactical nuclear freefall weapon which was maintained under strict US control. Each squadron had to maintain an aircraft fully armed at 15 minutes readiness to launch 24/7. These were the quick reaction alert (QRA) aircraft housed in revetments with an adjacent ready room for the crews. This was before the hardening programme had commenced to provide hardened aircraft shelters at RAF Brüggen. The weapon had a programmable yield depending on the target but could have up to a 130-kiloton yield which was about ten times the yield of the Hiroshima bomb, so although classified as 'tactical' they were seriously powerful weapons.

The nuclear-strike role introduced a whole new dimension for aircrew training. The delivery methods depended on whether a ground burst or an air burst was required. For a ground burst the aircraft would deliver the bomb in a low-level 'laydown' attack, overflying the target with a timed detonation allowing the aircraft to escape the blast zone. An alternative delivery involved releasing the bomb in a toss manoeuvre for an airburst. We practised both delivery methods at the local bombing ranges. The QRA aircraft were housed within a 'no lone zone'. This was a circular area around the armed aircraft guarded by a couple of US armed guards. Aircrew or engineers could only access the no lone zone in pairs to ensure that no single person could sabotage or interfere with the weapon. This rule was strictly enforced, and the US guards were instructed to shoot to kill in the event of any breach of these rules. This brought home to us all the very serious nature of nuclear-strike operations.

We were also now subject to the full force of the NATO Tactical Evaluation or TACEVAL. This was the annual operational evaluation to ensure that the squadron could meet stringent operational criteria. It would usually be triggered in the early hours by sounding the station 'hooter', a loud siren that could be heard from miles away. All personnel had to report to their place of duty and phase one involved the generation of serviceable combat-ready aircraft suitably armed and ready for war. There would inevitably be one or more aircraft on deep maintenance but generation of at least 80 per cent of the aircraft establishment was expected. Then followed phase two which was the flying phase. This would normally take the form of a conventional phase where our weapons capability was demonstrated on the range. The scenarios always assumed that however good our front-line forces were, they would eventually be pushed back by the overwhelming numerical superiority of the Warsaw Pact. There would follow a selective nuclear release 'S-hour' where tactical nukes would be used to slow or stop the Warsaw Pact advance. However, once the nuclear genie was out of the bottle, further escalation would be inevitable and 'R-hour' would follow, that is the general release of nuclear weapons – a truly horrifying prospect.

Those of us standing so close to the prospect became convinced that this would never happen for real. We were fully aware of the realities and felt that this no-win situation would never be embarked upon by any sane government on either side.

The whole gamble was on the deterrent effect of nuclear weapons giving 'mutually assured destruction', and it appeared to work in practice. Right through to the end of the Cold War there were people like us on standby waiting with our fingers on the trigger. This is something the general public nowadays have never experienced or perhaps have suppressed, and it is sometimes useful to be reminded by the Cold War warriors what it was really like back in the day.

BECOMING AN IRE

Early on in my time with 17 Squadron I was sent back to Coningsby to do the IRE course. Before doing this, I had to be checked out to fly the F4 twin-stick aircraft from the back seat. This was challenging at first because the view forward from the back seat was quite restricted. I had been an IRE before on the Canberra, so I was used to the job and what it entailed. It was to put squadron pilots through their annual instrument rating renewal test. This meant witnessing their flying on instruments to ensure they could operate smoothly and accurately to the limits of their rating – normally a Green or Master Green rating allowing approaches down to about a 200 ft cloud base in 600 m visibility. Over the course of two weeks, which included classroom work and some ten flights with OCU instructors, I was passed as an IRE and returned to Brüggen. Ironically one of my first candidates for instrument rating renewal was my immediate boss and flight commander Sqn Ldr Wratten. I was later made the 'Command IRE', responsible for rating all the other Phantom IREs in RAF Germany.

There were only a limited number of married quarters at Brüggen and there were none available for us new arrivals when we first got there, so we all had to look for private accommodation locally. The nearest large town to Brüggen was the Dutch town of Roermond just over the border. A new estate of social housing had just been built called the Donderberg on the east side of the town. These were rows of identical town houses on three levels. They were excellent houses and I am eternally grateful to the Dutch for allowing us Brits to rent them. They were unfurnished and we had to find our own floor coverings and furniture, but we were very happy there for the next year or so until a quarter at Brüggen became available.

The commander-in-chief RAF Germany and commander of 2ATAF was Sir Christopher Foxley Norris. He was a distinguished ex-Battle of Britain fighter pilot and a great character. His tour of duty was coming to an end and our boss, Paddy Hine, decided that a 2ATAF flypast over his Rheindahlen headquarters was called for. He duly organised a formation consisting of an RAF Brüggen nine-ship followed by formations of German and Dutch F104s. I was nominated as 'whipper in', in other words as singleton responsible for ensuring that the formations were well spaced and symmetrical. Paddy Hine was a very experienced formation leader and had previously led the team who had performed a loop with 21 Hunters at the Farnborough Air Show. The flypast went well on the day and was followed up with a formal lunch for the air chief marshal and his wife at RAF Brüggen. I particularly remember that Lady Foxley Norris, a tall and stately woman, took a full part with the boys in the schooner races (i.e. a beer drinking race) which followed the meal.

NO. 31 SQUADRON

After about a year on 17 Squadron I was told that I was to be promoted to squadron leader. I was both delighted and surprised as this had come much sooner than expected, but the question was what would happen next – a move away from Brüggen, when I had so recently settled the family into our rented house in Roermond? My boss, Wg Cdr Hine, intervened on my behalf. The last Phantom Squadron at Brüggen was about to form as 31 Squadron and he proposed that I be the pilot flight commander. This was a daunting prospect for me, but I was duly posted to 31 Squadron in July 1971.

My new boss as OC 31 Squadron was Wing Commander Chris Sprent. Chris had just completed a very successful tour in the MoD at air plans and was clearly a very capable staff officer. Prior to that he had been the boss of Aberdeen University Air Squadron, so he was about five years from his last operational tour. He had however completed flying refresher and the Phantom OCU and was keen to start his new command. There were three flight commanders, myself and two navigators. One of these had come from the Javelin and the other had a SpecN qualification which meant that he had a sound background in navigation technology and knew all about inertial nav systems, Schuler loops etc. The rest of the aircrew had a mixed bag of experience. But there was a big hill to climb and the other two Phantom squadrons at Brüggen had a head start. I had to organise a full theatre conversion for the new crews and most importantly introduce them to their new nuclear-strike role.

As part of the work up we had to prepare for our reformation parade on 6 October 1972. This would be a full squadron parade with the CinC RAF Germany Air Marshal Sir Harold Martin as reviewing officer. The CinC 'Mickey' Martin famously had been on the Dambuster Raid with Guy Gibson. There would be two flypasts, the first when the CinC reached the saluting base and the second as the parade took the general salute prior to the march off. Both had to be timed to the second and we had one rehearsal planned. I had the lead of our four-ship formation, and we entered a holding pattern out of sight at 420 kts adjusting our orbit as required. The time from the CinC leaving his car to reaching the saluting base we had calculated as 23 seconds and at that point we would be committed to the final run in. On the day, the CinC took exactly 23 seconds, and we passed over as he raised his hand to salute. We then held off to the south to complete the second flypast when the boss called the general salute which worked out to the second, and I finished with a pull up to the vertical in full burner whilst the others went left and right. I have ever since felt for any leader of a flypast and especially on major national events knowing how stressful those occasions can be. Achieving a fixed time on target is easy enough, but coordinating an arrival time with a parade of variable duration is another matter.

As soon as we were all qualified in the nuclear-strike role we had to place one of our aircraft on QRA with a combat-ready crew on 15 mins standby duty for a 24-hour period every day. This was a big commitment as we were already short of crews. The whole UK Phantom force reached a bit of a crisis in late 1971. Rolls-

Reformation flypast.

Royce simply could not keep up with the supply issues on the reheated Spey engine. With all the planned Phantom squadrons now up and running, it was decided to scale down 228 OCU at Coningsby and allocate all replacement engines to the front line, and at the same time reallocate all OCU staff to the squadrons. As a result, we inherited Trevor Natrass as our qualified weapons instructor (QWI) and Mike Flynn as our QFI. We also picked up Bill Freeman who had been the unit test pilot at RAF Aldergrove responsible for accepting all new UK Phantoms from transatlantic delivery by McDonnell Douglas. As all UK deliveries were now complete, Bill's job became redundant and we were glad to have him. Bill was the oldest pilot on the squadron at the age of 45 and took in good part a lot of 'grandad'-type ribbing from the young bloods. Someone decided it would be a good laugh for him to fly with our youngest navigator Jim Stuttard who was exactly half Bill's age, and Bill was duly brought out to the aircraft in a wheelchair! These were very non-pc times, and such merry japes would be frowned upon today. In fact, things have changed quite dramatically, and it can now take eight years from joining for a new pilot to reach the front line, so first tourists can now be in their late 20s or early 30s when they arrive on their first squadron.

We still had to achieve top marks in the annual TACEVAL and to achieve this the station commander would organise regular MINIVALs to practise the essential elements of the TACEVAL. This was supplemented by the occasional MAXEVAL organised by RAFG. This was all designed to keep us on our toes and ensure that when the real TACEVAL arrived we always got top marks as nothing less would do. RAF fighter squadrons are always fiercely competitive, and with no hot wars to test our capabilities, we were judged on how well we did on exercises and competitions. One such was the Salmond Trophy which was competed for annually by all strike-attack squadrons in RAF Germany. It involved finding and overflying a small target at a precise time on target (TOT), somewhere in the low-flying area then proceeding to the range for a series of weapon deliveries. We won the Salmond Trophy in June 1972 much to everyone's surprise. The hot favourites to win had been 14 Squadron at Brüggen who had a very strong team, but they got disqualified at the last minute due to a technicality, and because we were second, we won the trophy. This was not the best way of winning, but it still meant that we were better than all the other strike-attack squadrons in RAFG, Phantoms, Buccaneers, and Harriers, so it was quite an achievement for us as the new kids on the block.

In September 1972 Brüggen decided to field a team at the NATO Tactical Weapons Meet at Florennes in Belgium. The team was to be led by Wing Commander Derek

Bryant OC 14 Squadron, with me as his deputy. Crews across the three Phantom squadrons had to compete for places on the team. At Florennes we had an intensive ten days of flying and socialising with F4 crews from the USAF, F104 pilots from Germany and Holland, three and five Mirage pilots from France and Belgium. The flight profiles tested navigation and timing accuracy as well as weapons deliveries on bombing ranges. It was not officially a competition, but we all wanted to ensure that the collective scores of the 2ATAF teams beat those of 4ATAF. It was neck and neck until the final day when Flt Lt Paul Day of 14 Squadron came up with a spectacular score on the range, including an 80 per cent strafe score which was almost unheard of for the Vulcan gun. Paul went on to spend many years as an instructor at RAF Coningsby and also to fly with the Battle of Britain Memorial Flight where he built up a record number of hours in the Spitfire.

We had our first armament practice camp at the NATO base of Decimomannu in Sardinia in March 1972. Decimomannu or Deci for short was an Italian Air Force base situated about ten miles north of Cagliari on the island of Sardinia. It was the base used by many NATO squadrons who would spend a couple of weeks there to use the bombing range at Cape Frasca on the west side of the island. We would deploy with the whole squadron, aircrew, engineers, spares, tools, equipment and the whole caboodle, transported to and from by RAF Hercules aircraft. We even managed to persuade them to take out an old VW beetle belonging to one of our pilots and painted in squadron colours. It was our one opportunity of the year to have an intensive period of weapons training at a location with (usually) good weather conditions. We practised delivery of the ten-degree attacks using the four lb practice bomb to simulate the 1,000 lb retarded bomb and increasingly toss deliveries of the 28 lb practice bomb to simulate a nuclear delivery. The SNEB rocket pod was still our main anti-armour weapon and finally the SUU23 Vulcan cannon for strafe. There was always a sweepstake for who would get the best weapon scores which I won on this occasion, much to the annoyance of our QWI Trevor Nattrass who had originally taught me weapons delivery on the Phantom on the OCU at Coningsby. He got his revenge later of course. I also won the moustache-growing competition, so I had a good detachment overall.

My navigator throughout most of my time on 31 Squadron was Alan Evans. Alan was a quiet-natured and endlessly patient Welshman. He and his wife always fully supported social events, although Alan would often retire to the anteroom to read the papers when it all got too much. His wife taught me the words of the Welsh folk song Sosban Fach in a phonetic form of English. The social life at Deci revolved around lots of beer and singing songs which in today's world would be considered highly inappropriate and non-PC. The RAF Brüggen song was an adapted version of a German World War II marching song called 'The Flag'. It went like this:

The flag flies high at the masthead, we'll fight for the freedom of the Reich
No longer will we tremble 'gainst England's military might
So give to me your hand Fraulein, your lily-white hand Fraulein
For tonight we march against England
England, England's island shores, island shores, island shores

And if I fall in battle or sink to the bottom of the sea (big splash)
Remember this my Fraulein my blood was shed for thee
So give to me your hand Fraulein, your lily-white hand Fraulein
For tonight we march against England
England, England's island shores, island shores, island shores

This was sung with great gusto especially if our German allies were present. There was a loud exclamation of "Sieg Heil" at the end of each verse. Like I said, very non-PC.

By the time the glee club had finished, my navigator Alan Evans very sensibly had usually retired to bed, but undeterred, the glee club would head to his bedroom for a final goodnight rendition of Sosban Fach. I don't know how the poor chap put up with us with such good grace.

PRE-PLANNED TARGETS

We had pre-planned targets for both conventional and nuclear attacks. Our counter air target was the Soviet air base at Cottbus, some 50 miles south-east of Berlin. At the time Cottbus was equipped with the MiG21 fighter and the MiG23b fighter bomber and was in effect the Warsaw Pact equivalent of Brüggen. Our main weapon for counter air was the 1,000 lb bomb which for a low-level delivery was fitted with a retard tail. In this configuration it would not have the terminal velocity to penetrate a hard target. Trevor Nattrass came up with an alternative attack profile using the toss manoeuvre and the ballistic 1,000 lb bomb which had the necessary penetration, and which avoided a direct overflight of this well-defended target. The 1,000 lb bomb could be fitted with a variety of fuses for air burst, ground burst or delays of various lengths and would have been very effective at disrupting operations in the target airfield. Our weapons training increasingly focussed on the toss manoeuvre. This commenced at four miles from the target with a four g pull to a 45-degree pitch angle with bomb release by a timer. Then followed an escape manoeuvre back to low level.

NATO SQUADRON EXCHANGES

During my time on 31 Squadron, we had several NATO squadron exchanges, two with German Air Force F104 squadrons and one with the Canadians with their CF104s. For these exchanges we would split the squadron in half; one half would go to visit the exchange squadron at their base. The other half remained at Brüggen to host the visitors where we had a busy social programme to keep them entertained. It was always interesting to see how the other half lived. The German guys all spoke very good English as they had all done some training in the USA. They would generally be posted to a particular base, for example JG33 at Buchel, and remain there for their full flying career, unlike the Brits who got moved around every three years.

WINTER SURVIVAL TRAINING

Every theatre of operations for the RAF had a survival training programme appropriate to its climate and for Brüggen it was the winter survival school at Bad Kohlgrub in Bavaria. I attended with one of our squadron navigators, and there were aircrew from all over RAF Germany and from the UK. The first week consisted of ski training and some lectures on combat survival, escape and evasion and resistance to interrogation. The ski training was very good, but the instructors (all local Germans) took no prisoners. One of our group that was fairly new to skiing started to lose an edge on a long traverse. As he started to point more and more downhill gathering speed all the time, the only words of advice from our instructor were "auf wiedersehen". Ski training was designed to improve our fitness and provide some light relief before the second week where we had to survive for three days before undertaking the escape and evasion phase.

The weather conditions were dry but bitterly cold and we were in deep snow. We were operating as a two-man crew and had the contents of our ejection seat survival packs, a parachute, and dinghies. The principles of survival universally taught in RAF survival courses are protection (to gain protection from the elements in the first instance), location (to establish comms with the search-and-rescue services if appropriate at the time), water (to keep hydrated) and food (the last priority but important in the long term). To create some rudimentary shelter, we could use the parachute as a tent supported on a tree branch and using the partially inflated dinghy for insulation from the ground. For location we had a personal locator beacon which an SAR helicopter could home in on, and some mini flares for attracting attention, however none of this would likely be of much use if we had ejected in enemy territory. The next priority was water, and we were surrounded by the stuff in the form of snow, but we had to find a way of melting and ideally boiling it to sterilise it. This meant gathering firewood and starting a fire – easier said than done in these conditions. The third priority was food. We had snares for catching rabbits and fishhooks for catching fish, but we were either too squeamish or not hungry enough to be bothered.

After three days of survival came the escape and evasion phase. We were given a rendezvous point about ten miles away and had to get there by a certain time. Meanwhile there were German ski troops with dogs looking for us, so the odds were stacked against us. But the intention was that we should get caught anyway and experience the next phase which was resistance to interrogation. This was treated as useful training for skilled army interrogators. We were instructed only to state our name rank and serial number but of course the interrogators were not going to settle for that. They would attempt to wear us down with lack of sleep and fatigue, using stress positions like wall standing with a hood over our head and white noise to disorientate. This was much like the techniques then being used with IRA captives in Northern Ireland. But at least we knew it would not last and that the exercise would soon be brought to an end. It was all good experience, some would say a bit like practice bleeding, and we definitely had to pay for our week's enjoyment at ski training.

MISSILE PRACTICE CAMP

Practice firing of these very expensive missiles was very limited, and if you were lucky, you might get one live firing during a three-year tour of duty. My chance came when I led a 31 Squadron team to RAF Valley to fire a Sparrow and a Sidewinder missile on the Aberporth range in North Wales. The Strike Command Air-to-Air Missile Establishment (STCAAME) hosted visiting squadrons at RAF Valley and liaised directly with the range at Aberporth in Cardigan Bay, who in turn provided Jindivik drone aircraft as targets. These sessions were run for both crew training and trials, so they had a dual function. The Sparrow missile was fitted with telemetry equipment to feed back data about the firing.

The whole experience not only provided valuable experience for the aircrew but also for our groundcrew and armourers. We had to cope with the vagaries of

Sparrow firing November 1973.

the weather which caused many delays during our time at Valley. The airfield at Aberporth where the Jindivik drones were based was oriented north-south at right angles to the prevailing westerly winds and was subject to frequent closure due to low cloud. We did eventually get our missiles away successfully on 10 October, and it was a huge privilege for me to squeeze the trigger and watch my Sparrow missile perform like it was supposed to, shooting off at up to three times the speed of sound towards the target. It did not have a live warhead so the Jindivik drone (usually) survived, and telemetry would later tell the result.

During my time at Valley the Yom Kippur war in the Middle East started. I watched the reports on TV fascinated, as the Israelis desperately countered Syrian thrusts in the Golan heights using their recently acquired Phantoms in an anti-armour role. The Phantoms were superbly flown by their Israeli crews and were pivotal in turning the tide at a crucial stage. Whilst we were practising at Valley, the Israelis were doing it for real and fighting for survival.

ACCIDENTS AND INCIDENTS

Sadly, we had two major accidents during my time on 31 Squadron. The first of these happened during TACEVAL on 26 June 1973. We had a busy day flying under scrutiny of the TACEVAL team and all had gone well so far. We were tasked with a night sortie to the Vliehors range in Holland to deliver a simulated nuclear attack via a toss manoeuvre with a time on target of plus or minus five seconds tolerance. The task was given to Hugh Kennedy and his navigator Sqn Ldr Dave Hodges. They had spent the day on standby in the Brüggen ops centre whilst the rest of us flew the attack missions. Their sortie would involve a night transit to Vliehors at 800 ft using the mapping radar. The range is on the western end of Vliehors island and entry to the range involves transiting the Ijsselmeer and crossing the breakwater which carries the A7 road. Timing for the toss manoeuvre starts from here and the Phantom should already have accelerated from its transit speed of 360 kts to the delivery speed 500 kts at a height of 250 ft. During this transition the aircraft descended into the sea and both crew members were killed. After much examination of the circumstances, it seems the most likely cause was pilot disorientation. The rapid acceleration using burner could have created a false vertical giving the impression that the aircraft was climbing. Add to that the hazy night conditions and a lack of a clear horizon and disorientation was a clear possibility. We had all done similar deliveries at Vliehors before, so the situation was not new to the crew. The mission was incomplete, so my nav Alan Evans and I volunteered to do the same profile again the following night. This passed without incident and our bomb was delivered on time.

The second accident occurred on 11 October 1974 when one of our aircraft departed from the westerly runway at Brüggen and the wings folded when the aircraft got airborne. Both crew members ejected successfully, and both survived. This was a good example of what Professor James Reason later described as the Swiss cheese model of accidents where the holes on successive layers of defence line up to allow the accident vector to reach a conclusion. The Phantom was originally conceived as a fleet defence fighter and as such had hinges which allowed the outer-wing panels to fold using hydraulics for parking on a carrier. The RAF Phantoms were never going to be used on carriers (although the RN Phantoms were) so the hydraulic wing fold was removed from the FGR2 and crucially, the warning lights which would indicate when the wings were unlocked were also removed. Our engineers would still fold the wings to create more parking space in the hangar, but this was now done manually. When the aircraft were put back on the line, the wings were spread manually and a locking bolt wound down to secure the wings in place. When the wings were unlocked, the only indication for the crew was a small portion of the locking bolt which protruded from the top surface of the wing and was painted red. This red portion could often be covered in grease and grime making it less visible. The crew were allocated the aircraft at a late stage and probably in a rush, failed to notice the tell-tale red portion of the locking bolt during walk round. It was also missed by the runway caravan who do a last-minute check of the aircraft before take-off. As the aircraft got airborne, the outer wings folded and the aircraft pitched up.

Unable to control the pitch up, the crew ejected successfully. After a short stay in Wegberg Hospital to check for possible spinal injury, they were both declared fit. I still look back with regret at both these incidents wondering what could have been done differently, but hindsight is a wonderful thing. In the first accident I lost two good friends and in the second a young man was unfairly accused of not doing his checks properly when circumstances conspired against him.

This third incident had a much happier outcome although that was not what we thought at the time. It did not result in an accident but terminated a promising career prematurely. Mike Jones was a first tour pilot on 31 Squadron who was doing well and was very popular with his peers. His annual medical turned up a possible heart condition which meant that he lost his medical category. Mike was devastated and decided to leave the RAF to start afresh. He went back to his native Scotland and did a degree in law. He was called to the bar in 1977 becoming a Scottish advocate and later a QC. His stellar legal career continued, and he became a senior partner in his law firm in 2008. He later became an appeal court judge and as Lord Jones was a Scottish Senator of the College of Justice. Sadly, he died suddenly before his time in 2016. I and two of his old 31 Squadron mates attended his funeral.

31 Squadron F4s.

END OF TOUR

My time on 31 Squadron came to an end in November 1974. In fact, the era of mud moving in the Phantom was also ending as the Jaguar came into service and started taking over the strike-attack role, leaving the Phantom to take over from the Lightning in air defence. We moved back to Edinburgh and bought a flat there. Our eldest daughter had started as a boarder at St George's School for Girls in Edinburgh and our younger daughter was due to follow soon. Being Edinburgh based for a bit would mean being closer to our girls and stabilise our home life. I already knew that my next move would be to the RAF Staff College in Bracknell and that I would have to commute back to Scotland every two weeks or so.

I had been on the Phantom for five years and it had been an action-packed busy time. The Phantom was probably the best multi-role aircraft of its generation, but it still had much more to give in the air-defence role as we will hear from Alan.

CHAPTER 4
AIR DEFENCE AND THE PHANTOM

"The only real security upon which sound military principles will rely is that you should be master of your own air."

Sir Winston Churchill

ALAN

When it comes to defence, there are two immediate questions you need to answer. The first is: "What are we defending?" This could be anything – a single tank, a naval task force, or even the United Kingdom itself. Given the difference in scale, each of these requires a completely different approach. That leads to the second question: "What have we got to defend it with?" For the tank, it might be sufficiently armed with air-defence weapons itself, or may be accompanied by a small squad of infantry with surface-to-air missiles. The naval task force might be defended by frigates with anti-air guns and missiles. In 2026, Star Wars-like laser emitters have even been used for defensive purposes: the USAF Navy HELIOS laser gun has had some success against drone attacks.

But no matter the scale of what you are defending, from a tank all the way up to the United Kingdom, aircraft have a vital role to play. When the German army realised during World War I that their heavy bombers and semi-dirigible airships could reach southern England, it immediately prompted the Royal Flying Corps to withdraw pilots and aircraft from France to the east of England, where they played a defensive role. Not long after, on 1 April 1918, the RAF was formed.

The idea of aircraft as a cornerstone of national defence was cemented in World War II, with images of Hurricanes and Spitfires constantly patrolling along the white cliffs. With the advent of air-to-air refuelling in the 1950s, it became possible to keep these patrols in the air for far longer. But with that, fuel also became a sort of passive weapon: you never had enough. Currently the RAF has just 14 Airbus A330 Voyager multi-role tanker transport (MRTT) aircraft, of which nine are routinely available (one civil registered). They certainly have a vast fuel capacity and can be used for troop carrying or freight, but as a Phantom pilot I found it hard to imagine that a tanker would be available every time I needed one. As I write this, the Falklands tanker has been withdrawn to support the Middle East, just as the Argentinians are getting F16s and once again sabre rattling.

The alternative to AAR is, of course, to keep your fighters on the ground, ready to scramble as required. In peacetime, a small number of fully armed fighters are kept at readiness. In wartime, all fighters would be kept armed at various states of readiness. But planes on the ground are sitting targets. We may be able to detect ballistic missile launches with the updated golf balls at Flyingdales, but even that might not make it possible to intercept a submarine-launched ballistic missile.

That means we have to think about passive defences. This simply means all measures taken to protect equipment and personnel and aircraft on the ground.

A330 Voyager tanker/transport.

Glostor Meteor NF11 by Ad Meskens.

These might include bunkers, hardened aircraft shelters and even the humble slit trench, featured vividly in the film 'Battle of Britain'. With large aircraft the only option is to disperse them, even at another airfield, and consider camouflage.

Defending Britain is a three-dimensional area task. In the 1950s and 1960s that meant the creation of air defence lanes supported by a number of ground-control radars. In the 1970s the work horse was the Gloster Meteor, later supplemented by its night-fighter version, the NF11 and the NF14. The weakness of night defences in the early part of World War II is still engraved on the hearts of command and control. Even so, the NF Meteors had a useful radar range of about four nautical miles and needed close control from a fighter-control station to get them into an astern position, where the navigator might make contact and talk the pilot into a gun-firing position. There were around 70 fighter-control stations to achieve this.

The Javelin succeeded the Meteor, supported by the Hawker Hunter in its day-fighter role. Speeds and intercept heights were increasing as the Soviets introduced their jet bombers (with the Il28 Beagle entering service in 1950). The defensive weapon was still the gun, and 4 x 30 mm Aden cannons made for an immense firepower. And of course these were backed up by the Bloodhound missile engagement zones, essentially to protect the V Force. The Beagle was replaced by the Tu16 Badger, and then the Tu95 Bear.

The advent of tail guns brought the Javelin FAW9 into service with powerful engines that would allow intercepts to 50,000 ft (I've been there), and Firestreak

Gloster Javelin FAW9 XH890.

air-to-air missiles to counter the Soviet tail guns. Typically, a radar lock on a fighter-sized target might be expected at or below 20 nm range. At night a radar dot from a device called a Collimator would point at the target and deflection shooting was even a possibility. 436 Javelins entered service. Essentially the defences improved to counter the evolving threat.

COUNTERING THE THREAT

The two classic methods of countering an air threat are to have aircraft on patrol (ideally supported by AAR), especially if the threat is imminent, or on standby at varying degrees of readiness. Readiness might be anything from two minutes with crews in the cockpit to a week for an aircraft in deep maintenance. Posture will of course comprise the numbers and capabilities of defending forces. Air Vice-Marshal Park (as then), the commander of No. 11 Group in 1941, had 550 aircraft on a good day to defend against 4,500 bombers with fighter escort. He chose to scramble small numbers so that he always had fighters and undamaged aircraft in reserve. He almost ran out except that the Luftwaffe strategy was changed from attacking the RAF to attacking London. This brought the bombers within range of AVM Leigh-Mallory and No. 12 Group's 'Big Wing' of 100 or so fighters, led and encouraged by Douglas Bader. Would this have worked in No. 11 Group? Well, after Leigh-Mallory took over No. 11 Group, after the appalling ousting of Park and his master AM Trenchard, a paper exercise was run to show that the 'Big Wing would have worked'. The results were never published. Kenneth More has a lot to answer for. Even then, as the Luftwaffe switched to night attacks, the threat had never been considered to be realistic, so a defence had never been prepared. The results were devastating.

In defence, some form of early warning is critical. Towards the end of World War I, when the RFC realised that the Germans were using the Essex rivers as navigation aids pointing at London, large concrete earphones were built around Dungeness to pick up the sound of engines.

The French army invested much development to field portable versions of sound detectors. In World War II the Luftwaffe development produced two technically excellent radars, the rotating Freya for area coverage and the Würzburg for highlighting specific aircraft. They had no concept of raid assessment, and intercepts were carried out with one Würzburg tracking the fighter and the other the bomber, with a controller trying to bring them together. Later they developed a form of grid system, with a controlled fighter or free fighter inside each grid box. Drawn out, this grid looked like a four-poster bed – giving it its name, *ein Himmelbett.*

In 1940, No. 11 Group's secret weapon was of course radar. Watson Watt's genius was in seeing how the radio returns could not only determine the size of a raid but the distance away. This led to the plotting table where plotters (mainly WAAF) moved counters showing all the known raid characteristics. Feeding into this was the observer corps passing information on raids they could see. The plot allowed accurate assessment of when to scramble available fighters even down to a pair. The unsung heroes were the post office engineers sitting through raids with their legs in

World War I sound detectors, Dungeness.

World War II Chain Home radar installation.

the pavement access boxes, mending telephone circuits damaged by bombing. To the end of the war the Abwehr (German intelligence) never believed that our fighter control was most often in wooden huts while theirs were in concrete bunkers.

POINT DEFENCE

When I was lecturing a five-nation course at RAAF Butterworth, there was of course no obvious threat. I saw the Singaporean-Chinese exchange crafty glances with the Malays, and we had to settle for a fictitious island in the South China Sea, with fictitious forces. No threat no sweat, but it did lead to the point defence discussion.

A threat can of course come from 360 degrees, in which case ground readiness becomes the preferred tactic. Singapore, Cyprus, Malta and the Falklands all spring to mind, and some form of radar warning becomes essential, even if that was just the special forces ashore in Argentina radioing in when an Argentinian raid was getting airborne. Since fuel was critical this allowed the controllers on the British aircraft carriers to time the Harrier scrambles in order to meet the raids. Fuel was a determining factor, but for the Argentinian pilots even more so. The successful attack on the *Atlantic Conveyor* had the use of C130 tankers to allow the Etendards to attack from an unexpected direction.

On a massive scale, Stalin left the defence of the Soviet Union and the Rodina in good shape. Having pulled critical industries back into the centre of the country, at his death the Soviet Union was surrounded by buffer states, 4,000 radars and thousands of ground-to-air missiles. The threat was seen as 360 degrees and the MiG25 (then MiG27 two-seater Foxhound with the enormous ASH air-to-air missile) was developed to meet hostile aircraft coming from any direction, predominately over the North Pole. It was a monster, and a Vulcan pilot told me he was intercepted just round the North Cape by an armed Foxhound, with no waves, no smiles. It was the most terrifying experience he could imagine.

IDENTIFICATION

Early identification friend or foe (IFF) was introduced in 1940 as a part of Chain Home radar. It was problematic. For example, in 1941, when two Beaufighters intercepted a Stirling bomber, one of them shot it down, and then the second Beaufighter shot down the first. During the Cold War, the primary form of identification was a partly encrypted IFF. Codes changed every six hours, but an unfriendly response could render a radar contact 'hostile' and thus subject to attack. Just because an aircraft is coming towards you from the Badlands does not mean that it is hostile. It might be a friendly coming back home. The primary and best method of identification was, and still is, the Mk1 eyeball. Identification has become infinitely harder for aircraft that are equipped with beyond visual range (BVR) missiles. The shooter has to know if he can fire his missile before he becomes vulnerable to a hostile aircraft. We will return to this when we discuss pulse doppler radar.

Training could also be counterproductive. During an exercise, everyone was wearing the same IFF code. A friendly squawk on many weapon systems prevented accidental firing. The anti-aircraft artillery soldiers assured us that their procedures were infallible, since most pilots regarded the highest threat as a 19-year-old squaddie with a surface-to-air missile (SAM). During a fairly routine day at the tactical leadership programme a few years later, we had an exercise with a class attack on a HAWK missile complex. I usually had an excuse not to go out to the target with the cameraman, but on this occasion, I was handed the microphone with nowhere to hide. The attack from different directions was pretty impressive and of course I knew what each aircraft was planning. Then a young Dutch captain came out of the bunker, and I was able to do a 'News at 10' interview. He was highly articulate and described what they had seen on their radar and how many of our aircraft they had tried to engage, all on video.

Then from around the corner came a bedraggled section of British squaddies with a corporal in charge. He explained that they were a blowpipe team, a slightly obsolete SAM, with stern-on infrared tracking. They had been defending the HAWK site.

"Do you think we might have a demonstration corporal?"
"Certainly Sir. Private Smith, present the weapon." "Sah".
"Right two o'clock bushy topped tree, two aircraft right to left."
"Targets acquired."
"Targets hostile, override the IFF, engage, FIRE."
"Override the IFF two three, FIRE."
"And that Sir concludes the demonstration Sah."
"Why override the IFF corporal?"
"If you don't override, it don't work Sah."

There was clearly work to be done. A staff officer from the Royal Artillery was shown this film clip a bit later. He had no idea and was in fairness appalled. The army went on with the Rapier to develop a 'smart stick'. The battery NCO simply pointed the stick at the threat. The stick then slewed the battery and did the identification.

A modern-day Typhoon has only a few of these problems. Joint Tactical Information Display System (JTIDS) is the 'state of the art' identifier. Since many defensive systems are networked, radars, army commanders, ships and other aircraft may all have had a chance to identify hostile aircraft. A cockpit instrument would then display different contacts as 'hostile', 'unknown' or 'friendly'. This of course then facilitates the head-on attack beyond visual range. A long-range missile might then be fired at 20 or more nautical miles distant.

COMMAND AND CONTROL

Since the Cold War officially ended in the early 1990s, the number of radar and command and control (C2) stations in the UK has reduced to just one at RAF Boulmer near Amble in Northumberland. I once took a simulated SHRIKE shot on Boulmer from the back of an F4G Wild Weasel and it did all seem rather easy. RAF Boulmer now controls all RAF air activity, and unclassified pictures show vast banks of radar screens. Technology has allowed one unit to see everything that radars and satellites can see in order to focus threat response. Even if Boulmer were to lose its radar head, it would be business as usual.

On my first day on No. 111 Squadron a QRA Phantom landed less its fuel tanks and Sidewinder missiles. The crew had some navigation problems and realised that if they jettisoned external stores, they could reach Iceland with zero fuel. At RAF Buchan, a radar-control station which ran a plot of the North Atlantic not dissimilar to the Battle of Britain plots, half was dedicated to SACLANT (Atlantic command in the USA), and half to SACEUR (European command in Brussels). The Atlantic controllers asked what the problem was and heard about the F4 getting short of fuel. "Would you like to borrow our tanker?" The European side had no idea it was there but turned the fighter towards the tanker and saved the day. Divided airspace is the curse of air defence command and control, although data linking has vastly improved the situation.

The advent of the E3A AWACS, first to the USAF, then to NATO, then to the RAF with eight AWACS E3Ds changed everything. When I first encountered the USAF E3A, it was roaming round the central region, mainly working surveillance and downlinking to the sector sites via an early model tactical datalink (TADLA), but retaining a control bench with three fighter controllers. Their callsign was 'magic' and that's just what they were. They could 'see' way into the distance and give control advice to fighters. However, the E3 has retired, and after a gap of a couple of years the UK has committed to three Boeing 737 E7 'Wedgetails', with a boxlike phased array radar on top of the fuselage. The original order was for five AEW&C aircraft, then reduced to three. Three E7s to replace eight E3Ds? With one possibly on contracted maintenance? Seriously? And no refuelling probe?

All radars, including the AWACS, are 'force multipliers'. They allow a fighter or a SAM to do more, in the same way a tanker makes the fighter's airborne time longer. We will come back to force packaging later, but a fighter might also be deployed at sweep in front of an attack package to improve its chances of survival. The US Navy are masters of force packaging with the F18E/F and the EA18 Growler, whereby reconfiguring they can package bombers with fighters, reconnaissance and ECM. The Czechs, masters of ingenious systems, developed a system called 'RAMONA', consisting of groups of three radar towers, capable of picking up all transmissions in use at the time. I tried to find out if this could be used for alerting fighters and SAMs but nobody seemed to know (or cared much). After reunification I discovered that it could. There is an excellent radar museum at RAF Neatishead (a former sector operations centre near Norwich), well worth a visit.

So, we come to the Phantom. It cannot be over-emphasised that the difference that a pulse doppler radar made was exponential. Prior to the Phantom, all aircraft radars were pulse radars. If you looked above the horizon the only returns could only be other aircraft. If you looked down, however, all you would see would be multiple returns of ground features, like a ploughed field. It was virtually impossible to pick up an incoming aircraft. By introducing pulse doppler (PD) you were measuring speed differences (like listening to a car engine going past uphill).

The problems start on the beam when the target disappears, so the operator is encouraged to have switched to his pulse radar, with the usual clutter in the stern. Now when the MiG29 arrived in East Germany the Americans did not understand why he would switch to infrared on the beam. The F15 and F18 pilots had radars which would synthetically track a target through the beam, and they had never been taught about the old technology. Of course, the weapons would match the technology with the Sparrow/AMRAAM making the medium-range shot and the Sidewinder/ASRAAM using pulse radar for close-in work. The F16 was maybe the first fighter where the radar transmitted from a fixed plate making the beam sweep electronically. This is what happens in the E7 Wedgetail, and even in the golf balls at Fylingdales.

The Phantom was procured as a carrier interceptor for which the pulse doppler radar/Sparrow combination was ideal. However, it was a slab of an aircraft and had to be understood. In the early stages of the Vietnam War many Sparrow shots were missed because seven switches were needed to fire the missile. One crew was notable in kills because the pilot always insisted on full weapons checks being read out. The Sidewinder and the gun were not much better, so the F18 arrived into naval service with hands-on throttle and stick. One plunger switch gave the pilot all the switching he needed for the Sparrow including gunsight, then a second plunge produced the same for a short-range missile, then the third plunge for the gun. Then of course the

RAF E7 Wedgetail.

RAF Phantom with AN/AWG 12 radar.

F4 was a hard aircraft to manoeuvre. The Belgian Air Force solved this flying the F104 by disappearing vertically and then reappearing behind the target. This all led to the fighter weapons school for the USAF at Nellis AFB and to the US Navy's Top Gun. For the first time, low-wing loaders such as the F5 and A4 were introduced as simulated low-wing loaders. Talk to me, Goose. In the RAF we had occasional opportunity to train against Hunters and the USAF F5E Aggressors, and to our amazement found that we could win. Counter measures came very late on, with the Phantom's flares appearing just before the aircraft left service.

When a fighter is scrambled, the crew never knows what to expect from a target or multiple targets, who could be well armed. They might be high or low, fast or slow, so training is inevitably on a small part of crew ability, backed up by the simulator.

So, force packaging may use air-defence assets to sweep ahead of an attack package, or escort with an attack package. During one exercise we at Wildenrath were tasked with accompanying a large Tornado attack from Laarbruch against the German Air Force base at Wittmund.

I was handed the lead and chose to escort the advance Tornado pack who were going for suppression of enemy air defence. This worked well and if we hadn't lost a secret piece of paper, it might have been an outstanding success. However, in my first visit to headquarters at Ramstein a German four-star general handed me an A4 page with a 30-minute by 30-minute grid drawn over the central region. "See what you can make of that, Al." Actually, I discovered later that we were going to

USAF F5E Aggressor.

re-invent the Luftwaffe *Himmelbett* from 1940, but more of that later when we discuss force packaging.

George is a dyed in the wool mud-mover. They all believe that if you put a couple of air-to-air missiles on an attack aircraft you now have a fighter. I remember the debrief from the re-enforcement of Cyprus after the Turkish invasion. "Well, anyone can do air defence." It's not that straight forward, is it?

CHAPTER 5
THE CAREER PATH

RAF CAREERS

GEORGE

Towards the end of my time on 31 Squadron, I heard that I would be attending the RAF Staff College next, but before we discuss that, it may be useful to talk about the way that RAF promotion used to work back in the day.

Promotion was based on seniority in the present rank, on recommendations from one's current boss, and upon completion of certain promotion exams. Most junior officer aircrew were completely focused on their flying and paid scant regard to their future promotion prospects in the early years. In fact, it was considered 'cool' to be dismissive of promotion prospects, but then realities would kick in later when one realised that promotion exams would need to be confronted and passed in order to progress in rank. The first of these was the 'B' to progress from flying officer to flight lieutenant. After that the 'C' exam must be passed for promotion to squadron leader. This was a much more challenging exam which required a detailed knowledge of various admin manuals. Perhaps the most important of these was the *Manual of Air Force Law* which sets out the legal rules and regulations which apply to all RAF personnel, and which sit above the normal common law provisions which apply to everyone. So, for example an individual could be accused of assault under common law but might also be accused of 'conduct prejudicial to good order and service discipline' under Air Force law. An officer could be required to sit on an RAF Board of Inquiry or a court martial and had to be familiar with legal procedures and the rules of evidence.

Training in Air Force law started early for us. I remember that Alan and I attended a court martial whilst we were undergoing basic flying training at RAF Acklington as 'officers under instruction'. The case involved a young man from a well-to-do family who had been accused of low flying in a Jet Provost training aircraft. He had indeed made a proper job of this as he had actually done a thorough beat up of traffic on the adjacent A1 road. Proving that low flying had actually taken place was quite difficult for the prosecution as they needed to produce credible witnesses to the event and most civilians could not judge with any certainty whether an aircraft was above or below the low-flying limit of 250 ft. One such witness was asked by the defence how he could be sure that the aircraft was indeed below 250 ft. He replied by saying "when I saw the aircraft approaching me, he was at such a height that I didn't think my car would fit below him". That was a pretty convincing testimony and taken together with other factors the accused was convicted of illegal low flying and was dismissed from the service. It turned out that he had wanted to resign, but his family would not hear of it, so he took matters into his own hands by getting himself booted out.

Alan and I were fortunate in that we had been given a 'permanent commission in the general list' when we signed on after gaining our university cadetship in 1963. This gave us a career in the RAF to the age of 55 with the option of leaving after 16 years or at the age of 38 with a pension. It also gave us accelerated promotion to flight lieutenant, so we started out with a distinct advantage over some of our direct entry colleagues who often regarded our 'flying start' as a bit unfair. It did however reflect the fact that we had spent several years in the RAF volunteer reserve in the UAS and had already built up a lot of relevant experience.

I completed the 'C' promotion exam towards the end of my time in Malta and was promoted to squadron leader about three years later at the age of 30. To qualify for Staff College required completion of a correspondence course called ISS which culminated in a written exam. I did the ISS and exam whilst holding down a challenging appointment as flight commander on 31 Squadron and it was pretty hard going. Having passed ISS, you were then classed as QSS or qualified for Staff College and then had to wait your turn subject to ongoing recommendation by your current boss. My number came up after five years on the Phantom when I was posted to the RAF Staff College at Bracknell.

By the end of my Phantom tour in Germany, I decided it was time to get on the housing ladder. We bought a flat in Edinburgh to provide some stability while our daughters were at boarding school there, which meant that I would have to commute back when I could.

RAF STAFF COLLEGE

The RAF Staff College at Bracknell in Berkshire was where you went to prepare for the next phase of your career as a staff officer. We used to call it the "joined up writing course" as it placed a heavy emphasis on the ability to produce concise written reports on all manner of service-related topics strictly in the approved service writing format. It was also designed to broaden the education of candidates and prepare them for the senior staff appointments in command headquarters and the Ministry of Defence. There were corresponding Staff Colleges for the army at Camberley and for the navy at Greenwich.

The Bracknell Staff College was located at Ramslade House, a Victorian villa standing in extensive grounds in Bracknell. It had previously been home to the 2TAF in World War II. It had been much extended since then with dedicated syndicate rooms, a large lecture theatre and an accommodation block for the students. It was a very pleasant environment in which to have one's head sharpened for a few months in preparation for the next phase of one's career.

The Staff College course had previously been of nine months duration but had recently been reduced to six months, with no corresponding reduction in the syllabus. What previously had been a somewhat leisurely course had become much more intense. Students were allocated to syndicates of about eight members from a variety of backgrounds. My syndicate had a wing commander engineer from the staff in charge. I was the only fast jet pilot, but we had a mix of engineers, suppliers, a Nimrod navigator, a VC10 captain, and a Yugoslav exchange officer. This was all designed to give a wide variety of backgrounds to add to the mix. I learned a lot from my syndicate colleagues and especially from the Nimrod navigator who taught me much about anti-submarine warfare, a subject about which I knew little.

The commandant was AVM Alasdair Steedman (later ACM Sir Alasdair) who had been a World War II bomber pilot and had a chest full of medals including the DFC. He was a refined and erudite Scot with a love of Scottish country dancing for which he ran classes for anyone interested. He was a natural thespian and loved to take centre stage introducing guest speakers in the lecture theatre giving eloquent career summaries and flattering introductions, making them feel that their contribution would be the highlight of the week. He was a great role model in the art of public speaking.

We had guest speakers most days where we assembled in the lecture theatre in our best blue uniforms. The topics were many and varied covering the whole geopolitical scene with UK politicians of every hue and senior serving officers explaining their roles and responsibilities. At the end of each presentation, we were expected to raise a hand and ask an intelligent question on the subject matter, so you needed to pay attention and not drift off, as could so easily happen if the subject matter did not appeal.

Bear in mind that this pre-dated the internet by a couple of decades. The only hint of things to come was that the college had a remote terminal connected to a mainframe computer and you set up a simple spreadsheet to model repeat calculations on your latest project, or if you were a real nerd, write a little programme in Beginner's All-purpose Symbolic Instruction Code (BASIC) to wow your peers. PowerPoint had yet to be invented and slides for presentations had to be produced on 35 mm transparencies by the in-house art department.

We also had to prepare a lengthy paper on a subject of our choice, and I decided that my topic would be cockpit ergonomics. So many of our contemporary cockpit displays lacked coherence with many dials and switches added as an afterthought and located wherever there was a spare space. The Buccaneer cockpit was described by its own aircrew as an ergonomic slum. This all added additional workload to a hard-pressed crew. I sweated over this project and took advice from various sources and eventually came up with what I thought was a worthwhile paper.

The course also taught the basics of public speaking and how to give a presentation on a subject of your choice to the whole assembly of students and staff. I decided to do a talk about the F16 and the F18. These two American fighters were in the very early stages of development but were already showing great promise. They had been developed in the wake of American experience in Vietnam where they had no lightweight agile fighters that could counter even the much older MiG17 still in use with the North Vietnamese. These sessions taught us to thoroughly prepare both the subject matter and the visual aids, to actively engage with the audience, to move around, maintain eye contact, and not to be heads down in your script, clutching the lectern. You still needed a script in case you dried up, but you needed to be completely familiar with your subject matter whilst able to react to any real time feedback coming from the audience. We were then given an honest appraisal at the end from both staff and students. There were about three different sessions of these presentations, and I found them to be of very great benefit.

We also did exchange visits with our army and navy colleagues at their respective Staff Colleges. I particularly remember the visit to Greenwich and a formal dinner hosted by the Royal Navy in the Painted Hall. You could look up and admire the painted frescos mostly figuring voluptuous naked women. There were visits to other units from all three services all of which gave useful insights in how the other half lived, visiting army training sessions in Salisbury Plain or going aboard a Royal Navy destroyer.

JUNIOR COMMAND AND STAFF COURSE

ALAN

For those of us too young or stupid to attend Staff College, there was the junior command and staff course, held for two months at RAF Tern Hill near Market Drayton. This required weekly attendance and was heavy on Air Force law and sword drill. Friday afternoons were stage shows where the staff (and later students) dressed up to simulate orderly room situations. I shall never forget a staff wing commander dressed up as an RAF policeman, on being asked why as a Jew he had taken the oath on a bible. "Had my thumb on the Old Testament Sah." Totally believable.

Whirlwind training, RAF Tern Hill.

Most junior officers had been dragged there somewhat unwillingly. There was quite a lot of drill in which parade flights were simulated with a rope between the end markers. In fairness both subjects turned out to be essential when I found myself in charge of 150 RAF apprentices and a guard of honour. The most important lesson was probably that of double jeopardy, so that RAF and civil law could not overlap or be mixed.

The staff never found out that on Wednesday afternoon, traditionally free for sport, I was taking my flying kit to one or other helicopter training squadrons, whichever programme looked most likely to succeed. In this way I learned to fly both the Whirlwind and the Sioux, discovering in the process that I really did not like helicopters at all.

My posting was to No. 3 School of Apprentice Training, where I would be flight commander to a large number of administrative apprentices. Unlike George, I found myself totally unsuited to life on a ground station, where I became the only RAF pilot amongst 50 ground branch officers. I did manage to stay current on the Chipmunk both instructing at RAF St Athan with the University of Wales Air Squadron, and with the Air Experience Squadron at RAF Cosford. However, I lost all confidence, covered in my first book *Fast Jets on the Flight Line*, and got posted for the second time to Lightnings, despite my legs still being too long. The Phantom OCU had temporarily closed due to the Spey engine turbine problems, and I found myself on the Harrier with only half the weapons training I should have had and a very low self-confidence. 150 flying hours later after I made a mistake on the range in Decimomannu (Sardinia) I was quietly removed and eventually found my way to the Phantom. It was not really the way an RAF career was designed to work, despite getting the right answer eventually.

THE OPERATIONAL REQUIREMENTS DEPARTMENT IN THE MINISTRY OF DEFENCE

GEORGE

At the end of the Staff College course, we were given our new postings. For me it was to be on the operational requirements department in the Ministry of Defence main building in Whitehall. I felt that this was a good choice, as it meant having some influence, however small, on future aircraft design.

My family would continue to live in Edinburgh, and I would need to find rental accommodation in London. I started in a bed-sit in St Margaret's near Richmond

Tornado development aircraft.

which involved a lengthy commute into central London but later moved into a shared flat with a colleague in Kensington Church Street, a much more convenient location.

My official title was OR13b. The OR13 office was the project office for the new multi-role combat aircraft (MRCA). It was later to be renamed the Tornado which was to serve the RAF with distinction for over 30 years in various wars. When I joined the office in July 1975, the project was still in its infancy with just two prototypes flying and the future prospects for MRCA were far from secure. There were many opponents both inside and outside the RAF who would have preferred an alternative solution like the American F15 or even an updated version of the Buccaneer with modern avionics. We felt we were constantly on the back foot trying to keep the project alive.

The OR13 office was headed up by a wing commander with a Lightning background. There were three squadron leaders; an ex-Buccaneer pilot who was also a test pilot and myself who were responsible for the interdiction strike version (IDS), and a Lightning pilot responsible for the air defence version (ADV). Note that there were no navigators in the OR13 office and we had to get back-seat advice from elsewhere. We reported to a deputy director (DD OR1) group captain called Bob Simpson. He was a great boss, a former Canberra PR CO who ran his office like a squadron, always giving us full support and seeing to morale with frequent beer calls. He was an old and experienced MoD campaigner who knew his way around the system and could generate support papers on the fly. I had the greatest respect for him.

The backstory to the MRCA included a number of failed attempts to find a successor to the Canberra and the Hunter of the previous generation. This involved the TSR2 which was a hugely expensive and ultimately doomed project that was never going to succeed. Then followed the Anglo-French variable geometry project which was short lived. The modified Phantom was bought by the RAF on the back of an existing project for the Royal Navy and proved an effective stopgap in the strike-attack role before it eventually reverted to air defence.

It seemed to me that the RAF often over specified requirements at the expense of flexibility. Defining a requirement purely on the basis of what would be needed in the NATO Central Front involved unnecessary constraints affecting how an aircraft might adapt to future requirements. It would also limit the appeal to foreign markets as export potential would be important to an aircraft's commercial success. The Canberra and Hunter had enjoyed healthy export sales because of their adaptability. Future UK designs needed to have flexibility baked in, if they were to succeed.

MRCA was a tri-national programme with the Brits, Germans and Italians who all had to compromise on varied national priorities to arrive at a common specification. For example, the West German constitution prohibited development of a bomber aircraft with strategic reach which limited the size and range of the MRCA design. The British had the most advanced design and development facilities at the time and had design leadership in MRCA, but the other two nations were keen to catch up and saw this project as one way of doing so. These competing priorities made the overall management of the project a real challenge, and this was the responsibility of the NATO MRCA Management Agency (NAMMA) based in Munich, and the commercial organisation called Panavia who coordinated the manufacturing and development activities of the national companies taking part. You can see already how the tri-national bureaucracy was going to be a potential nightmare.

To add a further complication, the Brits had to scale down the potential numbers of aircraft for the RAF as fiscal realities started to bite. This would mean losing design leadership as they would no longer have the largest share of the programme. The solution the Brits came up with was to convert a number of the MRCA to an ADV. This was hugely controversial both at the time and subsequently.

Any variant of the MRCA was never going to match the latest generation fighters from the USA in terms of manoeuvre or agility. The UK argued that it did not need that level of agility as fighter v fighter combat was not envisaged. Instead, it would patrol the Iceland/ Faroes Gap where its long duration would be an advantage. It would have a brand-new air intercept (AI) radar capable of tracking multiple targets and updated Skyflash missiles. This was a good example of how political imperatives would trump operational requirements or indeed future commercial appeal.

The ADV required substantial changes to the base MRCA design. The fuselage had to be lengthened to accommodate four Skyflash missiles, necessitating a fuselage 'plug' giving an extra fuel tank. The elongated shape looked better in my opinion and would have been well suited to the IDS giving that version a useful range boost, but it was already too late for such a radical change. Ironically the testing programme showed that the IDS could not meet its design parameters for range. For example, it was required to do a low-level profile carrying four 1,000lb bombs at 0.9 Mach over a radius of action of 250 nm. It could only achieve 220 nm, so how to make up the shortfall? The fuselage plug on the ADV would have been the perfect solution, but as explained earlier that was not politically possible, so a decision was made to put a fuel tank in that enormous tail fin. That solved the radius of action problem but led to further issues downstream.

Overall management of the MRCA programme was the responsibility of the MoD procurement executive (MoD PE) based at St Giles Court in London. The OR13 office provided the specialist pilot advice and overall monitoring from an RAF perspective. We spent a lot of time attending meetings at MoD PE and elsewhere trying to clarify the aircrew point of view to engineers and contract officials. There were also frequent visits to NAMMA in Munich, an altogether more enjoyable venue than MoD PE in London. There were also visits to British Aerospace at Warton who were one of the main contractors, so I seemed to spend a lot of time on the road living out of a suitcase.

Much time was spent troubleshooting issues that were thrown up during flight testing. One must bear in mind that the level of technology for avionics design in the 1970s was light years behind where it is today and there were several upgrades during the life of the aircraft in service. One example was a unit called the stores management system (SMS). This controlled each of the weapons stations on the aircraft, allowing the crew to select individual weapons for single or multiple release. It was housed in a sizeable box with several printed circuit cards and the original contractor Marconi Elliott struggled with its development. It also required at least a duplex system to meet weapons safety requirements and Marconi Elliott managed to spend all the development moneys without producing a working system. I am sure that modern technology could produce a working system in about the size of a mobile phone, but that was yet to come and was not possible back in the day. The requirement went to go to competitive tender again and I spent a lot of time assessing the various bids, such were the joys of aircraft development.

Other development issues that involved me directly were the Mauser cannon, a very effective weapon which suffered from very short barrel life, and a newly developed 'crutchless' type of weapons release which did away with the drag-inducing exposed crutch systems for stabilising the carriage of bombs. The navigation and weapon aiming systems were far in advance of what we had in the UK Phantom but still had issues which needed to be sorted during development. For example, the main computer was originally specified with 32 kilobytes of magnetic core store memory, whereas the ADV version had 64 kilobytes. It was decided after much debate to update the IDS computer to 64 kilobytes. These are nothing when we currently measure computer storage in terabytes, but back then it was a big deal.

Another big development issue involved the integration of the JP233 runway denial weapon. This was developed by Hunting Engineering and included two different munitions, a runway cratering munition and area denial mines. There was much debate on how these devices should be packaged and carried on MRCA, but the final configuration was for two large containers to be carried on the shoulder stations of the aircraft. Each container was divided into a rear section with 30 runway cratering submunitions, while the front section carried 215 anti-personnel mines. Both types of submunitions were retarded by small parachutes and required the aircraft to overfly the target runway at low level. JP233 saw service in the first Gulf War against Iraqi airfields, but the low-level delivery made the aircraft vulnerable to ground defences. Once the allies had established air superiority, Tornado tactics reverted to medium-level deliveries of iron bombs for which the weapon aiming system was not optimised.

I used to enjoy the frequent trips to Munich. It is such a lovely city, and it was good for me to establish working relationships with the staff at NAMMA and Panavia. I even got to go on a Panavia-organised weekend skiing trip. I thought about joining the staff at NAMMA after leaving the RAF and was offered a good job, but the pull of another flying career proved too tempting.

During my ground tour at MoD, I did manage to keep flying with the Air Experience Flight flying Chipmunks. I would travel down to Hamble every other weekend when I was not otherwise commuting home to Edinburgh. Keeping the flying part of my brain active over a period of nearly three years was of huge benefit for when I eventually returned to flying and made the flying refresher course so much easier.

When my time at MoD came to an end, I was told that I would be promoted to wing commander to take over 6 Squadron flying the Jaguar. This was a wholly unexpected development, but of course I was highly delighted at the prospect. I was also so grateful at the continuity in flying that the AEF Chipmunk flying had provided which made the transition so much more straightforward.

FLYING REFRESHER

GEORGE

It was three years since I had last done operational flying, so prior to conversion on to the Jaguar, I had to do a full course of refresher flying. I went through refresher training with Wing Commander Bruce Latton who was due to take over the Jaguar OCU at RAF Lossiemouth. Bruce was a good friend and a very capable pilot who had been part of the Harrier conversion team when the aircraft first entered service with the RAF. Our refresher training commenced in May 1977 at the School of Refresher Flying at RAF Leeming flying the Jet Provost Mk5. I had of course flown the Jet Provost before during my basic flying training so getting used to the Mk5 was not a problem.

During my ground tour at MoD, I had continued to fly the Chipmunk with No. 2 Air Experience Flight at Hamble. This provided some important continuity and ongoing stimulus to the flying part of my brain which would otherwise have atrophied during my ground tour. I had a short conversion back on to the Chipmunk by the resident QFI which required amongst other things a climb to about 5,000 ft followed by an eight-turn spin. Bearing in mind I had just come from the Phantom where spinning was something we did everything to avoid, this was a bit of a revelation. I did a total of 40 hours of Chipmunk flying and gave 60 young air cadets their first taste of operating the flight controls under my supervision and maybe (if they asked) a few gentle aerobatics. It was great to see their enthusiasm and interest in flying.

My re-introduction to the Jet Provost was most enjoyable. It reminded me about just how heavy the non-power assisted controls were, and a full sequence of aerobatics required a bit of muscle power. The training was thorough and included shortened versions of the full basic flying training syllabus with general handling,

Hunter Mk 6.

formation, instrument flying including a rating, low-level cross country and a final handling test.

I then proceeded to RAF Brawdy in Pembrokeshire to commence the short Hunter course at the Tactical Weapons Unit. I had only ever flown the two-seat Hunter T7 in the past, so it was a great treat to be sent solo and get to fly the single-seat Hunter Mk6 and Mk9. After initial conversion which included an instrument rating test, the course mostly involved ground-attack refresher with practice weapons on Pembray range in South Wales. This included strafe with the Aden cannon and dive bombing with 25 lb practice bombs. Then followed low-level simulated attack profiles in the low-flying areas. It was a thorough work out with some very experienced Hunter instructors including 'Puddi Catt' who I had last encountered in Gibraltar when he and his wingman tried to bounce my PR9 soon after departure.

The Hunter is one of these iconic aircraft a bit like the Spitfire and is universally admired by those who have flown it, and I can see why. It handles so beautifully, the controls are so well balanced and responsive. It was soon to be replaced at Brawdy with the Hawk. Puddi Catt was given a demonstration flight in the Hawk whilst I was at Brawdy, and he came back very impressed by the new aircraft which is high praise indeed from a dyed-in-the-wool Hunter pilot.

CHAPTER 6
THE JAGUAR

GEORGE

The Jaguar was in service with the RAF for 34 years, so it was one of the longest serving aircraft types of this generation. I was very fortunate to serve as the CO of 6 Squadron operating the Jaguar GR1 in its early years of RAF service.

I am a huge fan of the Jaguar because it was so good at what it was designed to do, which was to take a load of bombs from the RAF clutch airfields near the Dutch border to targets as far away as the Polish border and to do that at high speed and low level. It had a small wing to give it low gust response and a smooth ride. Its Adour engines had just enough thrust to do the job, and its turning performance was not great, but the Adours were economical and reliable, and the Jag could go a long way on the fuel it carried. In its early years it was subject to various jibes like "only getting airborne due to the curvature of the earth". It was at its best whilst flying hard and fast under a low overcast and in poor visibility in what we used to call "Jaguar weather". As someone once said, "In typical northern European weather just try and stop a well flown Jaguar".

I had spent five years flying the Phantom FGR2 in northern Europe, so I knew the mission and the area of operations. Whilst the Phantom was magnificent in so many ways, it was a bit of an engineering nightmare. Spares and engines were always in short supply and accessibility for the engineers to fix stuff was poor. As a result, the night shift struggled to get at least five aircraft ready for the first wave. In contrast when I reported for work as OC 6 Squadron there were invariably nine or more serviceable Jaguars on the line. This made running a flying programme so much easier.

But before we go any further, we should have a look at the origins of the Jaguar and its development.

JAGUAR DEVELOPMENT

In the early 1960s both Britain and France saw the need for a new advanced tactical training aircraft. They eventually settled on a design based on the Breguet 121 concept put forward by the French. This design was much modified, and in due course morphed into what we now know as the Jaguar. It was to be built by a bi-national company formed by Breguet and BAC with the lengthy and mind-numbing name of Société Européene de Production de L'Avion d'École de Combat et d'Appui Tactique, or SEPECAT for short. It was also to have an engine co-produced by Rolls-Royce and Turbomeca to be called the Adour.

Received wisdom says it is unwise to develop a new aircraft and a new engine together, but that is what happened with the Jaguar, and it seemed to work out pretty well. This coincided with a period of turbulence in British aircraft development with the cancellation of the TSR2 and the F111K and the need to find a replacement for the stopgap Phantom in the strike-attack role. The RAF never did use the two-seat Jaguar as an advanced trainer and rejigged its order to a total of 200 aircraft of which 165 were to be the single-seat attack version with 35 as two-seat trainers.

A bi-national programme had the advantage of economies of scale, and it also made it harder for one of the parties to drop out if the political requirements changed in the future. There was also a desire for the two countries to launch another Anglo-French project in the wake of Concorde which was going well at the time. Production of the aircraft was split 50/50. Breguet were to build the front and centre fuselage whilst BAC built the wings, rear fuselage and empennage. Final assembly would be carried out in both countries, in the UK at Warton in Lancashire and in France at Colomiers near Toulouse. Likewise, the Adour engine would be assembled at Derby in the UK and at Tarnos in France. A French naval version was postulated, the Jaguar M1, but only one was ever built.

The RAF version of Jaguar differed considerably in avionic fit from the version specified for the Armée de l'Air (AdlA). RAF versions would have a navigation and weapon aiming subsystem (NAVWASS) by Marconi Elliott, a laser ranger and marked target seeker (LRMTS) by Ferranti, a head-up display (HUD) by Smiths Industries, and a fin-mounted radar warning receiver (RWR).

The Jaguar.

THE NAVWASS SYSTEM

The NAVWASS system fitted in the GR1 consisted of a total of ten modules housed mostly in the aircraft nose section. According to a Marconi Elliott sales brochure which I still have, the E3R inertial platform alone weighed 25 kg, the power supply unit 17 kg and the 920M digital computer 15 kg. The digital computer had just 8k

GR1 NAVWASS.

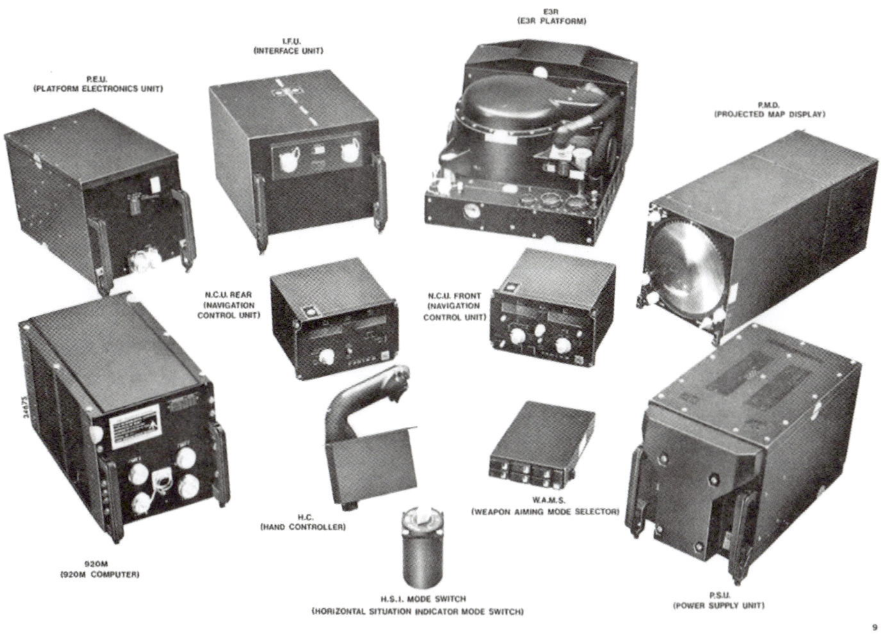

Jaguar GR1 cockpit.

of magnetic core store memory on board. That is 8 kilobytes, not the megabytes or gigabytes we are used to today. It is remarkable that the programmers were able to cram the necessary code into such a small space. There was a moving map display in the cockpit, a revelation at the time only previously seen in James Bond's Aston Martin. The moving map display was essentially analogue, with back projection of the map from 35mm transparencies. The Jaguar was the first RAF aircraft to have a proper HUD designed to be the primary source for aircraft attitude and weapon-aiming information. This was supplemented by basic head-down instrument displays if the HUD should fail. Fortunately, all were line replaceable units which could be pulled out and sent to the bay for servicing. Accessibility was good as the Jaguar had been designed from the outset with maintainability in mind.

The GR1 NAVWASS was state of the art in its day but had reliability issues throughout its service life. Like the little girl with the curl, when it was good it was very very good, but when it was bad it was awful. It could give the pilot good situational awareness of his position within about two miles over the course of a one-hour flight, but it couldn't be entirely relied upon. The pilot still needed to supplement this with good basic navigation skills using map and stopwatch, and we carried a 1:500 route map and 50k maps of the IP to target runs for each target.

If the IN platform failed, (or the kit dumped as we used to say), the HUD would occult and the pilot had to rapidly resort to the head-down instruments. Also, some of the display controls were poorly positioned in the cockpit low down behind the control stick. There were two fatal accidents in the early 1970s which were thought to have been caused by pilot disorientation for just these reasons.

The NAVWASS was replaced in RAF Jaguars commencing in 1983 by the Ferranti FIN 1064 navigation system featuring a much-improved inertial navigation unit (INU) plus a new computer and power supply with a single line replaceable unit (LRU) in place of five NAVWASS modules. This upgrade to GR1A standard provided a huge improvement in reliability and weapons delivery accuracy.

AVIONIC MID-LIFE UPDATE

The Jaguar had a mid-life update with further avionic system improvements, and the GR3 version entered RAF service in 1996. This provided GPS updating for the inertial platform, a terrain referenced system, a new head-up display and a new digital moving map. This transformed the capability of the aircraft in the final ten years of its operational life. You will see how radically the cockpit had changed in this image.

Jaguar GR3A cockpit.

THE ADOUR ENGINE

RAF Jaguars were delivered with the Mk102 version of the Adour engine which produced 5,100 lbs dry thrust and 7,100 lbs thrust in reheat. This small but rugged engine proved to be reliable in service. It had a modular construction which meant that engines could be stripped down for maintenance and repair avoiding the need to return them to the manufacturer. Later on, the engines were upgraded to the Adour 104 which gave a useful thrust increase to 5,500 lbs dry and 8,000 lbs in reheat.

Having two engines was always reassuring as you could always make it home if one failed. I was grateful for this when my starboard engine swallowed a seagull when I was doing 500 kts over the North Sea. After a loud bang and multiple warning lights, I climbed to a safe height whilst shutting down the starboard engine. I then returned safely to base for a single-engine approach, but I would undoubtedly have got my feet wet if I had been in an F16.

NO. 6 SQUADRON HISTORY

GEORGE

As deputy chair of the 6 Squadron Association and editor of their 'tin-opener' quarterly magazine, I have kept in constant touch with the current squadron and with past members. This has provided me with a wide perspective of both current and past history. I also run the association website. The 6 Squadron Association is very active and is open to all former members of the squadron or anyone who has been of service to the squadron in any capacity. It is an all-ranks association, and membership includes former senior aircraftsmen up to retired air marshals.

Let's take a look at the backstory of 6 Squadron and what makes it special in the overall history of the RAF.

THE FIRST WORLD WAR

The Royal Flying Corps was formed in April 1912, just nine years after the Wright Brothers' first flight, and three years after Blériot's first crossing of the Channel. Flying was still in its infancy, but some senior figures in the British army saw potential for aerial reconnaissance using these machines, and RFC squadrons were formed in numerical order. Pilots were initially recruited from the small number of adventurous young men who had learned to fly at their own expense. Volunteers were also sought, mostly from the ranks of cavalry officers who were considered to

BE2d.

have 'good hands', the logic being that if they could handle a horse, they should also be capable of handling an aeroplane!

And so it was that Captain (later Major) JHW Becke was ordered to carry out the formation of 6 Squadron, commencing 31 January 1914, at South Farnborough. Many of the personnel were transferred from the existing RFC squadrons, whilst others were new recruits.

6 Squadron deployed to France on 7 October 1914. The squadron settled into its main role of reconnaissance and artillery observation. It was during this period that the squadron was awarded the 'gunners stripe' which is still part of the aircraft livery, and the motto *oculi exercitus* which appears on the squadron badge meaning 'the eyes of the army'.

The squadron was operating BE2 aircraft at this time which were slow and vulnerable to enemy attack. As a result of mounting losses in 1915, the squadron was allocated some 'scouts'. These were single-seater fighters designed to engage enemy machines.

On one famous occasion, Captain LA Strange was involved in aerial combat with an enemy aircraft in a Martinsyde Scout. Whilst changing the magazine on his Lewis machine gun, the aircraft inverted and he fell out of the cockpit. He was left dangling as the aircraft descended in an inverted spin, and only just managed to recover a few feet above the ground. Captain Strange, a gallant and resourceful officer, survived active service in both world wars.

Another flight commander Captain LG Hawker was awarded the Victoria Cross, the first such award for aerial combat, when he engaged three enemy machines on 25 July 1915. In April 1917, the squadron was re-equipped with the much more capable RE8 aircraft. This two-seater had greater load-carrying ability and had a forward-firing machine gun. The squadron continued with reconnaissance, artillery support and bombing with great distinction until the end of the war.

THE INTER-WAR YEARS

In 1918, the RFC and RNAS combined to form the RAF and the total number of squadrons had grown to 176; a far cry from the four RFC squadrons who deployed to Flanders in 1914. After the armistice, many of these squadrons returned to the UK to be disbanded. But 6 Squadron was sent to Marseilles to embark for the Middle East, and commenced what was to be 50 years of continuous overseas service.

The Treaty of Versailles allocated the former Ottoman Empire areas of Mesopotamia (now Iraq) and Transjordan to Britain. Faced with the necessity of policing these vast areas, Lord Trenchard, the founder of the RAF advocated a policy of 'air control'. What would otherwise have required 10 divisions of 'boots on the ground' could now be managed by two RAF squadrons supplemented by some armoured car regiments. The policy was similar to what still happens today via drones and air strikes, except that in these somewhat gentler times, dissident villages were leafleted first to allow evacuation of civilians.

6 Squadron disembarked in Basra and the crated RE8s were reassembled. The squadron was based variously at Basra, Baghdad, Mosul and Palestine during a period of almost continuous action up until the start of World War II.

The RE8s were replaced in February 1919 with the Bristol Fighter F2b which stayed in service until being replaced by Fairey Gordons in 1931 and later by a series of Hawker fighter bombers. As war clouds gathered the squadron was based at Ramleh in Palestine, actively engaged in operations against Arab dissidents.

WORLD WAR II

Following the outbreak of war in 1939, 6 Squadron remained in Palestine for another year before deploying forward to Egypt in September 1940. At the time, the squadron was equipped with Gloster Gauntlet and Westland Lysanders and was dedicated to army co-operation. The squadron played a full part in the initial advance across Cyrenaica against the Italians. The first Hurricane Mk 1s arrived in February 1941.

The arrival of Rommel's Afrika Corps changed everything. At the same time, British forces and air assets were being diverted to stem the German advance in Greece and the Balkans. British forces were forced to retreat from their forward positions in Cyrenaica, and 6 Squadron fought long and hard in the defence of

Tobruk. The aircraft suffered heavily for lack of spares but not once was a request for reconnaissance turned down. Aircraft were often flying without tail wheels and Hurricanes without hydraulics. The situation at Tobruk had become untenable, especially in the face of Me109 fighter opposition, and the squadron was withdrawn to retrain and re-equip.

The Hurricane IId arrived in April 1942 and transformed the squadron's anti-armour capability. Armed with two 40mm Vickers S guns, these aircraft could destroy any German or Italian tank in North Africa. This is what led to the name tin-opener or can-opener.

The attack profile with the S gun was demanding. After patrolling at about 3,000 ft, when targets were sighted, a steep dive was started to increase speed to the maximum, levelling at just 20 ft before opening fire at close range. On one such occasion, Flt Lt Pip Hillier lost his tailwheel and removed half of his rudder on the turret of a tank.

A notable action took place at Bir Hachem in support of the Free French when S gun-equipped Hurricanes turned the tide of the action, inflicting heavy losses on enemy tanks and vehicles. The war was again fluid at this stage with rapid

The Hurricane IId in action (6 Squadron Art Collection).

withdrawals to other landing grounds being commonplace. Squadron groundcrew were magnificent in their flexibility and ability to improvise. The tank-busting Hurricane IIds of 6 Squadron operated with great distinction at El Alamein and throughout the subsequent advance through Libya and Tunisia until Axis forces were expelled from North Africa in April 1943.

The squadron then re-equipped with the rocket-firing Hurricane IV, and after a period of training deployed forward to Italy at Grottaglie in February 1944. The squadron's main role was to attack enemy shipping, as well as coastal targets, gun emplacements and the like.

POSTWAR

In August 1945 the squadron returned to Palestine to resume its policing duties. 6 Squadron was the last RAF squadron to operate the Hurricane, and these were finally phased out in 1947 as the new Tempest 6 aircraft arrived. This was the most powerful piston-engine fighter ever operated by the RAF, with a 2,500 bhp Napier Sabre engine, and capable of 450 mph.

The Tempests were soon to be replaced with the Vampire FB 5, and the squadron resumed its mobile role, moving between a main base at Habbaniya in Iraq, the Canal Zone, and Mafraq in Jordan. It was during a detachment to Mafraq that the squadron was presented with a personal standard by King Abdullah, and 6 Squadron continues to be the only RAF squadron with two royal standards.

The more powerful Venom arrived in February 1954 to replace the Vampire. The squadron moved to Akrotiri in Cyprus, and in October 1956 saw active service during the Suez crisis. Air strikes using rockets and guns were mounted against the Egyptian Air Force bases, and ironically, many of these were in the Canal Zone at airfields previously used by the RAF. The squadron also covered the allied landings at Port Said, and action continued until the ceasefire a few days later.

COLD WAR JETS

The Venoms were replaced by the Canberra B2 in July 1957 as 6 Squadron became part of the Akrotiri Strike Wing assigned to CENTO. For the first and only time in its history, the squadron had a nuclear-strike role.

During the next 12 years, the Canberras were upgraded, first to the B6 version and later to the B16. These aircraft were operated with three crew members: pilot, nav plotter and observer. As part of its CENTO commitment, the squadron did frequent training deployments to Tehran, and occasionally to Peshawar.

On 13 January 1969, the Standards were handed over to the new Phantom FGR2 squadron at RAF Coningsby, marking the end of the Canberra era, the start of an exciting new phase with the Phantom, and the first time the squadron had been UK based since 1919.

6 Squadron reformed at Lossiemouth with the Jaguar in October 1974, and after a brief run up, moved to RAF Coltishall where it remained for the next 32 years. With the Cold War still in full swing, 6 Squadron was NATO assigned with a forward war base at Tirstrup in Denmark. The normal rhythm of deployments included armament practice camps at Decimomannu in Sardinia, visits to Tirstrup, NATO squadron exchanges, trips to North America for Red Flag and Maple Flag, and 'flag waving' visits to Gibraltar.

Things turned deadly serious in 1990 with the Iraqi invasion of Kuwait. 6 Squadron was chosen as the lead element in the Coltishall wing deployment for Gulf War 1. This was to be the first 'hot' operation since the squadron's actions in the Suez crisis. Heroic efforts were made by the groundcrew before and during deployment, and many urgent modifications and updates to the aircraft were hastily implemented. The Jaguars completed 617 operational sorties with no losses and with an aircraft availability of 98 per cent.

There was some brief respite for the squadron until August 1991, when the squadron redeployed, this time to Incirlik in Turkey to police the no-fly zone. These were lengthy armed-reconnaissance sorties with in-flight refuelling, carrying the recce pod, with the real prospect of hostile engagement by Saddam's air defences. The Incirlik deployment was maintained on rotation until the Harriers took over in February 1993.

It was not long before the squadron was back on operations, this time to Gioia del Colle in Italy because of the civil war in Bosnia. There followed frequent returns to both Gioia del Colle and to Incirlik as the situation demanded. In between times, normal training and squadron deployments for other tasks continued. Throughout this period, the Jaguar underwent significant modifications and improvements, so that the final version was very much changed from the aircraft which entered service in 1974. Following a decision to draw down the Jaguar force, RAF Coltishall closed in 2006, and 6 Squadron moved to RAF Coningsby for the final few months before it too was made non-operational on 31 May 2007. Thus ended 93 years of continuous service.

Three years after its disbandment as a Jaguar unit, 6 Squadron re-formed at Royal Air Force Leuchars equipped with the Eurofighter Typhoon on 6 September 2010. In March, the squadron took over the duties of Northern Quick Reaction Alert from

The Typhoon.

the Tornado F3 thus becoming responsible for permanently maintaining aircraft at very high readiness to defend the United Kingdom's airspace. At a similar time, it also began to contribute to the enduring presence in the Falkland Islands.

Since then, the squadron has been in almost continuous operational deployments to Akrotiri for anti-Daesh operations, to Estonia for Baltic air policing and most recently in support of the operations against Iran. In 2024 the then government declared the Typhoon to be multi-role, well within the aircraft's capabilities but asking a lot of a pilot to be good at everything. The RAF's solution was to make each squadron a specialist in one of the disciplines required. This has worked well.

OFFICER COMMANDING 6 SQUADRON

GEORGE

To be the boss of a fighter squadron is such a huge privilege and to be given command of 6 Squadron represented the highlight of my RAF career. I had never been driven by ambition. My motivation had always been to fly interesting and exciting aircraft and to be the best that I could be in each role that I had been given. The fact that promotion often resulted always came as a bit of a pleasant surprise to me and I stepped up to the challenge as best I could.

I had watched over the years some colleagues who were completely obsessed with climbing the greasy pole towards the next highest rank and I saw how it came to affect every aspect of their home and professional life and I determined not to be like them. I think this attitude stemmed from when I first decided on the RAF as a career. My motivation had always been the flying, and I never nurtured the ambition of one day being the chief of air staff. I always envisioned that I would probably leave after 16 years and do something else.

Being given command of a squadron is one of the biggest challenges in the RAF and a crucial stepping stone to the higher ranks. If you make a success of it, you can expect to proceed to the next tier, but you are in no doubt that you will be under scrutiny the whole time. It is a bit like being a football manager where you can expect to be rewarded if you get results but can just as easily be sacked if you do not. One or two Jaguar squadron commanders had already lost their job for various reasons in the early days. Not having any particular ambition for the higher ranks is therefore an advantage as it stops you from constantly worrying about how your actions will be perceived and instead you just concentrate on the job in hand.

I took over 6 Squadron from Wg Cdr Neil Hayward in December 1977. Neil had a well-deserved reputation as 'Mr Jaguar', having worked on the Jaguar development project at MoD, followed by the introduction to service at RAF Lossiemouth. Under his guidance, 6 Squadron was already well set up when I arrived on the scene, and many of the initial teething problems had been overcome. We had a week together by way of handover before Neil moved on and I took over.

No. 20 Jaguar Course.

The Jaguar base at Coltishall had a great atmosphere and enjoyed the nickname of 'happy valley'. Unlike our Jaguar compatriots in Germany, we were free from the nuclear-strike role with all its attendant intensity, QRA duties, and life in hardened aircraft shelters. The city of Norwich was just ten miles away with its shops, entertainment and a first division football team. The Norfolk Broads were just down the road and the beautiful north Norfolk coastline close by. It was a very pleasant place to live. Sheila came south and we had a very nice married quarter on the base. Our two girls remained as boarders in their Edinburgh school.

There were three Jaguar squadrons at RAF Coltishall, 6 and 54 Squadrons in the conventional attack role and 41 Squadron in the reconnaissance role. There was a good deal of friendly rivalry between the three squadrons as we each tried to outdo each other. 6 Squadron was assigned to NATO's northern region at Tirstrup in Denmark, and we would deploy there for exercises and for real.

The 6 Squadron establishment consisted of 20 pilots and about 130 engineers. I had three flight commanders. Sqn Ldr Malcolm Bartle was the exec and my deputy; he was an experienced Hunter pilot and a QFI. Sqn Ldr John Pym was OC A Flight. He was our fighter weapons instructor (FWI) and was our most experienced Jaguar pilot having flown the aircraft from the very beginning. Sqn Ldr Doug Stephen was OC B Flight and had a couple of Phantom tours under his belt.

I also had a senior engineering officer and a junior engineering officer. We were very closely integrated with the engineers, all the more so because we lived and worked together closely on deployment. Our engineering was largely autonomous, a necessary requirement for our mobile role, and we did our own rectification and scheduled servicing up to and including minor servicing. For major servicing our aircraft were sent to Abingdon.

George as OC 6 Squadron.

Preparing for the chariot race.

The close ties, both professional and social, between the pilots and engineers were partly due to our frequent overseas deployments where we worked and played together. We had two engineering officers, a flight sergeant in overall charge of the troops, and chief technician trade managers for each specialisation. Flight Sergeant Hugh Brown ran a tight ship, and in charge of the line was a little Yorkshire ball of fire, Chief Tech Pip Curzon. The trade managers were all chief techs who took immense pride in their work. Out on the line in all weathers were the flight-line mechanics, refuelling, rearming, and turning round the aircraft.

I made a point of attending the trade managers meetings whenever possible so that I could hear at first-hand what the current issues were. I was constantly impressed by the quality of our engineers in all ranks and was in no doubt that our success was so very dependent on their efforts.

The close integration of engineers and aircrew in the Jaguar force was more than I had experienced in any other squadron and explained in many ways the high morale that was typical in Jaguar units of the time.

We were of course supported by the station engineering wing and the servicing bays, so that line replaceable units could be quickly fixed and turned around. When on deployment we were reinforced with engineers from the servicing bays who were fully integrated and considered part of 6 Squadron for the duration.

There was a tradition on station sports day that the three squadrons would compete in a chariot race. Our engineers designed and built a magnificent chariot which had as its chassis a bomb trolley. It was strong, probably over-engineered and would have withstood a nuclear explosion. It was also heavy, as we were about to find out. The idea was to beat the other participants in the chariot race using all methods both fair and foul. My job was to ride in the chariot armed with suitable weapons which included flour and soot bombs, water bombs and mops to repel boarders.

We got off to a great start and were soon exchanging ordnance with the opposition, but the heavy bomb trolley started to take its toll, and the opposition began to overtake. I had to dismount and help to push. We didn't win but came second and had a great day out.

RAF PUBLICITY

Operating the RAF's latest toy, I found we were in constant demand for visits and RAF publicity campaigns.

Jaguar four-ship (Richard Cook).

Two particularly handsome young pilots, Bernie Mills and Chris Daymon were in constant demand to star in RAF recruitment advertisements, a role that resulted in a great deal of good-natured teasing and banter from their contemporaries. Chris Daymon, a young fair-haired Adonis at the time, was also selected to appear as a sponsor on the Hughie Green talent show, which he did reluctantly but with a good grace. Two of our junior engineering officers, Richard Learner and Trevor Winn-Morgan also featured in recruiting ads.

We also developed a good working relationship with Richard Cook, a local photographer who specialised in dramatic air-to-air shots of aircraft. He had perfected a technique with a rear-facing camera mounted on a Folland Gnat in order to get head-on shots of aircraft. We duly set up a sortie with a formation of four Jaguars chasing the camera ship on a low-level flight which included some dramatic backgrounds from the Needles on the south coast to the low-flying area in Wales (opposite). These shots featured prominently in RAF recruiting ads at the time. 6 Squadron had its moment of fame until another outfit with newer equipment took over.

We also had our fair share of visitors keen to see the new jet. The Staff Colleges were regulars, and I worked up a slide show that showcased the squadron and its role. I was also invited to give a presentation at my alma mater, the RAF Staff College at Bracknell. I gave the usual presentation about the Jaguar, explaining its merits as well as its limitations. The commandant at the time was Air Marshal Sir John Curtiss, a navigator by trade. He had been the station commander at RAF Brüggen when I was there on the Phantom, and we had flown together a couple of times. During questions he asked me a loaded question about what was best, a two-seat aircraft or a single seat in the low-level attack role. A short answer to this is not possible because 'it all depends'. The navigator's role was changing. Modern avionic systems were taking over but there was still a need for a weapons system operator in the back seat to operate self-defence equipment on board, especially for deeper penetration as in the Tornado. But for tactical operations close to the front line a two-seat aircraft is probably overkill.

DENMARK

The routine of squadron life was frequently punctuated by overseas deployments. We had many visits to our forward operating base of Tirstrup in Denmark (now Aarhus Airport). It was a Luftwaffe airfield in World War II then postwar and throughout the Cold War it was a military air base for the Royal Danish Air Force and for NATO. Infrastructure funding had provided it with hardened aircraft shelters for the aircraft, but accommodation for personnel was in short supply. As a result, when we deployed in squadron strength, we had tented accommodation and catering was provided by a superb field kitchen giving the troops a plentiful supply of the kind of grub they enjoyed. The tented accommodation was shared by all ranks which again explains the close connection we had between pilots and engineers.

The base at Tirstrup was shared with a Danish squadron operating the Saab Draken. I remember particularly deploying there as part of our 1979 TACEVAL. The first phase took place at Coltishall with a no-notice call out and aircraft generation phase. The deployment to Tirstrup followed where we were scrutinised in our day-to-day operations by the TACEVAL team which included a young and very sharp Sqn Ldr Peter Squire who later rose to the dizzy height of chief of air staff. I took him on a familiarisation ride in our Jaguar T2.

We returned to Denmark in August 1979, this time to Karup in central Jutland. This was the main operating base for two Saab Draken squadrons. It featured famously in the immediate postwar period when the test pilot Captain Eric 'Winkle' Brown laid claim to a group of nine Arado AR234 jet bombers and transferred them back to UK for further study at RAE Farnborough.

We were there for a major NATO exercise called 'far event'. We were operating with mixed formations with other nations including an American detachment from Bitburg with their brand-new F15 fighters and a bunch of F5 Aggressors. As strikers, we flew anti-clockwise around Jutland ending up at a bombing range on the south-west coast. With the superb radar in the F15, they could always see us coming and there are few hills to hide behind in Jutland. We started to operate with the F5 Aggressor squadron in mixed formations with the F5s tucked in close formation with the Jaguars, so that only a single blip would show on the F15 radar. The F5s would then peel off and engage the F15s in close combat while we continued to the range unmolested.

We were joined on this detachment by our 38 Group AOC, Air Vice Marshal Joe Gilbert. He had always shown a keen interest in the Coltishall Jaguar squadrons who were his only fighter-bomber assets in 38 Group. I flew him in the T2 on one of the mixed formations which he greatly enjoyed.

An additional bonus for me was a flight in the two-seat F15 to see the operation from the fighter perspective. I found the F15 very easy to fly and much more forgiving than the Phantom, and its pulse doppler radar was a revelation.

DECIMOMANNU, SARDINIA

A regular feature in our calendar was an annual armament practice camp at Decimomannu (Deci for short) in Sardinia. The airfield was set up in 1960 by NATO as an air weapons training base for UK, Germany, Italy and the USA. Deci is situated about ten miles north-east of the city of Cagliari, and we used the bombing range at Cape Frasca to practice strafe, level and dive bombing and also toss bombing. I was very familiar with the base and the range having visited many times in the Phantom.

The Deci detachment was always popular as Sardinia is such a lovely island, especially in the spring with its abundance of wildflowers. For recreation we often visited the local holiday camp at Forte Village.

MORE SQUADRON EXCHANGES

We had two NATO squadron exchange visits during my time at 6 Squadron. These are usually quite convivial occasions aimed at promoting greater understanding between NATO units with similar roles. Such informal contacts provide a deliberately more relaxed forum for the discussion of common problems and for improving understanding through combined familiarisation sorties where the two units operate together.

The first of these took place in May 1978 on an exchange with the Canadian 441 Squadron based at Baden/ Sollingen in southern Germany. I had previously

Danish F100.

exchanged with 441 Squadron when on the Phantom and knew them to be hard flying and hard drinking.

I went south with four Jaguars including our T2 twin seater whilst a bunch of Canadians from 441 Squadron went north to operate with the other half of our squadron at Coltishall. Poor weather limited our flying but did not limit the hectic social life. We had a good time, learned a lot from the Canadians and vice versa, so the main aims were achieved. I had a trip in a two-seat CF104 in exchange for a flight in our T2. The CF104 was interesting, built for straight line speed with terrific acceleration, but with its tiny wings, not much good at turning. The Canadians knew how to get the best out of it, and it would have been hard for an air-defence fighter to stop it when it was flying low and fast.

The second squadron exchange took place in May 1979 with Esk 730 of the Royal Danish Air Force who were based at Skrydstrup in southern Jutland operating the F100D Super Sabre. This time I remained at Coltishall to host the visitors whilst the other half of our squadron deployed to Skrydstrup.

At Coltishall a varied schedule of flying and off-duty activities had been arranged for the visitors who were greeted on the afternoon of their arrival by 'Beers in the Line Hut' as a subtle acknowledgement of another notable Danish export. Day one of the visit kicked off next morning with a series of aircrew orientation briefings covering subjects such as local air traffic control, low-level flying routes, weapons ranges and other UK procedures. Sortie briefings were conducted by formation leaders in preparation for the start of flying on the afternoon of 9 May. The typical sortie composition throughout the exchange was a four-ship comprising national pairs. Whenever possible one of the two Jaguars in the sorties was to be a T2 with a Danish pilot aboard, such guest rides being supplemented by opportunities to experience the Jaguar simulator at Coltishall.

Much of the emphasis in the exchange sorties was to familiarise the Danes with the UK operating areas as their navigation had to necessarily employ the stopwatch and compass in view of the F-100's avionics limitations. The Esk 730 pilots know every square metre of their small country and relished the opportunity to fly over new territory. In fact, the scope of their mission at home is a broad one, linked to NATO's BALTAP (Baltic Approaches) Command. Esk 730's role takes in not only close air support for ground forces, but also maritime attack and air defence. At that time the squadron expected to be trading-in its veteran F-100s for F16s during 1981, and it would be the second RDAF unit to form on the F16. The first F16 was expected to be delivered to Skrydstrup in January 1980.

Flannery funeral party.

The visitor's boss, Major Henrik Vejen readily affirmed that we had "taken good care of them in the air and on the ground".

A 6 SQUADRON CASUALTY FROM WORLD WAR II

What follows was written by Flt Lt Tagg Taggart, who formed part of the 6 Squadron Guard of Honour and funeral party which I led.

"We were advised in 1978 that the wreckage of a World War II Hurricane had been found in the sea somewhere off the Italian coast near Grottaglie. Sadly, the remains of the pilot were still in the cockpit and through historical records we could verify that the aircraft was a 6 Squadron Hurricane that had been lost during the Allied drive north through Italy. A formation of two Hurricanes on a night shipping strike on 5 June 1944 had located some German F boats off the Italian coast and had attacked them. The leader pressed home two attacks but nothing more was heard from his number two (Fg Off Flannery) and despite extensive and repeated searches nothing was ever found."

The UK authorities managed to trace the sole remaining relative who happened to be the pilot's elderly mother who now lived in Portugal. When asked how she wished her son to be buried she indicated that it should be local, among the fallen and the pall bearers should be his squadron colleagues.

The pilot was to be interred at the World War II military cemetery at Monte Cassino where arrangements had been made by the British Consulate. An interesting feature of Italian bureaucracy was that the movement of human remains across Italy is tightly controlled by law and when the coffin arrived at the cemetery it was covered with official seals. When we arrived at the cemetery we gathered at the graveside for a quiet briefing on the procedure. While doing so, an RAF officer from the consulate expressed doubt at the length of the grave versus the length of the coffin. Sure enough, a length of string was produced and showed the grave to be 6 inches too short!! Time was also short; however, the gravediggers were summoned and all was well.

The mother was our VIP on this day, and she was not too steady on her feet. Many people were on hand for her support, and her son had a fitting funeral. Some 50 metres distant and discretely to one side there was an Italian Air Force band and guard of honour. One of our group whispered under his breath, "which side were they on at that time?" After the ceremony the mother was introduced to all of us. "Did you know my son?" was a question asked by a bewildered and distraught mother. What possible answer is there?

Humour, tragedy, courage and dignity all combined with a most beautiful spring day in that silent serene scene of the endless fallen. Up until now this pilot was listed as 'missing in action' some 35 years ago. It was a moving experience to have been part of the ceremony to have finally laid to rest a young 22-year-old Hurricane pilot who was now at peace and now listed as, 'killed in action'. Despite the grief, the mother seemed content. Fg Off Flannery died before I was born.

KEY PERSONNEL

I was very fortunate in having such capable people in key positions. My three pilot flight commanders could easily have been in my position under different circumstances. Sqn Ldr John Pym was our most experienced Jaguar pilot and was also a qualified weapons instructor. He was also a very loyal supporter of me throughout my time at 6 Squadron. He was a charismatic Australian, a gifted fighter pilot and also a bit of a maverick not averse to shortcuts and a touch of rule bending to get results, somewhat like the other maverick in the film of that name, so he needed some oversight with a light touch.

I had already learned that the best leadership style for me was to create a team, to delegate and to give individuals the authority to deliver their finest performance under my overall guidance. I had seen in the past individuals who could not resist the temptation to micromanage. It simply resulted in them getting overloaded and their subordinates becoming frustrated.

I had far more engineers than pilots and engineering is not my speciality, but I had a couple of engineering officers, a very capable flight sergeant and some splendid trade managers. I did my best to get to know everyone by name which was a bit of a struggle for me as I am not great at remembering names and faces but I did realise early on what a difference it made if the young SAC strapping me in could be greeted by name. We pilots get so focussed and obsessed with flying that it is easy to forget that without good engineering backup we are going nowhere. The engineering senior NCOs are the ones that make the difference, and if they are on side, the rest will follow.

It is worth also mentioning our ground liaison officer (GLO), Major Tyacke who had his own Land Rover and corporal driver. He was always a useful sounding board quite apart from his army specialisation.

And of course, we had our own exchange officers serving on 6 Squadron: Captain Jean-Marie Allier who had flown Jaguars with the French Air Force, and Captain Gys Schoor who had flown F104s with the Dutch Air Force. Both managed very well considering that English is not their first language and they had to get used to the RAF culture and way of doing things. They even adapted to our sense of humour which in those days was very non-PC. Gys was 'The Cloggie' and Jean-Marie 'The Frog'. Jean-Marie made his 1,000 hours on Jaguars whilst on 6 Squadron which was duly celebrated with champagne.

THE MERCERS LIVERY COMPANY

The Mercers rank first in the order of precedence of City of London livery companies. It was originally established as a trade association for merchants and especially for the export and import of wool and fine fabrics. It now exists primarily as a charitable institution supporting a variety of causes which include St Paul's School in London. They also sponsor units for all three services: HMS *Dauntless*, a Type 45 destroyer for the navy; the Mercian Regiment for the army; and 6 Squadron for the RAF.

The connection with 6 Squadron started during my tenure, and we hosted a large contingent at RAF Coltishall to look around the squadron followed by a formal lunch. Sqn Ldr John Pym flew Major Ide Smith, the master of the Mercers in our T2.

As CO, I was invited down each year to attend one of their formal dinners at Mercer's Hall in London, always a grand affair and full of the great and the good of the London scene. The connection between the Mercers and the squadron continues to this day and they have been very generous in their sponsorship.

ALAN

George didn't mention that he brought his squadron to RAF Wildenrath for a couple of weeks. They occupied the otherwise unused central dispersal. I visited one day when I had nothing on, said hello to George and was introduced to a number of his pilots. Sqn Ldr John Pym offered me a trip in the back of the T2, which was to be a flight over the Netherlands to the Vliehors range on Vlieland Island. The idea was to drop four retard practice bombs. They looked like large blue bean tins with fins on the back, but they simulated a 1,000 lb retard bomb, filled with a white powder so that the range officer could plot where it landed. John dropped three of the four bombs from quite low level and scored near misses. He then asked if I would like to drop the fourth bomb. Of course. The bomb sight in the back seat was the same as the front, and I had been watching quite carefully. I pressed the button on the stick and was delighted when the range officer announced, "direct hit". John was not amused and grumbled about it in a friendly way, all the way back to Wildenrath. Just saying.

THE 1978 TACTICAL BOMBING COMPETITION

GEORGE

The mid to late seventies were at the peak of the Cold War, and our training was directed towards the low-level attack role where our only tactic was high-speed low-level penetration, flying below SAM engagement heights and evading enemy interception. We became highly adept from constant practice, often in quite marginal weather conditions. Fortunately, in those days we didn't have any real wars to worry about – these came later. Instead, we had competitions both national and international, which were taken incredibly seriously. The RAF was expected to take on all comers and to win, nothing less would do! The Americans in particular were becoming thoroughly fed up with always being trounced by the Brits in NATO tactical weapons meetings.

When I arrived at Coltishall, the wing had been told to field a team for the 1978 tactical bombing competition. The other squadron commanders had a head start in figuring out pressing reasons why they couldn't do it. I ducked too late and was given what might have been a poisoned chalice. The CinC Strike Command of the day was Air Chief Marshal Sir David Evans. He was determined to show what the Jaguar could do, and he had declared a personal grudge match with his US equivalent in Tactical Air Command.

In fairness, we were given extra resources for the work up, including additional allocation of four lb practice bombs, extra range slots, and our own Marconi Elliott rep to help with tweaking the NAVWASS. The work-up period was run as a trial, and results were quantified in an attempt to identify the specific strengths and weaknesses of the Jaguar with a view to future modification programmes. The project officer for this was Sqn Ldr John Pym my OC A Flight, who was a qualified weapons instructor, and he ran the work up and the competition with great flair.

The engineers as usual were brilliant. The NAVWASS team in particular decided to keep the line replaceable units (LRUs) together as matched sets. The E3R inertial platform and the platform electronic unit were kept as a pair, so that if either had a problem they were both pulled out and sent to the bay for servicing. Much time was

Signed copy of the 23 TFW A7D Team.

spent on harmonising the aircraft after a gun change, laser change or E3R platform change. It was all time consuming but paid off in better scores.

For those who have not experienced it at first hand, it is worth considering the culture within a typical fighter squadron. There is a natural rivalry and sometimes intense competition between young men who want to be the best they can be, fuelled by testosterone and adrenaline. Your status in the hierarchy is determined by weapons scores and your combat ability in the air. The rivalry and lively banter continue in the debrief and later in the bar. Translate that culture into an international competition, where not only your personal reputation is at stake, but also that of your squadron and the RAF itself, and you will see that the pressure to succeed is immense.

Selection of the team for the competition was by a series of fly-offs, but the final six were selected for both ability and experience. We needed team members with big match temperament. We were required to field a four-ship and a pair. The four-ship was led by Sqn Ldr John Pym, with Flt Lts John Hodgson, Rick Lea, and Fg Off Bernie Mills. The pair consisted of Sqn Ldrs Russ Peart and Malcolm Bartle.

6 Squadron winning team.

The actual competition took place at Lossiemouth in July 1978. The teams were: 6 Squadron from Coltishall, 31 Squadron Jaguars from Brüggen under Wg Cdr Terry Nash, and three Buccaneer squadrons (15, 16, 208). The Americans had formed a special unit to take us on, from the 23rd Tactical Fighter Wing at England AFB, Louisiana, flying Vought A7s. Their team was selected from the best of the wing, and they were formidable rivals with a very capable aircraft. The A7 had a very good inertial platform based on the unit in the Minuteman Missile which had a level of accuracy far exceeding that of the NAVWASS in our Jaguar. The Americans we later discovered had a 'B' Team whose main objective was to waylay the Brits into late-night drinking sessions and nobble them for the next day's flying! The start of the competition was delayed due to poor weather, and with bad weather forecast for the following day we all retired to the bar where the beer and banter flowed freely. Later on, I went out for some fresh air to discover that the sky had cleared. On ringing the met office, I found that the forecast had improved and flying would be on the next morning, so it was back to the bar to shepherd my team off to bed – quite a challenge from a party in full swing.

The end result was that 6 Squadron won five of the seven available trophies so we had a good result. The team trophy went to the Americans who achieved a brilliant score on day two of the competition (although 6 Squadron had a better aggregate score over the three days). 6 Squadron also won the Marconi Elliott Trophy for best RAF team, and the Adour Trophy for best Jaguar team. The BAC trophy for best leadership in bombing and navigation went to Sqn Ldr Russ Peart of 6 Squadron, and the top gun trophy went to Flt Lt John Hodgson also of 6 Squadron who achieved a remarkable strafe score of 75 per cent. John was and is the complete gentleman, and the antithesis of the braggadocio and swagger of the Tom Cruise character of Top Gun fame. The weapons trophy for best bombing score went to Flying Officer Gary Rogers of 31 Squadron with an excellent 14 ft average. The poor old Buccaneer squadrons went home empty handed. With the Tornado on the horizon, this showed that it was no longer possible to compete internationally without a modern avionics suite.

The Adour Trophy for best Jaguar squadron was presented by Sir Stanley Hooker of Rolls-Royce. He had a hand in the design of the Adour but had made his name many years before in designing the supercharger which transformed the performance of the Merlin engine and in the design and development of the early jet engines.

The work up and the competition itself produced a host of data which helped define later improvements to the aircraft. It highlighted the limitations of the original NAVWASS in terms of accuracy and reliability, and it resulted in a new method for harmonising the Aden guns for better accuracy on strafe.

'FLAG' EXERCISES AND AAR
AIR-TO-AIR REFUELLING

GEORGE

I had to re-acquaint with AAR in the Jaguar having previously done a lot in the Phantom. The technique was essentially the same, except that there was no back seater in the Jag to assist with the line up, and the Adour engines tended to run out of puff above 25,000 ft when doing AAR, often requiring part throttle reheat to maintain contact. There were regular tanker towlines in the North Sea, and we would often top up from them before continuing north for low-level training.

We all had to qualify or re-qualify in AAR and I did a number of training flights in the T2 with some of our pilots who had never done AAR before.

The need for AAR became more important when the Jaguar squadrons started to attend the 'flag' exercises in the USA (more of which later). The Germany-based Jaguar squadrons were not AAR qualified, so we had to ferry their aircraft across the pond on their behalf.

RED FLAG

Exercise Red Flag is a realistic air combat training exercise hosted by the US Air Force at Nellis Air Base near Las Vegas, Nevada. It made use of an enormous exercise area in Nevada which was bigger than the whole of Wales and allowed realistic tactical flying with no restrictions. Red Flag had been started by the USAF as a result of their experience in Vietnam. They had found that aircrew who had survived their

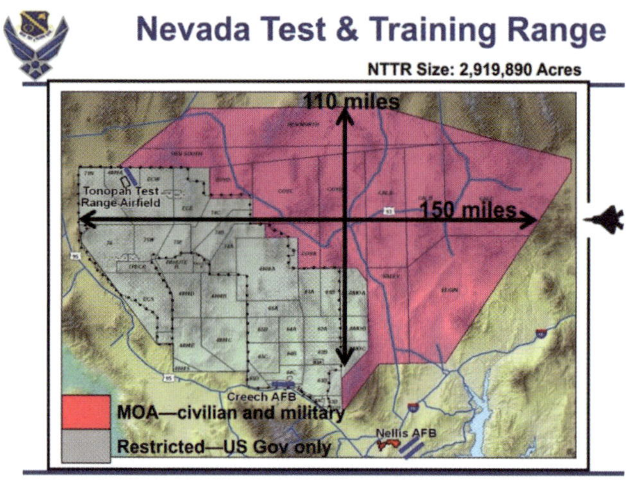

Nellis ranges.

The F117.

first ten war missions usually survived the whole campaign. Red Flag was designed to give that ten-mission exposure using the most realistic training scenarios possible. Captured Warsaw Pact equipment was used throughout, with radars, SAM sites, radar laid AAA, etc. all deployed and operating. They even had Aggressor squadrons equipped with the Northrop F5 fighter to simulate the Russian MiG21, painted in Russian colours and flown by elite instructors using Russian tactics.

My first visit to Red Flag was not as a participant. The Germany Jaguar squadrons had priority, and our job was to ferry their aircraft to and from Nellis via AAR as the Germany squadrons were not AAR qualified. Our full participation would come later, but it did mean that we were able to see how Red Flag worked and participate in the briefing and debriefing of sorties. I was immediately impressed by the full-on nature of the exercise and how the Americans had gone to extreme measures to make the whole training experience as realistic as possible. Although hyped up by Hollywood, much of what you see in Top Gun Maverick is representative of what happens in Red Flag.

Participation was initially limited to USAF units but was soon extended to allied air forces of which the RAF was first. A Buccaneer unit from Germany was the first

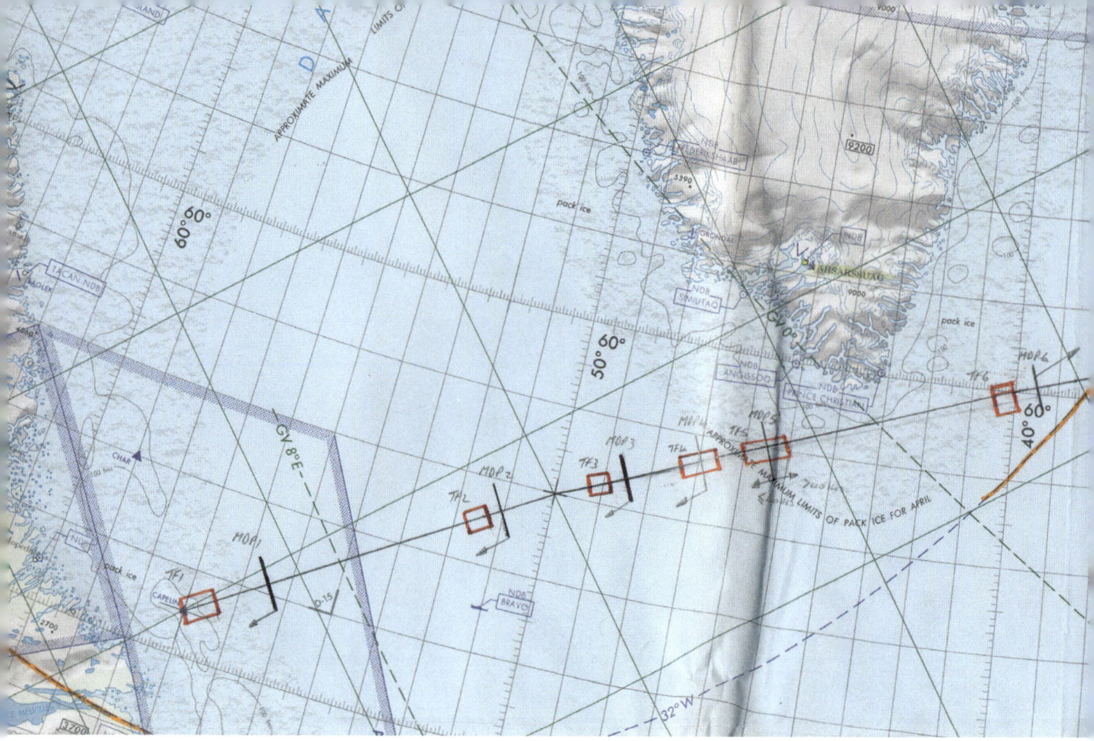

Refuelling brackets.

to take part and impressed the Americans hugely with their extreme low-level tactics.

Buried in the middle of the Nevada test and training range was Area 51, made famous by various conspiracy theories over the years as a possible site for investigating alien technology. This was nonsense of course but served as a distraction from what was really going on in Area 51. It was in fact a secret test and evaluation centre where the latest US technology was tried out.

This was the F117 stealth fighter which saw service in Gulf War 1. You can see why on a chance sighting during testing it might be mistaken for an alien craft!

At the end of the exercise, our job was to ferry the Jaguars back to RAF Brüggen in Germany via air-to-air refuelling. Each pair of Jaguars had a dedicated Victor tanker who took us across the USA and Canada for a night stop in Goose Bay, followed by the Atlantic crossing in one hop to RAF Brüggen.

Above is an extract from the actual map which I used for the return AAR sector from Goose Bay. The route passes just south of Greenland, and the refuelling brackets are marked, in each case with the option either to return to Goose Bay in the event of a failed fuel transfer, or to continue on to Keflavik in Iceland as our next diversion option.

The support from the tanker fleet was magnificent in shepherding and looking after their 'chicks' throughout this process. By now we were very experienced in AAR and were able to connect to the refuelling hose quickly and without drama. After our final refuelling bracket somewhere near Stornoway, we waved goodbye to our tanker and continued on to RAF Brüggen to deliver our two aircraft to 17 Squadron.

MAPLE FLAG

Red Flag had proved to be so successful that a similar high intensity training exercise was set up by the Canadians at CFB Cold Lake in Alberta and using the huge Cold Lake air weapons range for unrestricted low-level operations and live weapons drops. We took part during October to November 1979, positioning via AAR across the Atlantic.

For Maple Flag, we were authorised to fly down to 100 ft AGL, so as part of our work up, I had the job of clearing all pilots down to that height. This was done over the Welsh low-flying area on a special cleared route, and I flew multiple sorties with the nominated pilots at extreme low level until they were all cleared to my satisfaction as being safe to fly at this height.

The exercise itself proved to be of great value. The air weapons range boundary is about 40 miles north of Cold Lake and is huge at just over a million hectares of primarily tundra, pine forest and lakes populated mostly by Caribou, so noise complaints are few.

The participants included F104s and Voodoos from the Canadian Armed Forces, F4s, E3 Sentry aircraft and F5 Aggressors from the USAF. We started off doing some air combat training with the F5 Aggressors which as always was very good value. The Aggressor instructors were very experienced USAF instructor pilots. They replicated Warsaw Pact tactics whenever possible and although the received

Maple Flag.

wisdom at the time was that Warsaw Pact interceptors operated mostly under close control of a GCI station, there was also evidence that their 'elite' pilots were cleared to operate 'freelance' and could conduct visual CAPs independently. Our aim was always to avoid such engagements and proceed towards the target unmolested, but when intercepted to conduct effective self-defence manoeuvres to disengage as soon as possible.

The exercises progressed on to four and six-ship interdiction sorties. We had one sortie where we hooked up with an American RF4F whose job was to lead us into a pinpoint target which he marked with smoke. He did a good job in finding and marking the target resulting in a successful attack by our two Jaguars. The opportunity to operate at extreme low level making use of terrain screening wherever possible was one of the main training benefits of the flag exercises and such profiles were increasingly impossible to plan in UK and European airspace.

Debriefs were always thorough in flag exercises, but they insisted in brevity and concise and factual reporting. A debrief had to last no more than ten minutes and you were assessed on content and accuracy. An unofficial debrief would continue in the bar later and social life in flag exercises was always convivial.

Things have moved on since these early days, and air combat ranges are now instrumented so that the fight can be analysed later with 100 per cent accuracy.

Our station commander at RAF Coltishall, Gp Capt Tom Stonor (later Air Marshal Sir Tom) accompanied us to Maple Flag, and he was able to experience at first hand the great value to be had from this type of training. At the end of the exercise, we ferried the aircraft back via Winnipeg and Ottawa to Goose Bay and then via AAR back to Coltishall.

LESSONS FROM THE FALKLANDS WAR

GEORGE

I was very fortunate in that all my RAF service occurred during the Cold War. I was never involved in a real war and never had to fire a shot in anger. Nevertheless, you cannot spend your life training hard for an event you hoped would never happen without also wondering how you would have coped if it had turned hot.

Just two years after I left the RAF, we did see our first real war since Korea during which we operated autonomously and without the support of a coalition. This section is taken from an article I wrote for the 6 Squadron Association corresponding with the 40th Anniversary of the Falklands War. It concentrates on the offensive air aspects of the Falklands conflict and especially on the experience of the Harrier attack operations conducted by 1 Squadron and the lessons which were relevant to contemporary Jaguar operations.

THE FALKLANDS WAR

The Falklands War was the last time that our armed forces were involved in an operation without also being part of a wider coalition. It was the most remarkable undertaking at some 8,000 miles distant from UK. It required great courage, resourcefulness and determination by all concerned not least our political leadership under Margaret Thatcher with the robust support and guidance of Admiral Sir Henry Leach.

We all know the result, but at the time success was by no means guaranteed and our success was later considered to be a "close run thing". Just two years before, I had command of 6 Squadron at Coltishall with the Jaguar GR1. We had therefore been operating the same generation of aircraft and weapons that took part in the Falklands campaign, and the lessons learned would have been very relevant to our ongoing training and tactics.

Since then, many books have been published about the campaign by veterans of all three services. My main interest lies in the offensive air campaign covering both air defence and ground-attack operations by the Sea Harrier and the Harrier GR1s of 1 Squadron. On the face of it, the Harriers faced overwhelming odds, outnumbered 10:1 by the Argentinian air assets. The Carrier Battle Group had two embarked Sea Harrier squadrons: 800 on board *Hermes* and 801 on board *Invincible* but there was no airborne early warning capability. The type 42 and 22 escort destroyers provided radar cover and fighter direction which was limited to the radar horizon. The carriers were therefore kept well to the east of the Falklands and out of range of Argentinian attack aircraft which meant that the Sea Harriers had limited time on CAP.

The CO of 801 NAS on board *Invincible* was Commander 'Sharkey' Ward. He has written two books which give his own 'warts and all' view of the air campaign and are well worth a read. Sharkey was a very experienced operator who had flown Sea Vixens and Phantoms from the old *Ark Royal.* He had been desk officer in MoD responsible for Sea Harrier development and then commanded the Sea Harrier Trials Unit before taking over command of 801 NAS. He was therefore rightly considered to be 'Mr Sea Harrier' and knew more about flying and fighting the Sea Harrier than anyone else. He was also considered to be a bit of a maverick, and his book pulls no punches concerning shortcomings in the tasking and direction of the air war by the ‘flag’ on HMS *Hermes*. He is openly critical about his opposite number on *Hermes* who had differing views on Sea Harrier tactics. He also has some harsh words to say about the RAF, who he has never forgiven for the cancellation of the navy’s new carrier in the late 1960s on the spurious claim that the RAF could provide for fleet defence from shore bases anywhere in the world. He is also particularly scornful about the Vulcan Black Buck raids which succeeded in putting just one bomb on the Stanley runway.

The Sea Harriers gave a very good account of themselves with 20 kills for no combat losses against Argentine aircraft, but perhaps more importantly, their growing reputation resulted in many ‘soft kills’, where Argentinian raids jettisoned their weapons and headed home rather than face the Sea Harriers when their passive warning receivers detected the presence of a Sea Harrier CAP.

A number of factors contributed to the Sea Harrier success. The force was re-equipped in the nick of time with the Sidewinder 9L, a much more capable weapon than the 9G. The range from the Argentinian main bases was 300 miles which gave their attack aircraft minimum time in the target area and largely precluded the provision of fighter escorts. Finally, the navy engineers did a magnificent job in maintaining the aircraft and in keeping a high sortie rate.

The main ground attack and close air support capability was provided by the Harrier GR1s of 1 Squadron RAF. These aircraft did not sail with the task force but were later embarked on the ill-fated *Atlantic Conveyor* and were flown off to HMS *Hermes* when within range. Reinforcements were later flown out via AAR all the way from Ascension Island 3,000 miles away, a truly epic operation. In many ways the 1 Squadron GR1s had a harder task than the Sea Harriers. They were not trained for carrier operations and had to get up to speed very quickly, practising at RNAS Yeovilton with the ski jump and landing pads before embarking on *Atlantic Conveyer*. Their first carrier landing for real was aboard HMS *Hermes* on arrival in the South Atlantic. Their inertial systems could not be properly aligned on a pitching and rolling flight deck, so most war sorties were flown with standby instruments and using just map and stopwatch for navigation. The CO was Wg Cdr Peter Squire. I remember Peter well when he came to Tirstrup in 1979 as a Sqn Ldr on the TACEVAL team and he impressed me then as a very sharp operator.

Unlike the Sea Harriers, the GR1s had to operate over land in a very hostile environment against determined opposition from radar laid AAA, shoulder-launched missiles and a huge amount of small-arms fire. The GR1s suffered losses as a result. Both flight commanders and a squadron pilot were shot down (but ejected and survived) and Peter Squire only just recovered to the carrier after battle damage. The 1 Squadron groundcrew achieved miracles in maintenance and battle damage repair under the most trying circumstances.

The 1 Squadron A Flight commander, Sqn Ldr Jerry Pook, has written an excellent book about GR1 operations in the Falklands with lessons which are just as relevant today. There was much criticism that two of the shootdowns occurred on re-attacks, which of course ideally one should avoid. He talks about the extreme difficulty in acquiring well camouflaged targets at high speed and ultra-low level without proper recce coverage or expert close control and especially given the degraded nav attack system they had to work with. He mentions ineffective forward air control, something that we had also experienced in Jaguar operations. What was essentially a World War II technique involving a FAC talking the ground-attack pilots' eyes onto the target during the few seconds following pull up was always rather hit or miss, and so it proved to be. Also, the technique of running in from an initial point to pull up and tip in for weapons delivery would have been suicidal in such a high threat environment and 1 Squadron resorted to straight-in attacks at 500 kts and extreme low level with just a last-minute climb to 200 ft for weapon delivery to ensure that bombs would fuse. 1 Squadron achieved some notable successes in very challenging circumstances. An attack by a three-ship formation at Goose Green led by Peter Squire tipped the balance and led to the surrender of a much larger Argentine force to the 2 Para attackers.

1 Squadron was finally equipped with the Paveway 1,000 lb laser-guided bomb in the last days of the campaign and this proved to be a revelation. Finally, targets could be attacked with precision from a safe height, and this heralded the way ahead for future conflicts.

There are also lessons to be learned from the way the Argentinian forces conducted their air operations. Flying mostly Skyhawks and Daggers (Israeli-modified Mirage 5s) from bases on the mainland, the Argentinian pilots gave a very good account of themselves. By approaching at very low level over West Falklands, they could remain largely undetected until the last minute but had very little time for target acquisition as they crossed into Falklands Sound, so they usually went for the first target they saw which would be a warship rather than the ships unloading in the adjacent San Carlos water. They came in ultra-low and very fast with no regard for the correct weapon-release parameters, and as a result a high proportion of their bombs failed to explode. This was a mixed blessing because bombs delivered from 50 ft are more likely to hit the target than bombs delivered from 200 ft. A 1,000 lb bomb hitting a ship at 500 kts will do a lot of kinetic damage even if it does not explode, leaving the ship disabled and with the added problem of an on-board UXB to defuse.

The Exocet-equipped Etendard aircraft were the biggest worry for the task force as the RN ships had no short-range defences capable of shooting down a missile. Exocet attacks accounted for the loss of three ships of which the most disastrous was the sinking of the *Atlantic Conveyor* with its cargo of Chinook and Wessex helicopters, thus making the job of ground forces so much more difficult.

The on-board SAM systems on RN ships (Seawolf, Seacat, etc) took their toll but the short exposure time from the low-level approach over adjacent West Falklands meant that many Argentine attack aircraft got through. The performance of Rapier batteries on adjacent hills was disappointing as they struggled with the look-down scenario. Nevertheless, the Argentines suffered heavy attrition over the course of the war with over 100 aircraft losses from Sea Harrier, SAM, AAA and ground action.

There were important lessons too in the overall command and control of operations. There were separate commanders for the carrier battle group, the amphibious landing group and the army battle group, and with all three services involved and overall command at Northwood, there was plenty of scope for misunderstanding. Miscommunication was a factor in the losses of HMS *Sheffield* and in the losses of *Sir Galahad* and *Sir Tristram*. As joint operations are now the norm and communication systems much improved, most of these issues should now have been addressed.

So, given the experiences of the Falklands, how would the Jaguar force have fared if the Cold War had ever turned hot? We always tried to make our training as realistic as possible, and the Red Flag and Maple Flag exercises in USA and Canada certainly helped. The Falklands emphasized the need to keep exposure time down to an absolute minimum by making best use of terrain and flying at high speed and ultra-low level. Radar laid AAA took a heavier toll on UK attack aircraft than did SAM, and if we had persisted with pop-up attacks to 1,500 ft for ten-degree dive attacks we would probably have paid a heavy price. The Falklands War occurred at a transition where smart weapons were just entering service and in later campaigns as part of a coalition with local air superiority, smart weapon delivery from a safe height was the way ahead.

CHAPTER 7
AIR DEFENCE DAILY

29F SQUADRON

ALAN

Training was over (for the time being). No. 228 OCU had been fairly brutal. The OCU staff were utterly professional and the training was excellent. I was still feeling a little fragile from my missing years, so at the time when George was at Staff College, I was starting again, but it was a great feeling. Three crews were posted to 29 Squadron a few hundred yards from the OCU, so we collected our kit and wandered over. A new day seemed to have dawned. It was 25 November 1974 and the sun may even have come out. There was a lot of ground to make up though. I decided to stay in the officers' mess. Wendy was heavily involved as a five-county supply teacher, and she and I had agreed that I should commute from our house in Rutland to Coningsby as the programme dictated, just about an hour's drive. In fact, I grew to love Lincolnshire with its lack of hedges around the fields. You could see the seasons pass as the fields changed colour.

As a part of the great re-organisation, 29 was moving into what had been 6 Squadron. Our leader was the redoubtable Wg Cdr Danny Lavender, halfway through his own tour and claiming to know nothing about air defence. At the time he was in deep dispute with HMRC over a magnificent watch that was a personal gift from King Hussein of Jordan, which he won. The crews were mixed, some staying on from 6 Squadron with a role change, some posted in from 43 Squadron and some straight from training, like us. The engineers were largely unchanged, but with the addition of more radar technicians. I was crewed up with one of the two Canadian exchange officers, Gary Soule, who had learned his radar operator trade on Canadian Voodoos. He insisted that he didn't carry a map because he was a Fightergator. I knew that in practice all his documents were carefully lining his helmet bag.

We started training with a set target date for taking over our share of southern QRA as the Coltishall Lightnings stood down. Coltishall was going all Jaguar, so provision was made at Coningsby to make a new home for the Battle of Britain Memorial Flight. AAR from the Victor tankers was new to about half of us, and an entire AD infrastructure was required. An experienced fighter controller was posted in from sector operations at RAF Neatishead (near Norwich) to pave the way. Suzy Harrison did more than that. She owned two sets of campanologist's training bells which she would bring into the bar on Friday nights, and we became quite proficient bell ringers with a bell each.

Starting QRA was a big challenge. It was decided to park the two-armed F4s at the nearest point of the apron runway access. This was a short sprint for the groundcrew, and a bedroom was made for them, meals provided. For the aircrew, a storage room was available with access to the crew room one way and to outdoors the other. A Land Rover would be parked outside which the second pilot would drive. A telebrief was installed, a sort of open phone line which bleeped all day long through which sector and wing operations could talk to the crews. A hooter would announce an actual scramble. The officers' mess would feed us. It was all a bit Heath Robinson, but it worked and suited us well. However, the Russians rarely obliged with probes into the North Sea, so we felt that in many ways we were scaring off the elephants in Hyde Park. ("There aren't any elephants." "Effective, isn't it?"). It was before the days of terrorist high jacking which might require armed intervention, so the next event was to actually fire a missile.

A small number of aircraft were detached to RAF Valley to the Strike Command Air-to-Air Missile Establishment (STCAAME). A small team there had become experts at analysing missile performance and developing each weapon as it arrived in service. There were set profiles to be flown and practised in the simulator beforehand. We would send five aircraft with maybe six crews, from which Gary and I were allocated a Sidewinder AIM9G. The Sidewinder was an IR heat-seeking missile loaded with metal rods, but for STCAAME, these were replaced with a warhead that just went bang. For each firing, there would be a primary shooter, a backup shooter, and a camera aircraft for which they had adapted a forward-looking camera left over from the aircraft's mud-moving days. When George had attended a few years earlier their allocation was two missiles, but every firing was evaluated including theirs. The target was an Australian Jindivik drone towing a sort of sled with either flares for the Sidewinder or a radar reflecting lens for the Sparrow. Very occasionally the missile missed the sled and shot down the Jindivik, much to a team's jubilation.

It was our first time away from base as we got to know each other from which I only remember seeing the first *Star Wars* film in Holyhead. We got the job done, made new friends with the STCAAME staff, and were subjected to an hour's remedial formation flying by the boss on the way home. Danny, the boss, was generally happy with the 'can do' approach and would brief the next week's activities at a Friday afternoon squadron meeting. The Canadians would sabotage the event with unlimited gin supplies from the American BX at Alconbury, and on one occasion Danny briefed the week just passed. No one noticed. By this time, we had also adopted a navy drink called a 'chocolate spider', a vicious concoction that looked and tasted wonderful. The wives listened to the brief that it was a friendship drink that you sipped it and passed it on. Sadly, not everyone ever listened.

We had a squadron exchange with a Danish 726 F104 Squadron, during which I had my first Starfighter back-seat flight. In fact, the F104 turned out to be a pleasant aircraft to fly despite its 'bad boy' reputation. Of course, with tiny wings, its turn rate was a joke. Only the Belgians managed to get round this by taking the aircraft into the vertical, but that came later. I took one of the Danes flying in the back of an F4, not quite so exciting for him as there was no control column, but we flew the same

Danish F104D RT683.

aerobatics that I had seen in the F104 and compared notes. The 'away team' returned from Aarhus sightly bedraggled, and it seemed that 'what happened in Denmark stayed in Denmark'.

We sent three crews at a time to reinforce 43 Squadron at RAF Kinloss. They flew the FG1, or F4K, which was specified for the navy's carrier work, and came to the RAF after the withdrawal from east of Suez. We had a quick briefing in which we discovered that the FG1 did not have a battery or an INAS. However, it did seem to be slightly more agile and was a pleasure to fly. When we discovered that the wing fold still worked from a switch in the cockpit you could see a 29 Squadron pilot taxying with the wings going up and down. Back home in RAF Leuchars the F4 was just too big for the QRA hangars (constructed for the Lightning) so the northern QRA aircraft sat with the wings folded. Just outside the hangar was a large notice: 'SPREAD WINGS'.

Then sometime later, to our amazement, while we were settling down to Saturday daytime television back at Coningsby on southern QRA, we had a call from sector. Apparently, a Lightning from RAF Leuchars had made a mess of intercepting two Russian aircraft, and would we like the intercept? What a question. Sure enough, a commentary started on the telebrief, we rushed to get into our immersion (dry) suits and made sure we had everything including food and drink plus service and private cameras. The hooter sounded, the Land Rover behaved itself and the groundcrew were already at the armed aircraft. Ten minutes later we were airborne heading north. Gary, my Fightergator, then proved his worth, counting off distances from the TACAN (range and bearing), statements of the obvious. The last beacon at Saxavord broke lock and there was silence. I actually had a 1:600,000 map covering Iceland to Norway. My diary map. Gary asks, "Al, do you have your diary map?" "Well do you mind passing it back?" He really didn't carry a map.

By this time, we had refuelled from our very own Victor tanker and had been passed to the Danish fighter control station on the Faroe Islands, call sign Polestar, who steered us towards our targets. In fact, we had radar contact at around 70 miles. The two Tu95 Bear Ds were flying in trail, with the second aircraft a good deal lower and 20 miles behind the leader. When we got closer, we could see that he had an engine out, but he was continuing anyway. From the smiles on the crew's faces, this looked like a Cuba run, great sun, rum and girls, what fun after a winter on the White Sea, and where would they have diverted to? The Norwegians had made the first intercept as the Bears entered NATO airspace. We then picked it up, and we were surprised to be joined by two USAF F4Es from Iceland. Later, the Bears would

Bear D intercept near Iceland.

be accompanied by stateside interceptors, probably from the Air National Guard. In the meantime, we had our pictures and went home.

29 Squadron had gelled quite nicely. We had our own skiffle group (skiffle was a form of folk music in answer to serious rock and roll, a feature of coffee bars and the 1970s) running complete with washboards and tea chest base. We were doing well in the monthly station exercises, MINEVALs, and were quite proficient in

Post Bear intercept with groundcrew.

electric counter measures (ECM), provided by the Canberra T17s of 360 Squadron. It was time to find out about the gun, the SUU23/A. Up to this point, the aircraft's centreline hard point had carried a fuel tank. The armourers were quite excited. On the day we did a refuelling trail, two Phantoms to one Victor tanker, with a refuelling top-up on joining formation, and another over the French Alps. After that we did annoy the tanker slightly by having more fuel than we needed and accelerating to supersonic down the Med. We arrived in time to watch the XM645 Vulcan explode, not a great start to the detachment.

The grand plan was that we were the reinforcing squadron for the RAF Luqa TACEVAL, with tanker support. The bar duly closed so 57 Victor Squadron set up a bar in a spare bedroom and called in the skiffle group to perform. Three days later the exercise ended. 57 Squadron organised a grand parade up the officers' mess steps and we met a funeral party at the front door. The station commander declared that every dog has one bite and this was ours. Somebody bought him a chocolate spider and that seemed to smooth things down. However, despite problems using the air-to-ground gun sight for air-to-air, results were quite respectable. Don Oakden had taken over the squadron and he changed nothing. We were that kind of unit. Malta had changed little from George's time there, and we loved it. The buses were still

Restored single-colour Maltese bus — blue local line.

The SUU23/A cannon.

coloured according to their line to help illiterate peasants and RAF aircrew. You took a red bus to get back to the mess. Easy. Later the Prime Minister Dom Mintoff had all the buses painted muddy green, and everyone got lost. The blue bus pictured served the southern suburbs of Valetta.

We aimed to fly the aircraft up to four times a day. However, everything had to be serviceable, the gun, the radar, the gun sight and indeed the target tug. These were a three-aircraft detachment of Canberras from 360 Squadron. The minimum shooting range was, I think, 200 yards, not below 15 degrees angle off. Even so the crews complained of hearing bullets going past. The Canberra flew in an enlarged ellipse. The 20mm inert bullets were dipped in different colour paints so that up to five shooters might fire on one flag, and the flag was just that, about the size of a tennis net towed behind the tug. While the gun could fire out at 6,000 rounds a minute in about 12 seconds, the training shoot was done at 4,000 rpm. Even so, a touch on the trigger might fire seven or eight rounds. After the shoot, the tug would drop the banner on the runway where their ground party would take it to the squadron. A weapons instructor would then count up each colour, work out a percentage and record the shoot on paper. Competition was fierce, but, as ever, we got there. Though there was a slight altercation with an RAF policeman over our band instruments being loaded onto the return C130; apparently, we should not have recorded them as 'miscellaneous tuning equipment' in the load manifest.

There was a squadron exchange with the Dutch 322 Squadron at RNlAF Leeuwarden, and once again we came to appreciate their F104 Starfighters. RAF tradition was then deeply embedded in the Dutch Air Force, and of course, like the Danes, they all spoke perfect English. Embarrassing. Their mascot was a fairly vicious grey parrot that lived in the crew room and went home with one of the pilots at the weekend. However, we actually did some serious work with their fighter control at Nieuw Milligen, as well as getting to love that part of Friesland. We spent the weekend on the Dutch island Terschelling, actually sleeping in the SAR helicopter hangar. Gary had gone back to Coningsby with the boss because a wing had torn off one of our F4s performing aerial combat manoeuvres with the Dutch. The crew had safely ejected into the sea. After much research it seemed that McDonnells knew all about this possibility and had kept quiet about it. We spent a few miserable hours in the simulator learning what to do if it happened again. However, from the Dutch exchange I made a lifelong friend 50 years ago, Rob van de Pol, and we have had a lot of adventures together now, including weddings, funerals and even a divorce party. He even proofread this book! His daughter is the same age as our son. He went on to KLM and now lives in a perfect reconstruction of a Beemster Polder traditional house, a Stolp or old farmhouse. When it was being built, a local walker paused and asked if this was the new town hall. It's big.

After dinghy drills in the sea off Grimsby, numerous station exercises, aircraft and ship recognition training, we were on to the next major event, as we started to prepare for a visit to RAF Coningsby by HM the Queen, with Prince Philip. All the women involved of course had to have expensive new hats, and the rest of us got on with the spit and polish. First though there was to be a flypast as Her Majesty took the salute from a station parade. The

Royal Visit, 30 June 1976. Wendy dressed up.

Royal visit by HM Queen.

four aircraft would fly over the saluting base as the salute was taken, quite the hardest to organise. (An easier way, for example, is to run the parade to meet the flypast.) I was to fly as number five, the 'whipper in', making sure that the formation was perfect, then breaking off and meeting up later. The formation was a diamond box, and number four in the box was a reconnaissance Phantom from 41 Squadron. Her Majesty would be presented with a picture later.

The officers' mess got new carpets of course. On the day all those to meet the royal family formed up in ten person 'clumps' and I was the idiot of the day. HM asked me a question which I didn't hear. So I said "Yes, Your Majesty". It was the wrong answer, but I was saved when she spotted that my Canadian navigator's wife, Dayleen, was wearing an identical dress to herself. She immediately homed on to our minority commonwealth citizen, where they discussed dress shops in the dominions.

A few weeks later we were due for our annual inspection by the air officer commanding 11 Group. It was decided that as we were in practice we would fly our four-aircraft flypast once again. This time though there would be no 'whipper in', and I would fly in the box. After the salute, we continued for a while, and I saw out of the corner of my eye an airfield go past. "Yes, Al" said Gary, "that's North Luffenham" (i.e. Canadian). "In that case we're going to fly over my house." All I could actually see were the jet pipes of the two adjacent aircraft. "And that's Wendy standing in the garden," Gary added. She was holding James, our new baby, and they had decided to welcome him officially into the RAF as the squadron's very own 'air force brat', something to be really proud of. Very few babies get a flypast.

That was it. On 25 September 1976, I was posted to 19 Squadron at RAF Wildenrath, with a few other crews. Life would be a lot more serious and three months later more crews were posted to 92 Squadron. A few years later, as the Tornado fighter variants arrived, 29 became the OCU. We said our rather sad goodbyes, sent the furniture off ahead, rented out the house and packed the last few bags and the baby into our MGB. We took the hovercraft and arrived at our new house in the German village of Ratheim late that night. The baby was almost as excited as we were.

19F SQUADRON

Our eclectic squadron were half air defence experienced and half leftovers from the Phantom ground attack at RAF Brüggen, a few miles to the north. The boss was one Bugs Bendell fresh from a tour on the RAF Germany staff at nearby Rheindahlen. The main problem was that the ex-mud movers did not believe that air defence was difficult, and some were never convinced. Two Harrier squadrons were still at Wildenrath, which would eventually move to RAF Gütersloh. Actually, that made perfect sense. They were still flying GR3s with a limited range and payload and the move put them closer to the IGB and to their army customers. The Lightnings at Gütersloh would then stand down. However, while someone at RAF Germany was planning this slightly complicated move, someone else was planning the hardening programme. This meant building hardened aircraft shelters and a command bunker so that the aircraft and crews could withstand air attack. The dispersal allocated to

A painting of RAF Wildenrath, on the German Dutch border.

19 Squadron was just far too small, and the two shelters nearest the runway were allocated to Battle Flight, Germany's name for QRA, except that here the F4s would maintain a five-minute alert. 92 Squadron would form three months after us and they would man one of the QRA hangars and use the dispersal at the other end of the airfield. Together we would make up a wing of 25 aircraft, embarrassingly small compared to our NATO neighbours where 36 aircraft was the standard. Like 29 Squadron two years previously the focus was on getting ready to take over Battle Flight from the Lightnings.

I explained in depth in my previous book how 19 Squadron formed; essentially how we muddled through. The dispersal was never big enough, there were not enough hardened shelters, so maybe it was just as well that there were not enough aircraft. We could produce four serviceable aircraft for the morning wave only after the incredible groundcrew had slaved away all night. Radar serviceability was always a problem, so intercept tactics evolved assuming that one aircraft was radar blind. It was critical that we worked and trained to the same programme as 92 Squadron, as on exercises wing ops might have to scramble one aircraft from each squadron to make up a pair. The pair would be taking off on opposite runways and sorting themselves out as a pair once airborne, an air traffic problem.

We started with a site clearance. The German builders had left a terrible mess, so we walked the site collecting rubbish. It took all day, but we had to be impressed by the used condom found in one of the HAS's. We built an ops room from scratch and the army fitted out the communications (this was 21 Signals who had a resident company at Wildenrath) including a DC-powered standby phone network. We were starting to get the idea that survival to operate was a major aim. We drew our NBC kit from stores and reluctantly attended small-arms training and gas mask drills in a special tent. We had many intelligence briefings on the strength of the opposition and how they had incorporated NBC weaponry. Station exercises became a normal part of training. The happy days of 29 Squadron were clearly over.

Then by co-incidence the RAF Gütersloh runways became due for resurfacing and 19F Squadron (Lightnings) was detached to RAF Wildenrath. This was a great opportunity for them to hand over the squadron memorabilia including a moving ceremony for handing over the squadron standard. I flew a photo opportunity flight with an armed Lightning, and the photo will show the improvement in weaponry, two IR Red Tops against four Sparrow, four Sidewinder and the SUU23/A Gatling gun on the Phantom.

We were very much the new boys in Germany. Our air defence Sector 2 control at Udem, callsign Crabtree, had never had its own fighter squadron and they were intrigued. On our duty visit to them we discovered that the C2 was not that straightforward in that the NATO element occupied a gallery with a glass partition between them and the German national fighter control unit. It was something to do with the nationals not getting duty free. We were assured that it worked though. A further complication was that within Sector 2 there was a second fighter control in Belgium, callsign Efflux, who managed the Belgian Air Force fighter wing at

Increased weapons load.

Beauvechain, near Louvain. We were supposed to work together, and 19 Squadron was loosely paired with their 349 Squadron. We very much needed Belgian support or the use of the Ardennes low-flying area and for the use of their upper airspace for supersonic work. The Belgian population apparently liked jet noise. In fact, the Belgians were more like us than anyone else we met. As one of the pilots told me, "at the end of the war, the Belgian squadrons were totally modelled on the RAF, and nothing has changed". They taught us how to use the vertical to make up for our poor turning performance, and when they got their F16s they still let us lead mixed fighter force events. More of that later.

Back in Germany, Crabtree was still our scrambling authority and most of our flying would be over Germany. Here the day-to-day problem was all about noise, starting with our closest neighbour, Wassenberg. Then to the west, the Netherlands had put a blanket embargo on flying below 1,000 feet, and then only on agreed routes. Within Germany low-flying areas were defined away from built-up areas, where we might fly at 250 feet agl. Otherwise not below 500 feet was the rule. It doesn't sound a big difference, but the perspective is totally changed, and both flying and radar handling were more difficult. We had made serious capital from being the first with a 'look down, shoot down' capability thanks to our AN/AWG12 pulse doppler radar, and unquestionably our engagement tactics were curtailed by the noise and height constraints. Use of afterburner was prohibited below 3,000 feet, so we were invariably at a loss turning with, say the Jaguar or Harrier. After our first year the USAF F15s started to appear with a more powerful radar and more favourable rules of engagement. They were happy to sit at 15,000 feet and employ their own 'look down shoot down'.

A further constraint was the wartime airspace assigned to fighters, the Fighter Engagement Zone (FEZ). It was a mere 30 miles wide, surrounded by surface-to-air missiles and the army. We still saw the biggest threat to be the 19-year-old squaddie in the back of a lorry with a shoulder-mounted SAM, and fairly poor aircraft recognition. However, we were incredibly keen to make it all work, and generally it did. We were sure that it would be 'all right on the day'. We also joined the programme for cross servicing at other NATO airbases. We would land a pair, socialise with the aircrews and let their cross-servicing groundcrew deal with mainly fuel and oil. We quickly discovered that many plug fittings on the RAF F4 were incompatible with American fittings. When we started weapons cross servicing, we initially sent a pair to Soesterberg, near Amsterdam, host to a large USAF F4 Squadron. The AIM7 Sparrow, despite being a different mark from our own missile, fitted exactly despite a multipin connector, and tuned up with the aircraft radar. The AIM9L Sidewinder, however, could not be connected to the missile rail; the umbilical connector was different. This went all the way back to the F4B procurement as a navy aircraft while the USAF took a different route from the F4C. The RAF's F4K and F4M had been procured via the US Navy. The USAF armourers were shocked, and over a period new umbilicals were issued to all bases that might be expected to supply a Sidewinder to an RAF Phantom.

Our German neighbours were generally friendly and helpful despite the noise issue. My own village, Ratheim, had an exchange with the Hartlepool police, and we enjoyed the spectacle of a bobby patrolling side by side with an armed local policeman. They had brought their rugby team in the expectation of a game with the Germans who at the time did not know what rugby was. A demonstration game was quickly arranged with the Wildenrath first team, causing great excitement. My neighbour, Herr Klein, got tickets and kept asking me about the game right up to the day of the match. I forget who won, but Herr Klein came home raving about the game, and of course it is now a German national sport. I am not sure they are ready for cricket though. We did enjoy an excellent relationship with our neighbouring town of Erkelenz. Its population had run right down as the Allies advanced through the Netherlands in 1944 and then filled up again with refugees from the east. The mayor, one Willi Stein, adopted 19 Squadron as the town's own, mainly from the coincidence of having the same colours, blue and white. Our stuffed chequered dolphin received star attention at the Carnival Prince's breakfast and on the parade through the town. Our squadron layered blue and white cocktail, *der blauer delphin*, became the town speciality.

FAF Mirage 3, Wildenrath E dispersal.

The last hardened shelter, with bungalow.

We did have an international cricket match when we ran the annual Berlin corridor re-enforcement exercise from Wildenrath. This involved three transport aircraft, one each from the USAF, the RAF and the French Air Force, to be escorted by 19 Squadron, a USAF fighter detachment, and a French Mirage 3 team from Colmar. The transports would form up each day to simulate a flight up a Berlin corridor, escorted by the fighters. They would be attacked at some point by two make-believe hostile fighters. At the weekend we arranged an international cricket match, in which the French did rather well. The Americans failed utterly, insisting on dropping the bat before they ran. The French followed up at the evening party, opening champagne bottles with a butcher's knife, breaking a few hearts in the process.

We were getting used to the pace of being in Germany. Work hard, play hard. During time off at weekends and on leave, Europe was at our feet. Wendy and I made trips as far as Yugoslavia, Spain and Italy, also Berlin driving up the road corridor from Helmstedt. France and the German Eiffel and Rhineland were not too far away. We made frequent excursions into Holland, mainly shopping in Roermond, the nearest Dutch border town. The Wildenrath NAAFI was well supplied though, and the Rheindahlen NAAFI was a forerunner of the UK supermarket. We had the latest films at the Astra cinema and all-day broadcasting from BFBS. The vast majority serving there found life to be stimulating and rewarding. I finally traded my MGB in for a more suitable Peugeot 504. At home, social life could also be hectic, and when James was two, my dear friend, colleague and navigator Tony Parker arrived. I remember that on New Year's Day his wife, Miggy, put on a buffet lunch.

James distinguished himself by trying to eat their glass fruit, then apparently drank everything available as people went to the buffet. He ended up on his head giggling and slept for 14 hours after we got him to bed. I would like to think that this didn't affect him.

The main emphasis at work was still preparation for taking over Battle Flight (QRA). The two hardened shelters were modified with simultaneous door opening by wing ops if necessary. Missile racks were installed and traffic lights were placed where motor transport might be stopped to make way for scrambling aircraft. Then we had the full horror of where we would stay. Horrible wooden cabins left over from the days of supporting the Vulcans on the bomber alert started to appear. These would house five people, aircrew and groundcrew, with bedrooms, bathroom and toilets for 24 hours. Glamping? This was Glumping. The catering squadron was never able to solve meal preparation since officers, senior NCOs and airman all received different meal allowances. Eventually a bungalow got built beside each hardened shelter which were reasonably civilised. We were still on a five-minute alert and the problem of whether to sleep with flying boots on or off was never really solved. I became deputy OC B Flight under the fantastic Graeme Smith and was Battle Flight officer with the thorny problem of producing the schedule each month as well as the weekly flying programme. Graeme sadly contracted leukaemia and passed a few years ago. I saw him in Addenbrookes but sadly missed his funeral, working in the Middle East at the time.

Station exercises, the MINEVAL, were monthly events. Annually there would be a RAFG exercise called MAXEVAL, then also annually the AAFCE TACEVAL team would arrive. Frequently the first the base would know was a small team arriving at wing ops, stop watches running. The exercise would start with a general call out with a telephone cascade. The initial aim was to get all the aircraft serviceable and ready to go to war fully armed. Everyone would be wearing NBC kit ready to put on gas masks and keep working at any moment. Small arms were issued and kept close at hand. Once the flying started, everything was weather and daylight dependent. If suitable we would scramble to a combat air patrol in a low-flying area. Otherwise, it would be a climb to one of the German training areas for practice intercepts. Communication was via the telebrief, with each aircraft effectively on the end of a common phone line. It was easy to lose track of time, so that when the shelter doors opened you could be surprised by teeming rain or even darkness, and we flew up to four times a day. You could be scrambled with anyone, even the other squadron, so that training standardisation was critical. The week-long exercise simulated the predicted phases of a short war, with frequent airfield attacks, simulated gas releases and the need for NBC protection as events unrolled. At the end of the week, you were marked out of four, on four counts: readiness, operations, support and survival to operate. The last had never been awarded until the amazing station commander, Group Captain John Mitchell, achieved the elusive and well deserved fourth 'one' (the highest mark).

There was a missile practice camp (MPC), with a team departing to STCAAME at RAF Valley for two weeks. The crews who flew in, a few hours before the groundcrew arrived, had a misunderstanding with Welsh customs who insisted that their duty free should be in their aircraft rather than the following transport. I think they were just ignored in the end. We had two APCs at RAF St Mawgan in Cornwall. On the first one we had hopes that it might be fun. Actually, when we met up with Joe Brown and the Bruvvers it was for a few days. On the second APC we knew it could not be. The third time we went to Cyprus which was a total success. However, Wg Cdr Tim Gauvain had taken over as boss with a light touch. He was a contemporary of George and myself through flying training and was generally thought of as a future chief of the air staff. He had arrived via Lightnings and a tour as an ADC to a very senior officer, but it was not to be. Just after I left 19 Squadron there was a fatal

19 Squadron at RAF Akrotiri.

accident during a filming sequence for which Tim took the blame and was quietly removed. Shortly afterwards he contracted cancer and passed some years ago.

We had a squadron exchange, once again with the Dutch 322 Squadron from Leeuwarden. We took them to Brussels for the weekend and met up with some of the Belgians from 349 Squadron with whom they had trained. Tragically one of the Dutch pilots was killed in a landing accident after we got back. John Mitchell laid on a Pembroke to take some of us, including himself, to the funeral at Leeuwarden.

We had a further exchange the next year with the Italian Decimo Gruppo at Grazannise, near Naples. Their A Team had gone to Wildenrath with the full intent of shopping. That left the B Team who were a bit like us. We had a wonderful time flying cross countries the length and breadth of Italy at low level, eating unknown pastas and fishing for catfish. They even showed us how to fly their famous X formation. I took Wendy and James there a few months later. I just remember one of the Italian wives telling her, "I have been married 25 years, and this was the first time I have been out without my husband." "Why?" Wendy asked. "I have wasted 25 years!" We drove back via a few days in the Rome Italian officers' club, parking the car at the ministry of defence. The Italians explained that the armed sentry would prevent anyone stealing the radio. We stayed friends with the Italians for the rest of our tours with a lively exchange of our Moselle 'dolphin wine' with their white 'spider wine', thus named because one of the first bottles we opened had a spider in it.

Italian AF F104 at Grazannise.

All things come to an end. This had been a most fantastic hard working but rewarding tour. I was posted as a QFI to No. 228 Phantom OCU at RAF Coningsby but before then I squeezed in a long weekend in Cyprus, staging at Brindisi. Two of our Grazannise friends came over to help and we had an exchange of wine. I was starting to feel a bit like Milo Minderbender (Catch 22) as we arrived back at their base a few days later and exchanged our Cypriot Commandaria for more spider wine. We managed to fit in some skiing in Switzerland to make sure that the one-year car had been outside the UK for 365 days and took the Dover ferry home. It didn't work. HMRC's finest went through my diary and discovered a nightstop in the UK. He treated it as a great joke and let us off. Phew! We were exhausted.

Wildenrath is sadly no more. In 1992 the Phantoms flew out and German mining moved in with open-cast digging. Siemens Trains now own the site with two large loops, one for local trains and one for the higher speed tilting train, mainly around our perimeter road. From the air it looks like a model train set, and its great Cold War days will soon be forgotten. All the shelters except 19's Battle Flight have gone leaving massive nostalgia in all those who served at Wildenrath. I dropped a tear.

AAFCE/TACEVAL

ALAN

At the end of World War II, the Second Allied Tactical Air Force supported Montgomery's 21st Army Group through northern Germany and the Fourth Allied Tactical Air Force supported the American armies in the south. Postwar this command split proved unworkable and a combined headquarters was created. It was based at Ramstein but was always seen as remote from the front line. There were Americans serving in the north, mainly supporting the NIKE and HAWK SAMs and guarding any form of nuclear weapons, but AAFCE staffers tried hard to make a single combined force. Part of this was to descend on all air units once a year and run them through a week-long World War III scenario. Call out and aircraft generation might be separate from operations and survival, but they did their best to create realistic exercises and flew in two seaters to check airborne competence. While there was a small core of permanent TACEVAL team members, they also relied on co-opted members from other similar role units.

When the boss came into a briefing one day and asked if anyone was interested, I jumped at it. I believed strongly in Europe and NATO, and this had to be cooperation at its best. The pre-exercise briefing is held at a military facility within an hour's drive from the unit to be evaluated. To my amazement my first involvement was with my friends at Leeuwarden. The so-called in-brief was at the Dutch airfield of Deelen. When I walked into 322 Squadron, they pretended that this was a social visit, but we needed to see how they generated crews and armed aircraft. The flying phase was high level overland with their GCI at Nieuw Milligen and then low level over the sea. I flew a chase mission with Rob van de Pol in a TF104G through their low-level CAPs, then a second sortie on what's called 'vertical dispersal' where the airfield is presumed to be under attack, and all aircraft need to be airborne. There was an 'out-brief' with marks out of four when it was all over, then a long drive back to Wildenrath. The station commander wanted a report on everything that we might learn from them. I was invited back for a second TACEVAL under training. For the Dutch this was all routine. We were the new kids with a lot to learn.

The Dutch were able to assess a shoot on a Dart target towed behind one of their aircraft just out to sea. This was a half-sized aircraft covered in fabric and, like ourselves, their bullets had been colour dipped. The Dart arrived back reeled in under the tug's wing. Later models were able to count the rounds going through the Dart. This seemed to me to be a vast improvement, but we were unable to convince higher authority. Graeme Smith even took an aircraft to the Germans at Wittmund to investigate. Their Dart loaded onto an outer pylon but fouled the aileron. The headquarters will was just not there.

The next invitation was to the Luftwaffe air defence base at Neuburg an der Donau in Bavaria, with an 'in-brief' at Leipheim. Did the Germans cheat? Of course they did. We passed two coaches full of troops to be called in for guard duties a few hours before the exercise started. They pretended to be amazed when we walked in, but all their war kit was neatly bundled up under chairs. The German Phantom F4F was armed with a nose cannon and four Sidewinders so could be loaded up in a very short time. They had pulse radar, but none of the serviceability problems of our pulse doppler. They were ready to do well inside the target times to CAPs around the German Alps and used their Dornier 28 light transports to relay essential reporting between their aircraft at low level and their wing ops. However, this was a wing that had not yet got used to having back seaters in the F4 and had no idea how to get the best out of them. They were very much single-seat fighter pilots and very different from us. However, there was much to report back on their ground defence.

Shortly after this the next invitation was to join the team going to the USAF base at Bitburg in the German Eiffel (the German end of the Ardennes). The wing

GAF F4F Neuburg.

consisted of three squadrons and a total of 72 new F15s. Impressive would be an understatement. They also held both air defence and nuclear QRA. We questioned the mentality necessary to switch from one to the other. They also closed all cafes and restaurants and made no attempt to feed their visitors. I had with me a 92 Squadron navigator and the RAF had loaned us a Mini. We discovered that frozen pizza leftovers thawed out very well inside the engine. I actually flew four times in the F15B, and you immediately knew who its daddy was. It was a grand high performance, son of Phantom, grandson of Voodoo, and a delight to fly, if a little heavy on the controls. The pulse doppler radar was easy to use and tracked targets in the stern and on the beam, the next generation in fact. They took me on two ACT flights over the North Sea with AAR support from a Mildenhall KC135, and a gunnery sortie against a USAF Dart again over the North Sea.

Two more TACEVALs followed at the GAF F4F base at Wittmund, the Richthofen Wing, very much like Neuburg but with sophisticated use of the navigator, then finally at the USAF 32 TFS hosted by the Dutch at Soesterberg near Amsterdam. They fielded an embarrassingly large number of new F15s, (32 I think for a single squadron) and took me on a vertical dispersal with a vertical climb. They also practised 'hot pit' refuelling where a hydrant was plugged into the aircraft with the engines running. When I reported this the RAF view was that it was a highly dangerous procedure and had no place in our operations.

I subsequently did two more TACEVALs, one under AFNORTH at Skydstrup on their Danish F16s.They were excellent operators, but the event was beset with Danish politics. Then I was back at Soesterberg some years later to see what happened to a home-based USAF squadron when it re-enforced from the States, this time with F16Cs. Of course, they were operationally excellent but had little idea about survival.

It was generally thought that the way we did our gunnery was beyond the overview of AAFCE TACEVAL. However, a USAF full time member actually made his way to Akrotiri to see what we got up to, causing vast consternation at Larnaca Greek immigration by arriving in best USAF uniform.

228 OCU

An operational conversion unit not only converted pilots onto a particular aircraft and looked after standards but also acted as a reserve squadron. So, when Coningsby moved into a war footing, possibly monthly, the OCU stopped training, formed crews and generated armed aircraft. This was before any hardened shelters existed at Coningsby and there was really no space for dispersal. We ended up in a long straight line on the disused second runway. When not required for pretend war, I seem to remember flying a Chipmunk off it. 228 OCU became 64R Squadron while they tried to remember AAR technique and the students ran guard duty.

64 Squadron and Victor AAR.

Internally there was a gulf between the QFIs who ran the aircraft conversion up to high angle manoeuvring, and the QWIs who thought they were better and taught weapons and air combat techniques. The navigators helped out as required and various unskilled pilots were eventually called tactics instructors. The main challenge for an instructor was the conversion to the rear cockpit. The radar and its controls were wire locked in and the challenge became the INAS. A friendly navigator eventually explained that the radar's multi-function control switch was essentially on/off. The mysteries soon cleared and I discovered how to make a full alignment in under two minutes. We never explained this to the weapons instructors. I quickly renewed my IRE qualification and was confirmed CFS A2, an above average QFI.

I was sent off to London for a week to attend the flight safety officers' course and spent my time at Coningsby with an office in ops wing getting a sound grounding on how safety is managed; invaluable knowledge when I eventually moved into a safety business some years later via acting as FSO for my first airline. That all came much later. We moved into a married quarter which we actually enjoyed. In some ways Coningsby was Wildenrath without the overseas allowances. At the New Year I was promoted and awarded the Queen's Commendation for Valuable Service in the Air and had the little oak leaves sewn onto my uniforms. Nobody else knew what it was.

No. 29 Squadron, our neighbours, experienced a fatal accident when one of their experienced Phantom pilots, Steve Glencorse, disappeared with his navigator into the sea at night. I was called in as FSO and impounded all the operations and maintenance documents. The maintenance documents needed a lorry to deliver them to the Board of Inquiry and kept arriving for a week. A small amount of wreckage was washed up, but we could never be certain of exactly what caused the accident. We thought he had probably made a stern conversion in a practice intercept and had hit the sea when he was looking up at the target aircraft. I sent off the long signal to the MoD and had a wrist slap for writing 'presumed dead'. Apparently only the coroner can say that, and I should have written 'believed dead'. Who knew? I don't think Steve did.

There was fun to be had though, and shortly after my arrival there was a raffle for who would go where with the spare aircraft for that year's aerobatic show pilot. I won this by drawing the only overseas flight to the American air base at Aviano in northern Italy. We took a clean wing pair to Wildenrath for a refuel and then amazingly had clearance to overfly Austria. The Americans entertained royally and we flew back with great memories on the Monday morning. The French had started an air traffic control strike to the frustration of a Brüggen Jaguar team and a Canadian group based in Germany. We actually plotted to take one four-ship under my wing and the other under my leader's to make just two radar contacts. Unfortunately, Aviano ATC spotted this, and the others had to shut down.

It was always fun taking senior officers through either conversion or refresher flying. I managed to use a couple of serious expletives to AVM Harding on his way to run No. 11 Group, as he took me through Mach 1 pointing vertically downwards in maximum afterburner. We came out at 2,000 ft. He politely thanked me for an accurate description and went on to make a double killing in the 1 v 1 v 1 that we were a part of. He was a hero. He never forgot and repaid me twice in the coming years, even as chief of the air staff. You should never take over control too soon!

A year passed very quickly, then it was off to RAF Leuchars in Fife as squadron QFI on 111 Squadron.

111 SQUADRON CXI(F)

Treble One Squadron (nicknamed Tremblers) had a good and proud pedigree from its formation in Palestine in 1917. Many older folks can remember the Black Arrows 22 Hunter loop at the Farnborough Air Display, led by Sqn Ldr Roger Topp in a Hunter T7. 111 Squadron was the first to have an RAF crest on which all subsequent crests were modelled. The diary records that in 1936 one of the squadron's pilots had an uncle who was the Chester Herald. He apparently took an interest in the jumble of badges which identified a squadron and decided to do better. The current badge was approved by Edward VII and reflects the squadron's past in Palestine and defending London. They were sadly disbanded on 22 March 2011, when the Tornado F3 was stood down.

By the time I arrived the squadron flew the Phantom F4K, or FG1. These were the aircraft that would have made up a second carrier squadron in the navy had that carrier not been cancelled. There were small but significant differences from the F4M, to make the aircraft more carrier compatible, but most of them had been disconnected, including the ability to fold the wings from inside the cockpit. The most significant difference was that there was no battery which had a major impact on certain emergency drills, and no INAS. The navy had fitted a sort of cockpit position keeper which needed to be told its position at frequent intervals. It was a slightly nicer aircraft to fly. 111's aircraft were in fact from a mixed background, about a third each from the navy, the navy's Phantom Training Flight, which did only a small amount of carrier work, and the RAF, whose aircraft had never been to sea. The ex-RAF aircraft were twice as serviceable as the ex-navy machines, with the PTF somewhere in between. The navy expected a lot from their aircraft.

My job was squadron flying proficiency and standards, also instrument ratings. This meant sometimes 50 per cent rear cockpit work especially as, for a while, I was also doing our neighbour's, 43 Squadron. However, we also had a squadron pilot who was also a QFI and later an IRE. There was some urgency in getting me onto QRA, but I was surprised when my arrival simulator check was learning a STCAAME Sidewinder firing profile. I was on QRA in early April as Q2 with a Q1 who had recently fired a missile in the previous financial year. We were due another scramble to fire a live round from QRA, and in late morning I was scrambled to fly to the Aberporth range, check in with a photo-chase Lightning and fire from the profile I had practised. I saw the towed flare light up, the missile, an AIM9G Sidewinder, behaved perfectly, and I landed at RAF Valley to be debriefed and the missile rail to be inspected by the resident armourers. It did bring home the fact that we were routinely flying heavily armed aircraft.

Treble One was a maritime air defence squadron, with a lot of fighter-control work with the navy. This involved much study on ship recognition, and we quickly learned how to spot a ship's nationality. A navy exchange officer explained that British ships always had a lot of white paint because painting was a job that first lieutenants liked to give to defaulters. Exercises ran from NATO maritime events via Strike Command via HQ No. 11 Group to station events, with regular QRA scrambles to keep the squadrons busy. It was not always fun and games though.

On a night scramble Pete Barrett and I intercepted a pair of Soviet navy Bears at around 20,000 ft, and at the time intel wanted to know door numbers in order to track a deployment from the Far East Fleet to the Northern Fleet. We were equipped

Soviet Air Force Tu95 Bear D from QRA.

with an infrared reading device, but Pete just could not see the door number. The next thing was to move forward underneath the Bear's cockpit and light an afterburner. Just as I was about to do this, Pete said "Al, forget the door number and just ease back the way you came in." When we were safely back on the Bear's wing Pete asked me to check the altimeter. We were descending fast through 3,000 ft. Clearly the Bear's captain wanted to wipe us off on the ocean. The Soviet navy was the last formed of the five Soviet services: Gorshkov's navy. They had massive pride and were distinctly unfriendly.

In August 1981 I took two aircraft and a small groundcrew detachment to the German Air Force base at Jever in lower Saxony, near Wilhelmshaven on the North Sea coast. Getting there from Leuchars would be tricky so I phoned the admiral's Devon crew in Edinburgh. "Does the admiral need the Devon over that weekend?" "No, it's free." "Well, can I have it?" Amazingly they agreed. Our aircraft were delivered a week later. The tactical leadership programme, AAFCE TLP, was based at Jever, and eight times a year they hosted 18 mixed aircraft to give NATO crews a chance to get to know each other's capabilities and to fly together, six air defence against 12 mud movers. Everyone got a turn leading and it was an opportunity to try many and varied tactics to get the best out of each aircraft. George Lee, the world gliding champion, was the RAF's resident air defence staff member. Apart from being beset by radar problems, and my navigator going sick and having to be replaced, we saw the programme as pure magic. It lasted for a month and afterwards I had never felt so sharp, before or since. I decided that if I possibly could, I would take George's job when he was due to retire. Looking back, I suppose that was a bit of a cheek. I have described the four weeks in detail in *Fast Jets on the Front Line.*

Two months later there was a world leader meeting at the Gleneagles Hotel in Perthshire. They were all flying in via Leuchars and would park their various aircraft there. 43 Squadron were banished to their revetments on the far side of the airfield and since we had no revetments, we were sent to RAF Machrihanish at the southern end of the Mull of Kintyre. What a week – we did low-level air defence among the Western Isles, saw Fingle's Cave and flew right round the Summer Isles, total magic. I was crewed for convenience with Bob Crane, the squadron QWI, and I well remember rounding the end of the Mull round the rocks at very low level. Unknown to us, some of our groundcrew were busy scaling the cliff, and we were close enough for them to get the tail number. That cost us a lot of good-natured complaining; better than fighting over the piano. We never did discover why 200 US SEALs were based there, but we assumed that it was to service the SR71.

It had been decided that each fighter squadron should pair up with a Type 42 RN destroyer. We drew HMS *Southampton* and sent four aircraft to RNAS Yeovilton overnight so that we could take part in their commissioning ceremony in Southampton Water. It was all cleared with Southampton Airport, and the marine band played 'Those Magnificent Men' as we flew past. Then Southampton Tower piped up: "Hey what about us?" Well, it's a good job that nobody had a camera as we spread out and went over as low and fast as we dared. Then there was a base exercise which the station commander asked me to run, based on my AAFCE TACEVAL experience. The deal was that he would not get his copy of any signal I sent out, but that I would tell him if we intended anything outrageous. This included landing a US special forces C130 on the taxiway. A company of Royal Marines poured out to attack 43 Squadron, whose junior engineer boarded the aircraft and pretended to shoot the pilots. The Americans took his gun and told him not to be a stupid boy. They then took off with him on board, and he arrived back some time later, I think from Mildenhall.

In the middle of the week the real Strike Command TACEVAL team arrived to take over tasking the Victor tankers I had organised, saw how it was going and gave me total control of the tankers on our script. At times I felt like the sorcerer's apprentice, running a team of 30 and indirectly all the Scottish fighter-control units. We even had HMS *Southampton* stationed as a picket ship about 40 miles out with a free invitation to be attacked by our 'enemy bombers' on their way to Leuchars. We ended during the survival phase of the exercise with a recce Jaguar from 41 Squadron taking pictures of Leuchars to see who was still moving. When it was time for the vertical dispersal, I sent a Phantom into Coltishall for the pictures which were the hot topic of the out-brief next day.

Then of course the Falklands campaign started, and we were heavily involved teaching the Nimrod crews operational tactics. They were quickly equipped with AIM9L Sidewinders and became quite proficient at taking shots. We had to learn

Alan refuelling from a USAF KC135 via its four metre metal hose.

to take fuel from USAF KC135s equipped with the hose extension on the end of their more usual probe. It was not easy as you had to put a bend in the hose to open the refuelling valve, then stay perfectly still. Ripping the basket off was a distinct possibility. Later the modified Vulcans were introduced with a centreline hose, distinctly more popular. Sixteen crews across No. 11 Group had been nominated to man the eight Falklands Phantoms, should the Argentinians pursue the campaign from the mainland. I had a bag packed, but it never happened. For HMS *Southampton*, I went with another Phantom to Yeovilton and flew a number of sorties against the ship as it moved down the channel on its way south. We flew alternate attacks making the radar look like an Exocet radar signature, which allowed the entire defensive systems to operate together for the first time. We wished them godspeed and went home.

Then it was off to Decimomannu in Sardinia to work the air combat manoeuvring range (ACMI). The range itself was a series of aerials out to sea where unlimited air combat training might take place. Four nations shared the Italian base near Cagliari, the Italians of course, the Germans, the Americans and ourselves, and the main aim was the use of the excellent air-to-ground ranges. The ACMI was quite new. An American company ran the infrastructure, and just before a mission crewed up, they would install a pod on a Sidewinder rail. In the range the pods communicated with each other and with the ground station, plotting all the players and recording simulated kills. Fights against other nationalities were easy to arrange, in particular the USAF F15s. It was a steep learning curve, in particular when to leave a fight, usually short of fuel. The debriefing cabins featured large screens where viewers could watch the entire progress of a fight, and each formation's radio talk was recorded for subsequent evaluation. Unfortunately, the sea was quite rough at the time, and the buoys were unable to keep steady transmissions going. This wasted several sorties and I believe that it was some time before the problem was fixed. I managed to get struck by lightning returning from a sortie, and the ATC controller immediately took over talking me through a 'no compass, no gyro' recovery. He was brilliant and I met him later in the officers' club having alcohol poured down his throat by his friends. He was a 19-year-old Italian trainee with a great future.

In the autumn of 1983, we were off to Cyprus for our APC. The newcomers who had not shot before had the first week to themselves, so determined not to run the ops desk again I took off to 84 Squadron to learn to fly the Wessex helicopter. They were happy to see me as the CFS examiner had just arrived with ten hours allocated for refresher flying on the Wessex. He needed a pretend student and suddenly they had a real one. It was a great week with straight flying instruction, a trip into the UN Buffer Zone, the 'green line' delivering supplies to Danish and Swedish observation posts. We did some wet winching and some Northern Ireland situations with the RAF Regiment. It's a lot easier when you don't have to learn checks or worry about failure lights coming on.

It was a highly successful four weeks until the recovery home. In the meantime, I had picked up an aircraft that apparently could not fly straight, but I was happy to take it back to Leuchars via Brindisi. We set off in fours an hour apart and all went well until Brindisi. The first four had mistakenly joined for the wrong runway and got close to a civilian airliner. I had checked with the tower before joining and knew that approach was announcing the wrong runway. The entire squadron was lined up with our C130 support transport, and the Italian base commander had thrown us out. That meant a few days in Decimomannu before the European weather cleared enough to let us get to Wildenrath. There was some nonsense about a bonfire and burning down a cherry tree, so it was time to get out of Sardinia as well.

My aircraft was gently getting worse. I explained this to the boss on the ground at Wildenrath who gave me the option of staying there until the aircraft was fixed. He explained that his carpet slipper was from an accident when he landed in the bonfire. The Wildenrath cross-servicing flight was amazed. The next day we had a meeting with base engineering at Leuchars and raised 30-odd unserviceability items against my aircraft. I asked our squadron engineering officer if this could possibly be the aircraft that the navy had put together from two crashed airframes. "Yes, I heard the story and it's rubbish." The next day he told me that the aircraft had no records before 1976! When it reappeared a couple of months later it actually flew quite well. Guess who got to do the air test. Well, the following year, after I had left, they decided to take out a cherry tree sapling to make peace with management. This was put in a baggage pod and entrusted to the US marine exchange officer. He managed

RAF Akrotiri.

to divert into Nice and leave the aircraft cooking on the ground for several days. In any case the plan had always been to plant the tree and then set fire to it. At the last moment the tree pushed out a bud and the squadron was overwhelmed. The tree had earned its reprieve.

I had already received my posting to TLP, all very exciting. Either myself or 43's QFI still had to go to the Falklands, but in the meantime, I was tasked to take two aircraft and a small groundcrew detachment to join an American air defence exercise in Iceland. Our hosts were to be the 57th TFS, the self-styled Black Knights, flying white Phantom F4Es. The weather was lovely as we flew up to Keflavik but started to snow the next day for the rest of the exercise. The squadron had a small number of soft-skinned 'pods' where flying aircraft were sheltered during and after flight. Our hosts magnanimously gave us two of them. The outside air temperature was bitter, and we were jealous of their winter gear. Two C130s arrived in the evening with our third crew and our groundcrew, also with two life-saving Land Rovers. Social life revolved around a 'club'. By treaty, money could only change hands in the US navy facility, so all other 'clubs' were credit arrangements. The fighter bar was run by the flight surgeon, in other words the squadron doctor. "What have you got to join?" "A crate of Glenmorangie." "You're in. Welcome." Then we were into the massive speakers playing 'Bat out of Hell', a sort of rock opera from the 1970s. Everyone had to get feet off the floor and be a bat. Last one bought the round, except that you didn't have to pay. "Let's take an elevator ride!" and everyone jumped out of the window into a snow drift. Last one up the stairs 'paid'. When I got home, Wendy asked, "What, like MASH?" Precisely. It was the way the Americans had invented to survive the winter.

On Wednesday there was some chance of the weather improving enough to launch an exercise wave. By cunning negotiation with the forecaster, they were looking for a three-hour gap in the weather. Suddenly flying was on. I told the two other crews to get ready as fast as possible, but the groundcrew had gone to lunch. So Bob Lawley and I took a Phantom each and acted as groundcrew starters. It was total hell under a starting Phantom, and I never afterwards lost respect for the young lads who had to do the job. The weather held and Bob and I kitted up for a flight. This ended with a general recall and a landing in the next snowstorm. What a life. Iceland was beautiful, expensive and challenging. I got to love the place after four more visits later on, but what a start.

I tossed with my competition for who went to the Falklands. He lost, and then my posting officer called to ask if I could go direct to Arizona. Who could refuse?

THE AAFCE TACTICAL LEADERSHIP PROGRAMME
YUMA

ALAN

My poster called. "Stop the competition for who goes to the Falklands. You're to arrive in Germany and then go to Arizona." "Is that a code word, or Arizona in the good old USA?" I left 111 in indecent haste, got a trooper flight to RAF Gütersloh, who apparently hosted the small RAF presence at Jever, and started the arrival process. I met an end-of-tour leaver in accounts who wanted to sell his second car. Sold. The German bank welcomed a new account and was eager to lend the money for the car, and the MT section understood the problem and re-instated my German Forces driving permit. So, two days later I was on the autobahn heading for the Ruhr and then Wildenrath. I met up with the TLP RAF navigator, Roger Carr, and the next morning we reported to GAF Wahn, the German Air Force side of Cologne Airport where we met other TLP staff. Amazingly it had all worked. I gathered that the US Marine Corps had sent some pilots on a visit to TLP to see how NATO solved some of the same problems that they experienced, and that this was a return visit. The Luftwaffe would take us in their Boeing 707 freighter/trooper to El Paso and made sure that we had the funds to get from there to Yuma.

It nearly worked. We had tickets for Phoenix, but the entire flight programme was running an unpublished hour late. Shortly after take-off the flight attendant took our vodka martinis away as we were landing at Albuquerque where we were thrown off the flight. Our bags continued on to Phoenix. So, for the next six hours we sat around unshaven in our uniforms and finally got onto the last flight to Phoenix after Wolf Kloss, our GAF Phantom back seater had exploded in Bavarian, having had no sleep the night before. Wolf was a most enigmatic character, a displaced Prussian as a child, living in Neuburg an der Donau and distance commuting to Jever. In Phoenix, our bags were sitting on the pavement. The next day, after a four-hour drive, our Dutch close air support specialist, Peer Dekkers, summed up the Grand Canyon with "It is big isn't it". So, on the Monday we boarded a very small airliner to get to Yuma in Arizona. Some US Marines met us with, "quick, check your bags. The first officer unloads them and usually gets it wrong." Welcome to unregulated travel.

The US Marine Corps is just over 300 years old. On their birthday someone at Coningsby was unkind enough to point out that the UK Marines went back to Alfred the Great. The USMC is a self-contained tactical army dedicated to assault with an incredible history. However, their many disparate arms have to work closely together, and this was the marine air weapons and tactics (MAWTS) exercise, where air and ground were brought together at Yuma. Our visit was for a week and each day a marine department, or 'shop' would host us. We had a day with close air support, where I flew in a Bronco and various other flights were made available. We had a day with air defence, and on the Wednesday, we were with the AAR Team. I had already had a flight in an OA4 Skyhawk, famous for its snaking, and had a try at refuelling from a marine C130. The spokes on their drogue looked like a bird's nest, but my marine P1 insisted that this was one of their good ones. They took us to Miramar for a day out with a visit to Top Gun, which had absolutely no female psychologists, and a Wednesday night in the officers' club. If Tom Cruise had really sung there, he would have been straight out of the window. It was tough.

We had a day with the helicopters where Mumu, our Belgian interdiction specialist and I were taken into the desert in a CH53 to practise evasion against attacking aircraft, in particular pretending to use a Sidewinder against the fighter. We queried the lack of host aircraft launch speed, but they weren't too concerned. So, during the lunch break amongst the towering desert cacti, we could relax before the next session. Both pilots were involved, "I have it, you have it" and so on with crewmen hanging out of the sides and back joining in, all aiming to keep the fighter in sight and maybe get a simulated missile off against him. They let me fly this giant machine back to Yuma and taxi it in, actually surprisingly easy being totally stable.

The basic marine problem started to become clear. They were trying to do too much with what they had available. I already knew that they would land an F4 at a USAF base and pick up a new brake chute when theirs was in tatters. The USAF had put out an order to repack the marine original chute and return it to them. Then there were only so many Sidewinders in the inventory, unlikely to be released to the helicopters, but that did not stop them trying. They were desperately keen and proud. I seemed to remember that the Chaparral SAM system, essentially four Sidewinders, had rocket boosters to get the missiles to flying speed but they were undeterred. Then on this MAWTS evolution they were experimenting with ACMI pods on ground targets to see if they could accurately plot kill probability. This was an incredible week, with a lot of ideas to take home. The GAF obliged and diverted the El Paso Boeing 707 into Yuma, then straight back to Cologne. Welcome back to Germany.

In some ways the TLP was trying in miniature to do what the marines had shown us; to bring a number of disparate aircraft, nationalities and command structures together for mutual understanding and tactics development. It had at that time already produced the tactics for mixed fighter force from the time that the F4 was the

Flying with the Portuguese.

only aircraft with a 'look down, shoot down' capability, taking non-PD radar aircraft into a merge, for example an F104, and later the F16 as they started to arrive. TLP was first postulated in the 1970s when I was at Wildenrath, and initially it comprised two weeks ground school at Fürstenfeldbruck in Bavaria, with a very small staff arranging tabletop games. It was highly successful and moved to Jever to host flying courses in September 1979. There would be eight courses a year from the AAFCE member nations, with guest appearances from the Danes, Norwegians, French and Portuguese. It was very basic and had to contend with the growing noise resistance in Germany as well as a slightly Prussian attitude towards foreigners in the German officers' mess. The base commander was Oberst Klaffenbach, but surprisingly we quickly became friends which lasted until he retired.

I shared an office with a USAF F15 pilot, but we remembered his predecessor's advice: "Al, we have to reconstruct the merge." This was much harder than it sounded. We had to assess every gunsight or radar film from a number of different aircraft types, but thankfully this became a labour of love for a GAF F4 pilot who joined us, one Hupfi, from the Richthofen Geschwader at Wittmund. We got better at reconstructing the map of the area where a merge might have taken place and then putting together what had probably happened. In this way we could assess the success or failure of tactics used. We are still talking about six air defence aircraft intercepting 12 air-to-ground aircraft who had a target to attack. Occasionally we would arrange the merge off target so that the mud movers had light aircraft close air support, a full suite of self-defence weapons and hate in their hearts. The AAFCE rules for defensive turning and re-attack were quite sensible and we stuck to them, although this got much harder with the F16 that could turn on a sixpence.

So, the day started at 06:00 when I would meet the air-to-ground co-ordinator at the pilot breakfast facility. He had already gone to the Met Office and had a fair idea of what could be accomplished that day. They had a syllabus to accomplish for all the likely attack scenarios, and he already knew what could be done. I also had a list of scenarios, and we would haggle about what could be mutually achieved. Then by the time briefing started for the course, we already knew what might be achieved and what support assets we might bring in, for example helicopters, jammers, ground radars, AWACS and hostile air. We might even have to squeeze in two missions. On the last two evolutions, all 18 or later 20 aircraft would fly together against enemy air that we invited in. We always tried to bring in different aircraft types, for example the Hawks from the UK tactical-weapons units. Later on, the course was augmented with two recce aircraft, and a rotating staff position was established for a German, American or RAF staffer. I managed to scrounge an antique epidiascope from 2 (recce) Squadron so that we could project recce maps onto the screen. It was hard work but incredibly satisfying, and this was before the first computers had started to arrive.

Eventually of course noise triumphed. It was made quite clear that the German government would like us to shut down. Tentative moves were made to move us to Florennes in Belgium. It was said that the Florennes mayor called the Jever mayor and asked, "what's this TLP?" The answer was 3M Deutschmarks spent a year downtown. We countered with a scheme which we called 'tactics not politics'. These went on wine bottle labels, T shirts, key rings and stickers. All graduates in NATO staff positions were sent a little stack of stickers with instructions to put them on the back of toilet doors used by senior officers. The Germans actually saw the funny side of this and from that point on there was a move to save TLP. The move to Florennes took place and TLP was there for 20 years, with the French joining in as full time staff. The last move was to Albacete in south-west Spain. The make-up has changed significantly, and the emphasis has moved to asymmetric warfare. It now runs on a memorandum of understanding with quite heavy ground school and a variety of courses available.

In the early 1980s it was all quite primitive. The RAF staff were really not well looked after. All the other members had their TLP officers integrated into a staff structure of some sort. Flying hours were not established nor national career reporting. The RAF had set up a good administrative back-up, but really did not look after their officers. It was a classic bit of Brexit. It made me deeply unpopular when I arrived at Wildenrath and effectively stole squadron flying. They were quite happy that I should fly on exercises and TACEVAL but not training. I even took part in a tactical air meet in 1984 flying one of 92 Squadron's aircraft on a massive mixed-force sweep into France, but it was never an easy relationship. I was replaced by a Lightning pilot which really summed up the RAF's attitude to TLP membership. However, I did manage to put in a week's flying with one or other squadron, as well as a simulator trip for currency, an afternoon with the RAFG intelligence cell, and a NAAFI session to top up with all the essentials unavailable in German shops, then a 400 km drive back to Jever. I also passed the 2,000 hours on the F4 milestone, and 19 Squadron were kind enough to arrange for the McDonnell's certificate and badge.

2000-hour Spook.

The intelligence connection gradually led to my inclusion at the quarterly evaluation of Soviet and East German activity at the 6912 ESG, a large radar and listening post looking out over East Germany. It was actually perched on *der Teufelberg,* an enormous hill made from Berlin's wrecked buildings. This meant catching the overnight American military train from Bremerhaven to Berlin, getting on at Bremen. That way everything was laid on, travel orders, bus transfer, very nice accommodation at the military hotel, Columbia House, at Templehof Airport. In those days there were three other daily military trains to Berlin, an American day train from Frankfurt, a French train from Trier and the British train from Hannover, complete with its own wine label. I tried it once for the experience and still recall the British Army train commander exchanging salutes with the Russian guard commander, before they disappeared for a quiet vodka, all done so that the guards could see the train's happy passengers finishing off a sumptuous lunch.

With no prior intention, I gradually became the expert on what was happening the other side of the border. Initially there was a problem that the intelligence was either American or British and I was NATO. They finally decided that I was able to discriminate and I was welcome in Berlin. I even got to brief BRIXMIS and was appalled to find out that they were getting no direction at all on what information was urgently needed. I explained what we needed, but they had no idea. The resulting briefing, which could go anything from one to four hours, turned into a road show that was in some demand. When the Canadians requested it at Bad Sollingen in the Black Forest, I was able to trade for a CT33 taxi and a CF18 back-seat ride on arrival. All this led to an invitation to fly out to Tucson in Arizona to brief a tactics evolution which the US Air Guard were arranging.

At TLP we were well aware of the NATO plans for eight major mixed-force raids a day complete with fighter escort and SAM suppression. The Americans were increasingly sure that the front-line defences were so severe that low-level ingress was no longer a viable option. They were right of course, as the first Iraq war later proved. However, with the electronic support required for medium-level ingress, that would mean two raids a day, and no support for the other six. This was never really solved. The American asset that fascinated me was the C130H, which could jam just about anything. That vital jammer still exists in the form of the E37B Compass Call. At TLP we were of course able to match this kind of tactical thinking, but we did develop mixed-force tactics combining as many assets as we could with an increasing number of external players. We even integrated a NATO AWACS controller as a course participant and later on a GCI controller, all bringing in their own perspective.

Back to my second Arizona adventure in the job, my German colonel decided that it was essential for him to accompany me. I arranged a VC10 trooper flight from RAF Laarbruch to RAF Brize Norton, and the ANG arranged a KC135 flight from RAF Scampton to Topeka AFB, Kansas, followed by a C130 flight to Tucson the next day. It all worked out. The tactics evolution was in fact going to be at Davis Monson AFB, with flying in the TA7 and the F16. The briefing went well and I met Victor Belenko, the Soviet Foxbat defector. In fact, I was officer in charge of Victor for 24 hours when we must have visited every country and western bar in Tucson. I was able to find out a great deal about the make-up of a Russian pilot from Victor. I was left in no doubt that they were taught to fly from the heart, and that the tight control came later. The ANG obliged us with commercial tickets to Washington, DC and the GAF with seats back to Cologne.

Looking back three years, a German four-star general had put a piece of A4 paper in my hand which was essentially a grid of 0.5-degree (or 30-minute) boxes covering the central region from Denmark to Austria. "Al, this is a concept for integrating fighters, SAMs and airspace control in the Central Region. See what you can make of it." After we studied it for a while we thought it might just work, and thereafter we ran 'the grid' for a couple of missions on every TLP course. It was delightfully simple and over a period of time we were able to use it for air defence and air-to-ground, as well as integrating AEW and GCI. Its highlight came when we ran it on the tactical air meet 1984 at Kleine Brogel, using an air defence sweep ahead of an air-to-ground package of around 80 aircraft. The air defence aircraft were generally used to sweep ahead of the bombers and report back French Air Force activity as grid positions. (The French had put up 40 aircraft.) This produced an immediate air picture and over the week proved the concept. The AAFCE staff were delighted. We eventually submitted a comprehensive report to my air marshal, who passed it on to his staff, and that was the last we heard. However, my dear friend and colleague Tony Parker saw the air defence plans for the First Gulf War. "Al, the only thing missing was your signature at the bottom." You win some, you lose some. Later I discovered that our box was not too different from the various box concepts used by the Luftwaffe in 1944.

In the meantime, I had been asked if I would like the new post of opening a British evaluation unit in Berlin, similar to the 6912 ESG. What a question, and I jumped at it. However, my Ramstein air marshal had been busy. I had a call from him to say that he had arranged a posting for me at the Department of Air Warfare at Cranwell. I tried to explain about the Berlin job, but he was adamant that Cranwell was the right job for me and I should be grateful. That was it then, back to the UK, which we did in November 1986. Actually, nothing ever happens for the worst. We were able to sort out our house, stabilise James' education after attending one American and two German schools, and pave the way for him and Wendy to do degrees at Nottingham University. At one stage to his intense embarrassment, she was in the year below him meeting in secret for an exchange of money and laundry. He ended up with a 2.1 in Russian, and Wendy a 2.1 in art history and German.

I loathed the job at Cranwell though. I was the RAF air defence specialist with lecturing duties covering central and northern Europe. The problem was that I knew that my information

SEAAD RAAF Butterworth, Malaysia.

was probably 10 per cent out of date, and in the service audience there would be at least one person with the actual facts. I missed the next round of promotions, later explained to me that my board simply did not understand a NATO report, covered in red ink. I would go up next time, but it was not to be. I had a misunderstanding with an RAF policeman after I failed to lock up properly, and that was it. Cranwell did have its moments. I was able to fly ATC cadets in the Chipmunk at No. 7 AEF RAF Newton and flew as many weather checks as possible in the Jet Provost T5 with a Cranwell instructor. I went back to Wildenrath twice a year to fly the Phantom for a week, and I made two visits to Malaysia to lecture to the south-east Asian air defence course, as we settled back into the local area.

What follows is the statement by the nearly 50-year-old Spanish TLP at Albecete. It would seem that we got it right all those years ago.

> 'TLP is a multinational headquarters based at Los Llanos Air Base, Albacete. We are composed of military and civilian personnel from the 11 NATO nations participating in the programme. Our main objective is to increase the effectiveness of our air forces in the field of tactical leadership and conceptual and doctrinal initiatives in support of the Supreme Allied Commander Europe (SACEUR), Supreme Allied Commander Transformation (SACT) and National Defence Forces.
>
> Throughout our 46-year history in Germany, Belgium and now in Spain, TLP has become the focal point for NATO's Allied Air Forces tactical training and development of knowledge and leadership skills, necessary to face today's air tactical challenges. This is being achieved with the effort, dedication and professionalism of our staff. TLP prides itself in having a diverse and talented work force.
>
> TLP is a programme of excellence and will remain aligned and relevant. We are ready to adapt to the pace of change and to achieve our goals we follow a five-pillar strategy based on:
>
> - The integration of 4th, 5th, and Xth Generation platforms
> - The adoption of the Agile Combat Employment concept
> - Live-Virtual-Constructive training
> - A state-of-the-art Contested-Degraded Operations environment
> - The introduction of Joint All Domain factors in the challenging air scenarios, in both the academic and the flying courses.'

CHAPTER 8
THE RAF TODAY

GEORGE

My RAF service was during the peak years of the Cold War. To most people the last Cold War is a distant memory, but we are now facing what amounts to a new one. Putin has ambitions to extend the Russian area of influence back towards what existed with the USSR. He has ambitions in the Baltic which have prompted NATO to deploy troops and aircraft in support. Baltic states like Finland and Sweden are sufficiently concerned to have applied for membership of NATO and of course, we are now in the fourth year of his war in Ukraine, where he has publicly stated that if he is in danger of losing, he would not hesitate to go nuclear.

As I write this, we have a new war against Iran initiated by the USA and Israel. My old squadron, No. 6, is undoubtedly now somewhere in the Middle East providing defence against incessant drone attacks.

I am still in regular contact with 6 Squadron who are based at RAF Lossiemouth in the north of Scotland operating the Typhoon and responsible for the Northern QRA. It is one of our few remaining fighter squadrons, and from what I can see is very overstretched, being away on deployment for much of the year.

The RAF has largely been hollowed out following the end of the Cold War, in common with the Royal Navy and the army. When I joined the RAF in 1963, the total RAF strength was 144,000, now it is just 30,000. The change has been dramatic, as shown by the graph overleaf.

According to the very latest statistics in March 2026, we have 137 Typhoon FGR4s and a growing fleet of about 47 F-35B aircraft operated jointly with the

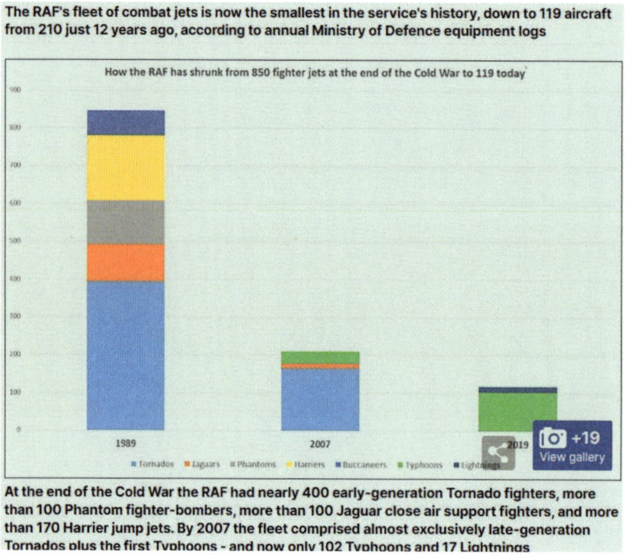

RAF strength.

Royal Navy. The Typhoon fleet is currently undergoing a series of upgrades costing £650 million. The MoD is facing a funding 'black hole' of about £28 billion over the next four years. We are committed to increasing defence spending to 2.5 per cent of GDP by 2027 with an "ambition" to reach three per cent of GDP in the longer term, but it will not be enough unless our commitments more closely match our capabilities. We still seem to think we are a world player, but the fact is we are now much diminished. We need to acknowledge that and cut our cloth accordingly.

Of the four other squadrons I served with, this is where they are now.

- 39 Squadron – now disbanded and standard lodged at RAF Cranwell
- 54 Squadron – now the ISTAR conversion unit at RAF Waddington
- 17 Squadron – now the test and evaluation unit at Edwards AFB for the F-35B
- 31 Squadron – now operating the Protector RG Mk1 drone at RAF Waddington

The Royal Navy is in an even more parlous state having spent billions on two aircraft carriers which seem to be white elephants, and where there are not enough fleet defence vessels to keep them safe when at sea or to form two carrier strike groups.

The training system for RAF pilots is now radically different from what we experienced. Alan and I progressed through basic and advanced flying training and on to operational conversion and our first squadron in the space of two years. Now it can take eight years to reach the front line, so we are seeing first-tour pilots on 6 Squadron arriving in their late 20s.

We now have the UK Military Flying Training System (UKMFTS) which is run by a civilian contractor called Ascent Flight Training. This is a joint venture between Babcock International and Lockheed Martin. Ascent is now responsible for all military flying training for all three services. It was awarded a 25-year PFI contract in 2008 valued at £3.2 billion for the provision of aircraft, simulators and personnel training for the British armed services.

There was clearly a need to upgrade RAF training in the light of modern aircraft like Typhoon with digital avionics, but there have been some 'bumps in the road' due to aircraft technical issues like the engine faults on the Hawk T2 which halted training for fast jet pilots for a while. There were other bottlenecks caused by infrastructure and capacity constraints, instructor shortages, delays in equipment programmes and the like.

I feel for the current generation of trainee RAF pilots. They are often faced with lengthy holding periods between courses sometimes for as much as a year due to capacity issues. It must be very difficult to maintain morale and motivation in such circumstances. When they do make it through to a front-line squadron, they will be joining a unit which is frequently overstretched and overcommitted.

In such circumstances it is surprising and gratifying that our armed forces are still so highly rated and perform so well.

LEAVING THE RAF

I have mentioned before that it was always my intention to leave the RAF when I reached my option point, in my case after 17 years of service. I struggled with this decision because I had been very lucky, and things were going well with my career, much better than I could ever have hoped or expected.

You have to declare your intention a year before your leaving date and are entitled to attend a career review at the RAF air secretary branch to have your 'palm read' prior to making the decision. I was duly interviewed by an air commodore who went through my annual assessments and other documents from my file. It was all very positive, and he indicated that I would be on a fast track for early promotion. That did not make the decision any easier.

But there were other considerations I was struggling with. My future career would involve a succession of command headquarters and MoD jobs, albeit at higher ranks, so I would be flying desks rather than aircraft. There would be regular moves involved for the family and I needed to consider the ongoing impact on them. My two girls had been given a very good education at a private school, subsidised at about 50 per cent by the RAF, but had also missed out on home life. My wife had been denied a career of her own and had spent the last few years as an unpaid welfare assistant looking after squadron personnel and families. That was not likely to change with increasing rank. Also, RAF pay was not generous compared to the private sector, and I approached my last few months at Coltishall with a substantial overdraft. As the boss, you are expected to push the boat out on social occasions, and it all adds up. The resettlement terms were generous, and on retirement after commuting some of my pension, I could expect a tax-free lump sum of £20,000. That was a lot of money in 1980 and equivalent to about £100,000 in 2026. It would allow me to more than clear my overdraft, secure the private education for my daughters after the RAF subsidy stopped, and still leave enough for an upgrade to our house, so the financial arguments were in favour of leaving.

Job prospects in the airline sector were good at the time, and I had offers from Britannia Airways, Air Europe and Dan Air. I also had a very attractive offer to work for NAMMA in Munich with subsidised housing and school fees covered.

But it was still a difficult choice. Being in the armed forces is more than just a job, it is membership of a brotherhood, and the pull to remain is enormous. I discussed the options with the family who were supportive but nervous of such a huge change. I also felt a sense of obligation to the many people who had helped my career so far. Interestingly my three flight commanders had all reached the same conclusion and had decided to exercise their option to retire. They were all aware of the struggles I was having with my decision, but I had not tried to influence them in any way. In the end the balance for me tipped towards leaving, and I informed my station commander and filled in the necessary forms.

There was just one cloud on the horizon. The Thatcher government was determined to confront the unions and there was the threat of a recession. Up to that point the airlines had been booming, but would it last?

There was an immediate reaction of anger and disappointment. The AOC 38 Group, AVM Joe Gilbert, was furious with me. He had been very supportive in the past, saw me as a bit of a 'poster boy', and was rightly concerned about the outflow of talented people from the RAF.

The fact of my upcoming retirement did not change my commitment to the job of running 6 Squadron and I worked as hard as ever in the last few months. My final day at work arrived, and I had one last flight in the Jaguar. I did some aerobatics, flying upside down a lot, and knowing that I would never be able to fly a fighter aircraft like this again. I ended with a low pass over the squadron and a final break into the circuit.

After landing I noticed that the fire service had deployed. I thought it strange as I had not declared an emergency, but the real reason soon became apparent. After getting out of the cockpit I was picked up by the local search and rescue helicopter and dangled in front of the fire engine whilst they gave me a thorough soaking with the fire hose.

The whole squadron turned out, and I was presented with a glass of champagne and a group picture of the squadron. With me was my successor as OC 6 Squadron, Wg Cdr Mel Evans.

And so, I rode off into the sunset to start a new career as an airline pilot with Britannia Airways.

But there was a final coda to my RAF career, again very welcome and unexpected. I was informed that I would be awarded the Air Force Cross in the 1980 New

Last flight and a dowsing.

Year's honours list. I would wear my RAF best blue uniform one last time to attend an investiture by Her Majesty the Queen at Buckingham Palace. My wife Sheila and my two daughters Patricia and Susan attended, and it was one of the proudest moments of my life. The AFC is the RAF's highest peacetime award and although I had feelings of imposter syndrome, the actual citation which I obtained years later is very complimentary. Here is the text:

> "Wing Commander Robertson filled the appointment of officer commanding No. 6 Squadron from December 1977 until March 1980. During his time in command, he led his squadron with style and distinction, applying his particular brand of leadership to outstanding effect.
>
> "In 1978 he commanded the Strike Command Jaguar team in the Strike Command tactical Bombing competition and achieved notable success when his squadron won five of the seven trophies. The following year he led No. 6 Squadron to Cold Lake in Canada to take part in Exercise Maple Flag. During the exercise his squadron performed extremely well and most effectively, and in the final debrief the Canadian defence force commander referred to it as being 'the epitome of professionalism'. The unassuming yet so effective leadership shown by Wing Commander Robertson both in the air and on the ground was exemplified again in 1979 when his squadron operated under adverse conditions and achieved outstanding results in their tactical evaluation from a deployed overseas base. Following this evaluation the station was awarded the George Stainforth Trophy for the best performance in Strike Command.
>
> "Wing Commander Robertson inspired the very best efforts from his men both in the air and on the

AFC Investiture.

ground. In addition to showing leadership qualities of the highest calibre, he demonstrated that he was above all an outstanding pilot and first rate weaponeer, and he was held in the highest regard as a tactical air leader. His proficiency and competency, allied with his outstanding personal qualities have made him an impressive and successful Jaguar squadron commander. In recognition of his considerable personal contribution to the efficiency of the Jaguar force, I strongly recommend that he be awarded the Air Force Cross in the New Years's honours list 1981."

GEORGE ROBERTSON – RECORD OF SERVICE

DATES	UNIT	COURSE OR ROLE	RANK
Nov 1959 – Jul 1964	Edinburgh University Air Squadron	Elementary flying training	Officer cadet, acting pilot officer, pilot officer
17 Aug 1964	1 ITS South Cerney	Initial training course	Pilot officer
10 Nov 1964	RAF Acklington 6 FTS	Basic flying training Jet Provost	Pilot officer
27 July 1965	RAF Valley 4 FTS	Advanced training Gnat	Flying officer
08 Feb 1966	RAF Bassingbourn	Canberra conversion 231 OCU	Flying officer
09 Jul 1966	RAF Luqa, Malta	Pilot	Flying officer/ flight lieutenant
30 Jun 1969	RAF Chivenor 229 OCU	Pre Phantom Famil	Flight lieutenant
17 Jul 1969	RAF Coningsby 228 OCU	Phantom Conversion No. 3 Course	Flight lieutenant
05 Jan 1970	RAF Coningsby 54 Squadron	Pilot	Flight lieutenant
30 Sep 1970	RAF Brüggen 17 Squadron	Pilot	Flight lieutenant
06 Sep 1971	RAF Brüggen 31 Squadron	Flight commander	Squadron leader
16 Jan 1974	RAF Staff College Bracknell	65 advanced staff course	Squadron leader
18 Aug 1975	Ministry of Defence	Operational requirements OR 13a Tornado	Squadron leader
16 May 1977	RAF Leeming	JP refresher course	Acting wing commander
04 July 1977	RAF Brawdy	44 short Hunter course	Acting wing commander
10 Aug 1977	RAF Lossiemouth	20 Jaguar conversion CSE	Acting wing commander
16 Dec 1977	RAF Coltishall	OC 6 Squadron	Wing commander
28 Mar 1980	Pending retirement		

CHAPTER 9
COTTESMORE

TORNADO TRIPARTITE TRAINING ESTABLISHMENT

ALAN

I was in a job which was supposed to be a career enhancer, but after the misunderstanding with the RAF police and a new easily upset boss, I was going nowhere. I was commuting 35 miles each way daily, and as I sat in road works on the A1, I watched the Tornados doing circuits at RAF Cottesmore. The penny dropped and I asked to switch to specialist aircrew. I was immediately summoned by the posters who thought I was really daft. They explained why I had missed the last promotion list, and told me, "not to worry you'll be on the next one". They hadn't heard about 'the incident'. "You're right, he'll never forgive you. We'll post you to the Tornado F3 OCU at Coningsby. Sorry, Cottesmore is now closed to air defence." We haggled for a bit, and they finally agreed to send me to the Tornado tripartite training establishment (TTTE) at RAF Cottesmore, but only after they had identified a replacement. I called them with a name of someone who was delighted to have the job. With a sigh of relief, I reported to the TTTE on 18 March 1988.

TTTE had been running for around ten years at that time. It had a badge and a motto, *E Tribus Tornado* (Latin for 'out of the tribe of the tornado'). Who knew? The MOU was signed in 1979. I well remembered intercepting a Tornado over the Wash in late 1980 on a 228 OCU exercise, actually a pilot we knew on his first Tornado flight. They were as surprised as we were. This was to be the first part of

Tornado training for the RAF, the German Air Force, the German navy and the Italian Air Force. The training would cover handling the aircraft up to formation tail chasing, and the use of all its systems, including simulated weapons delivery. Forty-eight Tornado GR1s were established, and everything was shared on a split of 40/40/20. The students would go on to weapons training, the RAF at Honington, the Germans at Jever and the Italians at Rieti. It worked well but eventually with the aircraft's mid-life updates approaching, the services were going in different directions and the TTTE was disbanded in 1998. RAF Cottesmore was handed to the Harriers returning from Germany.

The Cottesmore Tornados would fly 'clean wing', the RAF providing 19 of the Tornados ordered. RAF Cottesmore would provide normal base support, but the instructors would be mixed nationality from the four services. All aircraft servicing would be performed by the RAF, and a little house was built for the German and Italian logistics clerks who would translate the servicing paperwork. Aircraft exchanges were quite frequent when deep maintenance was due. The working language would be English, and the post of chief flying instructor would rotate. The Germans and Italians also provided a senior officer equivalent to the RAF station commander to take care of national matters.

The GR1's empty weight was 13,065 lbs, and its powerplant was two Turbo-Union RB199-34R Mk101 turbofans at 8,475 lbs. Wingspan was variable, with sweep manually selected at 25 degrees, usually circuit work, 45 degrees for general-purpose flying or 65 degrees for high speed, which was rarely needed at TTTE apart from demonstrating it. One got used to the variable sweep very quickly, as well as the powerful reverse thrust which could be preselected, giving the Tornado a short roll out. The clean aircraft was fine for the TTTE mission. Most of the British Isles could

TTTE Tornado GR1.

be reached either directly or by a hi-lo-hi profile, and the British aircraft also carried fuel in the tail, ideal for an extra five minutes. The INAS was fully digital and, with the help of Kalman filters, incredibly accurate. The radar had been subcontracted by the Germans to Texas Instruments and was very readable and reliable. All the information was presented to the pilot in a very pilot friendly head-up display, day and night and a map display that was invariably very accurate. In other words, the GR1 was a delight to fly; if you like the sports model. However, its star quality was the terrain-following radar, the RAF's first, so that flying low level at night in cloud became a possibility, even fun.

It was an ugly aircraft though; the proverbial horse designed by a committee producing a camel. For weapons, it was not short of pylons, four under wing and three on a vast flat underside on which could be hung a wide variety of stores. The aircraft had fittings for two 27mm Mauser cannons, and for self-defence might carry a Sidewinder or an ASRAAM. A wide range of air-to-ground ordnance was available including the ill-fated JP233 runway denial weapon. Laydown bombing, dive and toss bombing were all available and tied to the weapons in use. At least that's what they told me and later sent me to Honington to drop a bomb. The gods of war clearly did not approve. They filled all the UK ranges with sea fog for the two days I was there, but honour was satisfied. Missions were planned by taking a mouse over the route on a flat table and then recording the route into a giant clanking first generation computer. A route could be stored on a large >B drive eight-inch floppy disc. Actually, the aircraft computer memory was 64k, loaded by cassette, all designed in the era of the Commodore 64.

TTTE was run via three training squadrons, A, B and C. A Squadron had a German boss and a number of German pilots. They had built a crew room like a Bavarian drinking hall, with a firm rule of 'No drinking until the last aircraft's down'. B Squadron was British with an RAF boss, and C Squadron with an Italian boss, and a very Italian flavoured crew room. There was also a standards squadron to convert instructors to the back seat and teach instructional technique where required, not forgetting the tri-national ground school which ran pilot conversion lectures and the simulators. When a student arrived at a flying squadron, he would be well versed in flying systems and emergencies. There were no QFIs as such; everyone on the staff was C to I, or competent to instruct. The RAF 'proper QFIs' kept quiet about it but funnily enough when a student was having difficulties, he was always referred to one of this group. It was not RAF exclusive, and one German had been accepted who had done a tour instructing on T37s in the USA.

Ground school complete, I joined the very Italian C Squadron, and I flew my first Tornado flight with an Italian instructor in a German aircraft. The sixth flight was a check before 'solo', which was really a flight with a staff navigator. I can remember hurtling round Wales and loving it. Then there was an instrument rating to complete followed by half a dozen weapons trips from low-level cross countries, including loft attacks simulating nuclear-bomb delivery. My student navigator, a young German, was introduced quite early on. We then moved on to terrain following and getting to trust the aircraft 'hands off'. The RAF Tornados had an E Scope radar display, which allowed a sideways look at what the radar was painting. Later on, I found this to be invaluable flying from the back, when I could crank up my seat and peer over the student pilot's shoulder. This was one of the few small differences between the national aircraft which were deemed to be safely ignored. On into night flying and night TFR, then pairs attacks onto targets chosen mainly for the weather that day. Typically, planning started four hours before the flight.

Then, after three months, we said goodbye to our new friends who disappeared to their various national weapons training arrangements, and I reported back to TTTE

TTTE Tornado GR1 formation.

Alan at A Squadron TTTE Cottesmore.

ground school. There was a week of instructional technique, then to the back seat of the simulator with an introduction to actually working the rear-seat navigation and weapons systems. It was all starting to make some sense, before the next move to the standards squadron and a month of flying the course lessons from the back seat. I was crewed with Bryan Murphy who was just back from Germany, and over the next few years we flew a lot together. I did my check flight with the Italian chief instructor, then moved with Bryan next door onto A Squadron. The Germans gave us a guarded welcome, actually waiting for us to accept them. In due course it was a happy place of work.

After that we had a new intake of students every two and a half months, and it was always a surprise. I was intrigued to know what the Italian students were like, but I need not have bothered. They were invariably excellent to the point of Italian perfection. Even the young back seaters sailed through the programme despite having only flown 100 hours training with the USAF in the back of a Boeing B737. The RAF students were a solid cross section, but the Germans surprised us. The youngsters were in the main underconfident which they displayed in the number of cloth badges sewn onto their new grey leather flying jackets. I would meet them at the post ground school barrel in the officers' mess and count the badges. Then I would note the name and ask to fly the Tornado conversion with him, because he was bound to be the biggest challenge. On the first few trips we needed an extra 45 minutes with the beginner pilots in order to complete all the cockpit checks required. I once burnt out an ejection seat 'up and down' motor trying to amuse the freezing groundcrew. The armourers were unamused. The courses rolled on, with the staff taking turns to run each course.

There were some lovely high spots though. Each nation showed off to the others with special nights. The Italians produced their night focusing on one area of Italy, the food, the music and the decorations. We have a souvenir plate from each year with recipes for polenta. The Brits ran a Burns Night also in the officers' mess featuring the excellent volunteer pipe band. The Germans and Italians loved it. Then the Germans emptied out the MT hangar and recreated a Munich beer hall, and this one was for all ranks to enjoy. Beer steins were topped up from watering cans and Schnapps from large jugs into miniature steins hanging round the neck. They had flown in a professional military band who delighted the good people of both Oakham and Stamford with serious band concerts. On the night, they had changed into lederhosen and marched in led by the traditional glockenspiel who was in turn following the German oberst and a wheelbarrow with an enormous German cheese. I thought it was better than the Munich version.

The flying was actually fun, the hours were reasonable, and Cottesmore, thanks to the MOU, was always fully manned. RAF sportsmen gravitated there because there was no chance of a quick few months in the Balkans or the Falklands. There was adequate spare flying for staff continuation trips to brush up skills. On one of these my German navy boss taught me how to loop a Tornado using 67-degree sweep. Essentially you used the same speeds as an F104, and I can remember going in at 5,000 feet with 500 knots, and over the top at 18,000 feet. A steady family life was assured. I also re-qualified as an IRE (including airways) and was a paid-up member of the secret QFI club. Then there were the exchange students who were always fun to fly with. One of them was a French navy Etendard pilot on his way to an exchange post with the German navy. Our Italian CI asked me if I would be happy to fly with him and just keep the French speaking on standby in case it was needed. In fact, he was totally excellent.

We did have a wartime role though, to deliver Tornados as required. That involved an annual civil airways flight, which meant a weekend abroad, just as

Above: Tornado GR1 over the Alps.

Below: TTTE Staff 1990.

Spain and Portugal opened up. The Germans and Italians were not interested so the RAF instructors took their slots. That meant a weekend to somewhere nice every three months or so. Bryan and I decided on Portugal because at the time nobody knew anything about flying there. We decided to refuel at RAF St Mawgan on the Friday morning in case there were air traffic problems and took RAF jets with the extra fuel in the tail. The destination was Monte Reale, home of the Portuguese Air Force A7 fleet, where Tito, my friend from Jever, was now base commander. It was a lovely weekend assisted by the totally professional Portuguese pilots, venturing as far as Lisbon, being dragged in to a wedding, and visiting the Portuguese Air Force museum. Later on, we went to Montijo on the south side of Lisbon's River Tagus, which was home to the G91 and frankly less interesting, apart from watching a G91 jettisoning his fuel tanks into the river. Italy was always a favourite, and I fondly remember weekends in Rome, Pisa, Rieti and Villafranca (for the opera at Verona. We saw Aida and I still remember the Egyptian slaves' chorus).

In the end after four years of serious but happy training, I was threatened by my poster with a ground posting and so it was time to leave. I was nearly 50 and when a young German student lost control on a toss manoeuvre as a part of his instrument rating it was time to go. TTTE lasted until 1999 and RAF Cottesmore was handed over firstly to the Harrier squadrons returning from Germany, and after

their disbandment to the army. It is now Kendrew Barracks, and Rutland lost its last RAF airfield. However, the RAF still uses the runway for low visibility training. The Tornado was finally withdrawn from RAF service in 2019, although it remains in service with the German, Italian and Saudi Arabian air forces.

ALAN'S RAF CAREER IN BRIEF

George and I were the first two would-be pilots to enter the RAF on university scholarships, and they were not quite ready for us. However, we were eventually joined onto the appropriate short-hour university course. We had considerable seniority when we made flight lieutenant at RAF Valley, but nobody ever explained the full significance. We were made painfully aware that some of our Gnat instructors had only just made that rank on a second tour. George's start in the RAF suited this seniority perfectly as he swiftly rose through the ranks. At one point I saw his name on a list of squadron leaders whose careers should be managed for further fast promotion.

The picture is of a starry-eyed university acting pilot officer, escorting the then Queen Mother before the award of degrees at the Albert Hall. He fully believed that the career path stretched out in front of him. It did not quite work out that way.

I did love the Javelin and my time on 60 Squadron, but when our opposite number, 64 Squadron disbanded, choices had to be made. I applied for the Central Flying School partly because I thought it would help my career and partly because I wanted to teach anyway. Everyone including the boss said I was crazy. They were right.

ULAS degree ceremony.

After two years flying the Jet Provost at Linton-on-Ouse teaching navy pilots, the prime minister declared that Britain would pull out of our bases East of Suez. The RAF realised that they suddenly had too many flying instructors and grounded 40 of us in a mid-point experience bracket. So, after two years instructing, I was posted to No.3 Apprentice Training School at RAF Hereford as an apprentice flight commander. This was not just a no flying job; there were not even any aircraft. I could not possibly get the reports I needed for promotion as I slid gently out of the promotion bracket.

I then spent two years with the Harrier and was then posted to the Phantom OCU as the engines were modified enough for air defence training to restart. So, after refresher training on the Hunter at RAF Wittering, when I finally arrived on 29 Squadron at RAF Coningsby in 1973, I was effectively starting again. At the time, flying this brilliant aircraft as a fighter was all I had ever wanted. After two years I was posted to 19 Squadron at RAF Wildenrath where I spent the next three years flying Cold War air defence. I became Battle Flight officer, deputy flight commander and representative on the NATO TACEVAL Team, and I qualified as a French linguist. It was all happening at last.

I then spent a year, from 1980-81, as a Phantom QFI at the Phantom OCU (64R Squadron) – at RAF Coningsby. The picture below is of a 'clean' Phantom at the USAFE base at Aviano. (I had won the raffle to fly the spare aircraft for the Phantom aerobatic display.) I was promoted to squadron leader.

F4M 228 OCU Aviano.

With the ANG at Davis Montan.

Next in 1981 was a posting to 111 Squadron at RAF Leuchars as squadron QFI followed by one to the NATO tactical leadership programme at the German Air Force base at Jever in Lower Saxony in 1983. The picture above is from a visit to the US Air National Guard at Tucson, AZ.

The RAF then claimed me back with a posting to the Department of Air Warfare at RAF Cranwell lecturing in air defence. I hated it and applied for a transfer to what's called specialist aircrew in 1988 with a posting to instruct on the Tornado GR1 at the TTTE at RAF Cottesmore. Actually, this allowed my wife and son to complete their university degrees from home and at last gave us some welcome stability. I resigned in 1992 after the young German student pilot mentioned earlier tried to kill me. Fortunately, he failed. Nothing ever happens for the worst, but what a strange and incredibly satisfying career.

EPILOGUE

FIGHTER PILOT TO AIRLINE PILOT

GEORGE

I left the RAF at a break point just after my 38th birthday and entered the world of civil aviation. Making the transition is not as easy or straightforward as you might imagine, as the two jobs are profoundly different. Fighter pilots consider themselves to be the top dogs, the cream of the crop during training and deemed good enough to step into a fighter cockpit which demands the highest-level stick and throttle skills. Lesser mortals end up in larger, slower aircraft like transports and bombers. This is the received wisdom they have grown up with, which feeds the view of an arrogant and aggressive fighter pilot, but this is often far from the case. In fact, the two roles are different and require different skill sets, so making the jump from one to the other is not easy and can be underestimated. You go from getting kitted out in all the fast jet paraphernalia G-suits, bone domes, etc. flying short, adrenaline-charged sorties, pulling lots of G, managing a formation, dropping weapons etc., to a much calmer and slower environment flying in shirt-sleeved comfort but for longer periods. Your performance is judged by different standards: safety, passenger comfort, knowledge of routes and destinations, crew management etc. But aircraft handling and accurate flying is still important, and the fighter pilot is usually good at that.

COMMERCIAL LICENCES

The first step in making the jump is getting the commercial licences. I had started this process in my final year in the RAF by doing a correspondence course for the written airline transport pilot licence (ATPL) exam. This covers all the essentials including aircraft systems, technical knowledge, aviation law, radio equipment, morse code and in-depth knowledge of navigation and related avionics. There is a separate exam on aircraft performance. This teaches how to use specific type-rated performance charts to determine safe speeds for different aircraft weights and runways. I then had to do an instrument rating test with a CAA examiner, which I did in an Aztec light twin, so there are quite a few hoops to jump through before you even get close to a commercial airliner.

Meanwhile we had vacated our married quarter at RAF Coltishall and returned to our Edinburgh flat. I had already been interviewed and accepted by Britannia Airways for a job as a first officer on their Boeing 737 fleet. Britannia had a good reputation as an employer and many of the senior training captains were ex-RAF, which made the transition a little easier. I did however have to wait for six months for the next available course.

During this period, I got a job to exercise my brand-new commercial licence as a freelance Aztec pilot for a small air taxi company in Glasgow. They specialised in short flights for up to five passengers around the highlands and islands. This served to keep me in flying practice and also provide some cash flow, but it also emphasised the dramatic change in status and prestige that came with my new role. It was a bit like changing from being a formula one racing driver to driving a black cab.

JOINING BRITANNIA AIRWAYS

Britannia Airways was a charter company based at Luton Airport and it was on a bit of a roll at the time. It was now owned by Thomson Travel and was therefore vertically integrated with a major tour operator. The British holidaymaker had moved on from the traditional UK holiday destinations like Skegness and wanted more and more to go abroad to Spain and the Mediterranean for sunshine, warm seas and beaches. Britannia had been early on the scene and was by then well established and expanding its presence to other UK airfields like Gatwick, Manchester and Birmingham. It had made the shrewd decision to invest in new aircraft instead of older hand-me-downs from scheduled carriers and had chosen the Boeing 737-200 for an all-new fleet. It was the first UK operator of the 737 which proved to be a winner and was soon to be widely adopted by others including British Airways. In fact, BA came to Britannia for 737 training when they first ordered the aircraft. The 737-200 was a robust and reliable aircraft of 130 seats and ideal for the charter market as seat/mile costs were low. Britannia had enjoyed several years of expansion and had recruited heavily from

Britannia Boeing 737-200.

RAF retirees so that when I joined, roughly half the pilots were ex-service. They had recruited across the board including transport and bomber pilots as well as fast jet, and with a few from the Red Arrows. Many of the senior training captains were ex-RAF. Britannia therefore felt a bit like a home from home, but the transition was still difficult.

TYPE CONVERSION

Britannia provided a full type conversion course to the Boeing 737 for people like me joining with a full ATPL licence. This involved a couple of weeks of ground school, learning about the aircraft, followed by a technical exam set by the CAA. We then moved on to simulator training in Britannia's own 737-200 simulator at Luton Airport. This was a very thorough grounding in all aspects of flying the 737. Each session started with a detailed briefing lasting about an hour and a half, followed by four hours in the simulator. We were organised in pairs, taking turns to fly the aircraft whilst the other pilot handled the non-flying duties. After about two hours in the sim, we took a short break then swapped seats and roles.

I found the 737 to be straightforward to fly but it did have its quirks and idiosyncrasies. It had underslung engines which meant that the nose tended to rise when power was increased and then lower when power was reduced. You had to ensure that you kept the aircraft fully in trim using the powerful stabiliser trimmer otherwise flying accuracy would suffer. The simulator by today's standards was pretty basic. It had a monochrome visual display and was driven by a DEC minicomputer occupying the equivalent of two filing cabinets. The computer had a bit of a lag between control inputs and seeing the result. The simulator sat on six jacks giving full motion, and gave a realistic impression of pitch, roll, yaw and heave. We spent a lot of time dealing with failed engines and flying on one engine. In that respect it flew a bit like the Canberra I had flown years before, but with one important difference.

The 737 is what is called a 'Performance A' aircraft, which means it has the capability to continue the take-off under certain circumstances following an engine failure. Part of our preparation involved calculating take-off speeds for the day, based on the runway in use, the surface wind, temperature and the aircraft weight. A load sheet giving the weight of passengers and bags is given to the pilot by the aircraft despatcher. The pilot then has to complete a load sheet to determine take-off weight and the weight and balance for trim settings. The pre-departure period can be very busy, and it is important for all calculations to be cross checked by the other pilot. Having completed the load sheet, we then consult a performance table for the runway in use, entering with aircraft weight, surface wind and temperature. From this we extract three speeds. V1 is the decision speed below which the aircraft can stop in the remaining runway length and above which it can continue in the event of engine failure. VR is the rotation speed where the nose is raised to get airborne, and V2 is the safe speed for climbing away on one engine. These calculations are crucial and must be completed carefully.

One final consideration for take-off calculations is the need to save wear on the engines by using reduced power whenever possible. On a long runway and with favourable weather conditions there is no need always to take off at full power. Part of the take-off calculations involves looking at the option of reduced thrust take-off whilst still satisfying all safety criteria.

During type conversion you look at all possible failure modes, working through the emergency procedures in real time as a crew with one pilot handling the aircraft and the other pilot reading checklists and cross checking all actions. I had flown in two-person crews before, but this was subtly different with the two pilots side by side and able to closely monitor what each was doing. The type training completed with an instrument rating and a formal handling test.

LINE TRAINING

After completing the simulator tests, it was time to fly the real thing. The first session involved 'base training' where a 737 empty of passengers but with the trainee pilots on board was flown (in our case) to Shannon Airport in Ireland. Shannon was chosen because it was a quiet airfield where we could fly around the circuit undisturbed.

With a training captain in the left seat, we each took turns to fly in the right seat as first officers flying visual circuits, take-offs and landings, and single-engine work.

We were accommodated near the airport but spent the evenings in 'Durty Nelly's' pub in Banratty, a lovey old Irish pub with live music. It was a good way to spend a convivial evening getting to know new colleagues.

After that, line training began in earnest. This involved flying a normal line flight with real passengers on board as a first officer in the right-hand seat, with a training captain in command in the left seat. We flew 'leg and leg about' which meant one leg as the pilot flying (PF) and the next leg as the pilot not flying (PNF). PNF duties include the radio calls with ATC, for the navigation, for updating the met information and for maintaining the nav log.

This also allowed us to get to know Britannia's route structure and bases, and we spent a lot of time living out of a suitcase as we were rostered for flights from all UK bases and to all overseas destinations. Airline pilots become good at what they do because of constant repetition, so for example once you have flown to Alicante ten times, you knew the route and the approach pattern, the airfield layout, the parking area, the local handling agent, the usual departure route, etc. and you therefore became quite slick. In contrast, in the RAF each sortie was different, and the skill was in adapting to new situations quickly.

You had to get used to working with a crew, liaising with the cabin crew, doing sensible and informative PAs to the passengers, working quickly and accurately in everything, making sure your flying prioritised safety but also having an eye to the commercial realities. There was a lot to think about and the fact that you were once a hot shot fighter pilot was quite irrelevant.

BEING A FIRST OFFICER

I found it best not to talk about my previous RAF background unless someone asked. Some of my civilian colleagues had preconceived ideas about the RAF. They sometimes felt that the RAF guys had an easy passage with all of their training so far having been paid for by the Queen, whereas they had come up the hard way having paid for their own training, maybe serving their time in smaller regional airlines before progressing to the Boeing, so one had to step carefully. War stories about what you did on Red Flag and your good weapons scores were not appreciated.

Promotion in the airlines is largely governed by seniority. When you first join the company, you start at the bottom of the seniority list and progress upwards with the turnover of pilots and as new people join behind you. For promotion to captain, you will be looked at in seniority order and selected on the basis of your training reports and assessments. Your six-monthly visits to the simulator were therefore important in order to establish a good training record, which would eventually be used to assess your suitability for command. At the time, the training department in Britannia had a fearsome reputation, and especially when it came to command selection and training. Years before they had lost an aircraft at Ljubljana when a Bristol Britannia aircraft they were operating at the time flew into the ground with the loss of all on board. The enquiry into the accident determined that the captain had mis-set his altimeter to the wrong pressure setting. In Britannia there was much soul searching and the consensus was that the captain should never have been promoted in the first place. From then on, the command selection and training process had become a sequence of hurdles for you to clear, looking for ways to fail you rather than a means to assess your command potential. People would report for their annual base or line check in fear and trepidation which is not how things should be. I am pleased to say that things improved considerably in later years.

For me and my family the change in lifestyle and status was abrupt, but not unexpected. A first officer in the airline business is a lowly creature compared with an RAF wing commander, but equally the demands made upon you are so much fewer. As OC 6 Squadron the job never stopped. Even the social life was hectic and at the end of the three years I felt exhausted. We now bought a house in Bedford mainly because it had a good selection of schools, and my younger daughter Susan stopped boarding in Edinburgh and became a day pupil at Bedford High. Her elder sister Patricia was too close to her A levels to risk a change of school and stayed as a boarder in Edinburgh. My wife Sheila was at last able to start a career of her own and worked for Bedfordshire County Council, eventually progressing to a senior post as a local government officer.

In the years before I joined, Britannia had been expanding with new additions to the 737 fleet every year. This required a continuous recruitment process and new command opportunities. It had been common for a suitably qualified ex-RAF pilot to progress from first officer to captain in two or three years. The early Thatcher years changed all that as the UK went into recession, the unemployment rate soared and people had less discretionary income to spend on package holidays. Britannia's expansion stalled and with it command prospects. As a result, I spent eight years as a first officer in the right-hand seat before my number came up for promotion.

This illustrated the cyclical nature of the airline business as boom followed bust. Many old established airlines went to the wall, including Dan Air and Air Europe, both of whom had offered me a job. I had clearly made the right choice with Britannia, who were very sound commercially. The flag carriers like British Airways were not exempt and the time to command for a BA first officer was about 16 years.

From what I recall, my final year's salary in the RAF as a wing commander in 1980 was £13,000. My first year's salary in Britannia as a first officer was £10,500, so when you add on the RAF pension of about £2,000, the difference in my total income was not huge. However, the pension contributions in Britannia were eight per cent of gross and that did make a difference. Promotion to captain would mean a big jump in income of about 35%, so the fact that I had to wait eight years in the RHS was significant. The work in a charter airline is very seasonal, busy from April to September then slack in the winter months. As a result, I was able to supplement my income working as a consultant on MoD contracting procedures and making use of the skills I had picked up in RAF Staff College and the MoD. Over the course of the next ten years this grew to a substantial business and made a big impact on our lifestyle. Another substantial perk with Britannia was the provision of two Thomson holidays per year subsidised by 50 per cent. We made full use of these and did skiing holidays every winter as a family until the girls finished full time education.

BECOMING AN AIRLINE TRAINING CAPTAIN

Soon after I became a captain on the 737, I was invited to join the Britannia training department to help them develop their first crew resource management (CRM) course. This idea started in the USA in response to an increasing number of aircraft accidents which were directly attributed to aircrew error. There were many reasons for this trend, but one common factor was that many captains were unable or unwilling to take advice from a subordinate and insisted on running the show as a one-man band, in other words of not making full use of the many resources of information, advice and assistance available to them. Also, first officers could be reluctant to step up and challenge the decisions of the captain or offer alternatives when they could see problems ahead. The aircraft themselves were becoming increasingly reliable, and it was time to look at ways of improving the reliability of the crew.

This project appealed to me, and my psychology degree finally had some relevance in helping to understand the underlying human factors and explaining this to a pilot audience. Britannia was an early adopter of human factors training for all aircrew, pilots and cabin crew. We were helped in the early days by Professor Helen Muir of Cranfield University who was one of the early pioneers in this area. Britannia started doing human factors training before it was mandated by the CAA and our course material was made freely available throughout the industry.

I moved on to become a line training captain and later a type rating examiner (TRE). I had been an IRE in the RAF, but a TRE in the civil world is a step up from that. A TRE wears two hats, is responsible to the company for training standards of its pilots but also directly to the CAA for ensuring that pilots meet the proficiency standards laid down for their licence.

Britannia was also continuing to expand and over the course of my 21 years with the company I moved from the 737-200 to the 757 and 767 with a mix of both short-haul and long-haul flying.

I moved back to the 737 in 1999, this time onto the new 737-800 which was just entering service. I attended a conversion course with Boeing in Seattle and then had the job of converting our own pilots to the new jet. This involved not just our UK-based pilots but also the pilots for our subsidiary in Scandinavia, so I spent a lot of

George in the 767.

EZY 737.

time in Norway and Sweden flying with local pilots who were always pleasant and very capable colleagues.

But my time with Britannia was running out as the retirement age then was 60. However, easyJet had recently started and were making rapid strides. They were desperate for experienced trainers on the 737 NG, and their retirement age was 65, so I made the jump coming straight in as a TRE.

When I joined easyJet they had just 30 aircraft, but when I left in 2012, they had 220, and that massive expansion had to be fed with a huge amount of pilot recruitment and training. I was involved from the outset in the selection process for pilot recruits and in setting up training programmes for new pilots to progress through simulator and line training to a new type rating. Soon after I joined, easyJet decided to go for a complete change of fleet from Boeing to Airbus and I carried on working for easyJet well past my normal sell by date as a TRE and pilot training manager until the 737 fleet phased out, right up to my 72nd birthday in 2012.

I carried on flying light aircraft as a hobby for a few more years. This was mostly in a Cessna 172 four-seater aircraft based near Edinburgh. It was good to be able to fly friends and family around southern Scotland for sightseeing and to give all seven grandchildren the chance to handle the controls. In 2016 though I felt it was time to hang up my wings. By then I had been flying for 57 years, and my enthusiasm had never wavered from when I was a 2-year-old with model aircraft suspended over my cot. The job as a pilot has changed over time, but it is still a wonderful career. I hope the latest generation of pilots have as much fun as I have had.

ALAN

I soldiered on to see Wendy and James safely through university and because I enjoyed what I was doing in a great team at the TTTE at RAF Cottesmore. I was also flying cadets at No. 7AEF, RAF Newton. I left the RAF aged 50 when there was no pension deduction and unexpectedly had three further careers. It is rarely an easy transition and should be of interest to any young person thinking about a military flying career. We both left the RAF in the era of charter airlines, before the low-cost airlines got started.

As I could feel my time as a Tornado instructor coming realistically to an end, I had become involved with a commercial pilot who flew a Cessna 425, which was called an 'entry-level turboprop'. Neil flew parties of businessmen regularly around Europe and I flew a trip with him to Nantes. It was his idea that I might like to get another small twin and we could help each other. I actually got quite a lot of interest from firms around the Midlands until I had a fatal phone call with one of the directors of a large manufacturer in Peterborough.

"You have convinced me that it would be cheaper and easier for me to hire your proposed aircraft to fly mechanics around Europe. However, I just laid off 72 staff, so I can't realistically take on an aircraft." It was the 1992 recession. "Would I get the same answer everywhere, do you think?" "Yes".

In the meantime, I had trained very much like George but on the Grumman GA7 Cougar at Cranfield. I can never forget my instrument-rating test, after getting up in the small hours, driving to Cranfield then flying the entire practice test for the first time. I was exhausted. However, a sub-tropical rainstorm started, and the CAA examiners arrived. One of them had a reputation for being very hard on students and the CFI decided that I should fly with him in the afternoon. We stood by the aircraft under his golf umbrella, and he asked if I had flown this aircraft that morning. "Good. In that case you may perform the outside checks as fast as you wish while I stand here." He didn't seem that bad. In fact, as we flew up the nearest airway, he was telling me stories about flying the Swift and asking me about the Javelin. The students couldn't believe that we had been chatting. As we shook hands he advised me to find out how to synchronise the propellers. I then sat the exam for Performance C and was ready to go.

Flying career dreams shattered, I was wondering what to do next when the phone rang. It was a fellow AEF pilot who had been an airline ops director. "Al, we're forming a new airline, do you want a job?" "No thanks, I really don't want to fly airlines. By the way, what aircraft are you getting?" "The A320". "When do you want me to start?" The lure of the first fly-by-wire airliner was irresistible, and the next thing was that I was on a flight to Toulouse with a group of new colleagues for two months training at Airbus. It was hard to believe that I was still in the RAF on terminal leave. In fact, I left the RAF as the city clocks were striking midnight on 2 April 1992, in a rooftop bar opposite our hotel. My new friends supplied the countdown and there was a mighty cheer at midnight. The waiter rushed out to see what 'les ooligans' were up to. "He just became a civilian." "Ma fois, we 'ave a procedure", and he produced a foaming two-litre beer mug, "compliments of le direction" (i.e. management).

After that, training was much as George described, except that some of it was space age and other bits seriously out of date. After the two-week computer-based ground school, we had a tour of the Airbus assembly. The hangar foreman explained how half the fuselage was made in Germany, and the other half in France. I asked if they always made a perfect fit. He said that about 99 per cent did. I asked about the other one per cent and he just said, "oh my God". We were training in pairs, and each pair was given a little car. We had a lot of fun exploring the local area as far as Andorra, and Wendy came out to join me for a week. We had time for some adventures in between simulator trips.

Back in the UK, we picked up our fairly revolting grey uniforms, and the new airline 'Excalibur' gradually took shape. We met the new cabin crew, which was a total culture shock for those of us from fast jets. The difference between the Gatwick and Manchester cabin staff was a real surprise. I was appointed flight safety officer because of my RAF experience, and I managed to squeeze another £2,000 a year out of the CFI. My line training was at Liverpool under Gordon Corps, the late well-known Airbus test pilot. He managed to prove to us four fast jet pilots convincingly that if the computers start to play up, dump the offenders, and fly it like a Hunter. My first flight was from Manchester to Tenerife South with Doug Gillanders, one of our excellent base training captains. He gave the aircraft to me to fly home, and after we were relaxing in the cruise he told me to put away the TFS airfield plates (one-page maps) alphabetically. I sat there for some time thinking, "silly sod, they all start with T". After a while I realised that there was page numbering, but this was a prize example of what the new first officer was supposed to know.

On another occasion I was flying the aircraft into Bournemouth from the direction of Paris. Something was happening around Southampton and London radar was turning us tighter and tighter on Bournemouth, until it was too tight to pick up the ILS approach. My line training captain (a sort of junior being who could only do flight training, not simulator) asked me what I wanted to do. "Call the Bournemouth Tower and tell them 'initials'." "What's that?" "You'll see". So, I turned onto the Bournemouth runway heading and gently dived the aircraft to about 1,200 ft. A very gentle pitch into the circuit and Bournemouth Tower cleared us to land. You could hear the controller chuckling. I then talked my LTC into the downwind vital actions and landed off a visual turn. I could see that he was unhappy about something. As we were standing in stony silence outside the airport waiting for the cabin crew, the first passengers started to appear. One of them approached LTC. "That was brilliant. Everyone loved it. Why don't we do that every time?" LTC pointed at me, and I got a further burst of praise from other passengers as well. After they had gone, LTC turns to me, "OK you're off the hook, but don't ever think of doing that again." A classic mismatch of fast jet and heavies.

Overall, I started to dislike the long night flights intensely. I didn't really like being a first officer aged 50 plus. After a few years I was in a strange way 'saved' by a medical problem which grounded me into the hands of the CAA doctors. I lost my job and two hobbies on the same day (instructing at the Leicester Aero Club, and flying cadets at No. 7 AEF, RAF Newton). They were thorough and after a fairly painful time I was given back a licence that said I could fly 'as or with a qualified pilot'. This was enough for Air 2000's ops director to offer me a job as his personal first officer flying once a week, generally to Funchal in Madeira. This was ideal as by now I had established a consultancy to advise on and help with a new set of regulations called JAR-OPS which applied by consent to all the countries that agreed to common air regulation within Europe. I teamed up with a quality expert called Nigel Bauer and with him ran courses in many different parts of Europe and beyond. In honesty we didn't get it quite right and were naive enough to think that airline managements would appreciate the opportunities that quality management offered them. Two airlines, maybe three, took in part of quality and never looked back, of whom the star was Ryanair. Don't laugh. They did exactly what they say they will do; cheap flights on time. George's Britannia were pretty good but kept their methods secret. Of course, I was now a member of the UK flight safety committee and found out most of the airlines' secrets. Most airlines settled for the compulsory part of quality management, namely safety management, and ignored quality entirely.

The Irish company, Transaer, gave me a real break in taking me on as their quality and safety consultant. This involved multiple trips to Dublin, and I quickly came to love the staff there and the country in general. Wendy came over several times; the trip around Galway was unforgettable. At one stage I remember offering the taoiseach (prime minister) a beer to which he answered, "very kind of you but I'm getting a round in". So much for politics. I had a call from Transaer's ops director, "Al stop messing around as a first officer and come and fly for us". I could do that with a licenced first officer, with an endorsement from the IAA. I sewed on my fourth stripe and trained on a contract with Airtours and discovered via a group of drunks that the management representative on board was in fact the Airtours CSD. "They're not bad lads Al. If we were boys, we'd be them. They just misjudged it and we've got spare seat covers where they were sick." She was the boss, but I'd like to think that they are still a bit frightened even now.

Then I was onto the roster with the contract Transaer had with Turkish Airlines based in Istanbul. They were evaluating the A320, and in the end bought some. I loved this contract, even though I kept getting the slightly tricky Athens flight. The

With Turkish Airlines.

Turks were charming and helpful, the flights were mainly around two to three hours, the Irish CSDs were delightful and competent, as were the Irish engineers who were with us. I can even laugh now about the toy poodle loose in the cabin running round barking at everyone. Of course, his mummy had bribed the agent who eventually gave in and produced a doggy box.

It all came to a stop when I was on the Novair contract flying out of Stockholm Arlanda. This had been quite a difficult challenge, with flights into the Arctic snow and ice. The Swedes took it all as quite normal. Can you imagine seeing the lights before the Lulea runway? But the previous SAS flight had just done it, so I had no choice. Amazingly it worked. After I had flown a scheduled flight to Gatwick, I swapped with another pilot and went home. Another medical grounded me and this time it was for keeps. The CAA gave me a PPL 'as or with'.

After that I took up gliding and flew just under 700 hours. I could also fly the tug and did some very interesting air-to-air photography on gliders and difficult types with Keith Wilson taking the photos from the left seat of the Eurofox and Dave Unwin flying the unlikely type of glider or motor glider. Invariably I retained a share in various aircraft to fly the £100 hamburger – plan for somewhere say half an hour away with the best restaurant. Including the burger it costs about £100.

Eventually it was time to go after more than 60 years in the saddle and start writing. I also picked up a job instructing on the F4J full motion simulator operated

Our Robin share – the £100 hamburger.

Above: Full circle.

Below: In Portugal for our 60th anniversary.

by aerospace experience flight simulators in Peterborough, who also have a Boeing 737-400 for serious instrument training and a 737-200 for fun. In fact, it flies like a PA28. The instructors are from very mixed backgrounds and never failed to impress me with their charm and instructional ability.

Then I read George's notes from a PowerPoint presentation he had given and had the inspiration for a second book. I do hope you have enjoyed reading it.

And of course, my dear wife Wendy and I were still travelling as we passed our 60th anniversary, this time on the Portuguese River Douro.

APPENDIX

"HUNTING BEAR" BY LJK SETRIGHT

GEORGE

In the early years of the Jaguar, we often had requests to promote the RAF's new jet, and we received a request from the motoring journalist LJK Setright who some readers may remember. He wrote for *Car Magazine* for many years, and his articles were always interesting. He revelled in technical detail unlike his successor Jeremy Clarkson who was dismissive of such information. You will see that LJK had done his homework on the Jaguar, and his article is well written, factual, full of good information but also humorous. He was a Latin scholar and a man of great erudition and wit, although physically rather frail. He had spent his national service as an air traffic controller in the RAF, so he knew a bit about aircraft. LJK had been commissioned by *Penthouse* magazine to write an article on what it is like to be a fighter pilot in the RAF's latest jet. He came to 6 Squadron to fly in our T2 in March 1978. Here is the text of the article he subsequently wrote for *Penthouse*.

Born of an understanding between the British and French defence ministries on 17 May 1965, brought up at Toulouse, Biarritz and Preston, and spread out into places as near or as nullabouts as Germany, Ecuador, India, and Oman, the Jaguar is a unique once-and-for-all breed, not just a swell cat or any old hellcat. It is a SEPECAT. You think that sounds Egyptian and antique, some bellicose brawlpuss bred of Bubastis? You should know our allies: think of NATO, the

Jaguar photographed by LJK Setright.

nattiest thing in alliances since the Peloponnesian League back in the days when Nahum reckoned that 'Pharaoh King of Egypt is but a noise'.

Don't dismiss NATO too lightly. It must be the best-organised alliance ever. When I went flying in a Jaguar, I was given a NATO vomit-bag; what other league would ever have thought of that? The lettering on the side was printed large, that he might run who reads it: BAG, AIR NATO STOCK No 1-40D-8105-130 2180. That's what organisation really means. I used the bag for exposed films.

The SEPECAT Jaguar is another and rather bigger number in the NATO stocklist, at the service or at the mercy of all the member nations. Think of Germany, which gave us Hieronimus Bosch; think of France, which gives us acronymous bosh. They love their acronyms do the French, and SEPECAT is one of them.

It stands for Société Européenne de Production de l'Avion École de Combat et Appui Tactique. If they had called themselves the firm that 'makes a dual-role aircraft of light weight and high performance to serve as an advanced and operational trainer and as a tactical support striker', they could hardly have made it much worse. In fact this Anglo-French company was formed in 1966 specifically to produce the Jaguar for the French services and the Royal Air

Force, bits of it being made in France, other bits in England. Partworkers and partners were the British Aircraft Corporation, which has since become British Aerospace and Breguet Aviation which suffered a take-over by Avions Marcel Dassault since when the French have been keener to sell their own Mirage than to share any Jaguar profits with the British. It is all as silly and as nasty as business can be when it grows international, full of government overseers and management committees and jobs for the boys at Rolls-Royce and Turbomeca, at Fairey and SNECMA, and all the waters of bilge and gripe flowing foully together; but out of this broth of business interests, this festival of political shinhacking, came a splendid aircraft. It has the blood of the Breguet 121 in its veins, the TSR2 and the Taon imprinted in its genes, the vigour of the English Electric/BAC Lightning in its loins. There were men behind it who knew all about the flight of paragons: cast an eye down the list of SEPECAT directors and it may stop at the name of Jeffrey Quill, the man who flew the first Spitfire.

There's a Spitfire! Not an aerial miracle anymore, but an ancient monument, and as gorgeous a gate guardian as might mark the entrance to any RAF station. So here am I at last, after a beastly long slow drive in another kind of Jaguar, an XJ12 that did 140 mph whenever the chance was there and still I'm an hour late, but there's the blue board announcing Royal Air Force Coltishall. How weary, stale, flat and unprofitable to me do seem the plasterboard plains of Norfolk, but what a place for airfields, and they're plastered all around Norwich, stuck there on its hill like a wizened nipple on the dry flat bosom of East Anglia. I don't think they're all operational now, but surely Coltishall will never close (didn't I think that about Tangmere?) and I suppose the guardroom is just past the Spitfire and Lightning, set up on struts to play Magog to the Spitfire's Gog, another monumental fugitive from the breaker's yard. A Lightning, of all things, the finest Double Derringer ever to take wing, still flying daily gravity-frazzling sprints from places like Leuchars up in the lorn lands, blowtorching up into the Bear-hunting skies where the big Russian surveillance planes might come snooping too close if not warded off more or less politely with a waggle of hypersonic wings and a flourish of two fingers – one for each of the Red Top air-to-air missiles waiting primed on the Lightning's flanks. And yet that blessed blastpiper must be a quarter of a century old.

They lead long lives, do modern military aircraft. In the days of dope and castor oil, the decade of wire and spruce and simpleton biplanes looping and spinning over Hendon on Empire Air Day, the defence of the realm was handed on from Grebe and Gamecock to Siskin, to Bulldog and Fury, to Gauntlet and Gladiator, before the Hurricane and Spitfire brought us up to date in 1937. The Spitfire lasted well; and the Mosquito was reckoned very old when the last fighting version watched over us through the nights of 1952. Then the jets came, and they grew much more costly, and much more complex, until it might take longer to make one fly than it took to defeat Hitler. Once serviceable, stuffed with sub-systems and bursting with black boxes, each costing a taxpayer's ransom and taking as long as his children to develop, such an aircraft has to remain in service for long enough to make it all worthwhile; so, the Jaguar, conceived in 1965, will probably be with us until 1990. The first of eight prototypes flew late in 1968; by 1972 they had flown more than 1,600 hours, the Rolls-Royce-Turbomeca Adour turbofan engine had run 20,000 hours, and the first of 200 Jaguars went into service with the French Armée de l'Air. In 1973 the Royal Air Force received the first of its 200; today it has eight operational squadrons of them. Two of those squadrons specialise in reconnaissance, the remainder concentrate on the Jaguar's forte, the low-altitude tactical strike.

That is what they do at Coltishall. A practice mission could take a pair up to Yorkshire one day, searing through the dales below Buckden Pike or lifting to scrape over Great Whernside at sheepshearing height. The next day might take them blasting through the granite folds of Snowdonia, or up to the Scottish border country to reive through the Cheviots. This day, I was to fly in one that might do any of these things; three dozen of the RAF strength is in two-seaters, 28 inches longer and one Aden gun less but otherwise much the same as the single-seater that would come along for company. After half a dozen years in service, the Jaguar is still something to show off.

It would hardly matter if it were half a century old. Cross the threshold of any RAF aerodrome and time is suspended in nostalgia, a return home to the same timeless wherever, the middle-class formality of garden suburb brick and greensward for the messes and admin buildings, the huge hangars looming near the perimeter track, the same special indescribable quality of the light which scrubs the whole place clean and bare like an old kitchen table. Never mind that the kite coming over the hedge is the latest laser-chasing whooshbang; it could just as well be a Beaufighter whispering in behind its two big Bristols, 40 years behind the calendar, or a tentative Avro 504 thumb-buttoned in on its stuttering rotary a generation earlier still. Coltishall is like all the other stations, all the other years, only the people have changed; and not just in the subtle alterations to that most understated of uniforms – the men themselves are different, healthier, cleaner, quieter, more purposeful. In the old days there were always the disillusioned and the dreamers. Now I can see no sign of either; instead, within a couple of minutes of reporting at the guardroom I am joined by the man who will fly me, Flight Lieutenant Hannam, obviously fairly young but not very (he has had too much to learn) and very fit but not athletically hard, a man who talks and moves quietly, economically, smoothly, quickly; if we rush straight to SSO there may yet be time for me to have my medical so that I can fly despite my late arrival.

A nurse takes my name, my blood pressure, my urine, my height – why should it matter to her that I am six feet four? Oh yes, there were lots of chaps who were too big to suit the cramped cockpit of a Spitfire, but surely the service does not play Procrustes nowadays. There are posters on all the walls warning of the dangers of flying with a cold, and the MO has a good look in each ear to see that the drums are clear and clean – I'm glad he looked into both – with an undertone menacing with direst consequences anybody who suffers altitude with his Eustachian's choked. Another moment of terror, the old bogey that has always turned up in my service medicals ever since the first time I had to cheat my way through Ishihara and the rest of the colour-vision tests; they are giving me an eyesight check. I stumble through, having concealed my monocle in a pocket, and am pronounced fit to fly. Forget about lunch, make do with a cup of coffee, let's look at the plane and find out how it works.

Walking under the little chisel-pointed tip of a single-seater's nose, I am shown that behind its optical glass is a laser rangefinder. It also works as a marked target seeker, so that some army man on the battleground can identify with a laser beam the target he wants attacked and the Jaguar can lock onto the reflection. There are many more ways of finding and hitting, for up in the cockpit the pilot sits alongside a couple of computers. He is there to do what they cannot, but what they can do is beyond any man, so the combination of man and machine transcends the merely mechanical to attain the electronically superhuman. A three-gyro inertial platform senses every change of speed and direction to keep instantaneous tabs on the Jaguar's position, with the surrounding area mapped on a screen between the pilot's knees. If he feeds the computer with co-ordinates for the position of a known target, the computer can compare the two plots and when appropriate mark the target on the head-up display, a jade screen slanted before his eyes like a teleprompter, with figures and symbols focussed at infinity for him to read whatever he wants to know, from speed and height to the time of high water in the Solomon Islands. An artificial horizon, a sight for the 30mm Aden guns, these things are easy and old-fashioned; but the computers can do much more. Tell them what bomb you propose to drop, and they will dredge up their memory of its ballistics characteristics, relate that knowledge to the Jaguar's position and speed, and predict exactly what the bomb's trajectory will be. A line of sight will be projected on the head-up display: it represents the path of impacts of an infinite succession of such bombs, as if they were to be released all the way from here to the horizon, and if that line passes through the target marker the Jaguar is well on the way to a successful strike. Across the line appears a horizontal bar: it marks the impact of 'the bomb of the moment', the one you are releasing now; and if you press the bomb-release when the bar coincides with the target-mark, the bomb will strike home. Ask the computer, and it will do the job for you; for certain types of bomb hurling, involving violent manoeuvres out of harm's way, it will do the job better.

The entire nose of the Jaguar is packed with electronics. Smith's, Plessey, STC, Ferranti, Marconi Elliott, Sperry, all the big names are represented. The work of these black boxes may be revealed on the head-up panel, or on the head-down navigation display or on the instruments (which thanks to all this automation, are surprisingly few and simple), or it may be more remote, as in the electronics counter-measures aerial high up on the tail fin where it can detect that the Jaguar is being picked up on some hostile radar.

Computers cannot do everything. They cannot save me when the plane breaks down, so I have to be guided through all the drill of ejection, including what to do if the automatics fail to separate me from my seat after ejection, or fail to deploy my personal parachute thereafter, or to inflate my flotation jacket. I have to learn where and how to clamber aboard the dinghy that should materialise if I come down into water, when and how to use flares and sea-dyes. In fact we will not be over water for more than few seconds, so it will not be necessary to wear the rubberised suits that protect against immersion, exposure, or some of the nasty side-effects of high-altitude decompression. Nevertheless, it is time I were properly dressed.

Get undressed first. The outfit starts with long underwear, snowy white and soft, to keep me dry and insulated. As in a racing car, it is unwise to wear any thermoplastic fibres such as nylon next to the skin, for in a fire it melts and takes the skin with it. I wonder about a G-suit to prevent all my blood being drained from my head and dumped in my toes in hard turns or pull-ups, but it turns out that the standard outfit is a pair of g-trousers. Breeches, more like, with air tubes strongly stitched into the cloth down the outside of each leg, and air passages across the lower belly, all fed through a rubber pipe with a quick release coupling on the end. When inflated, these will squeeze the nether Setright so tightly that no slump of blood will be possible. They will also press on the bladder, so I am told to make sure it is empty before flying, and that is not the sort of warning one ignores. Next, a pair of overalls, all set about with thigh pockets; the pilots of No. 6 Squadron all have their names embroidered on the breasts of theirs, as I note when we are joined by a wiry young flight lieutenant whose blazon declares him to be Steve Morgan. He will fly the single-seater, and bubbles with enthusiasm for its performance.

What about acceleration? How does the Jaguar compare with a good motorbike, or a racing car, from standstill to 700 mph, say? Probably not at all badly, reckons Mr Morgan, but where the acceleration is really impressive is from 400 to 600. I am going into a whole new realm, but I feel in this company more like an incomplete old cripple with my g-trouser inflation tube hanging out through a slot in the front of my overalls, as though I had undergone some ghastly colostomy. More rebuilding follows, with an inflatable jacket, really a waistcoat cluttered with attachments of which most notable is a small black boxy contrivance in the centre front, with a length of convoluted hose hanging free. It is a miniature regulator that will feed me oxygen to breath from the Jaguar's liquid store, and this tiny lightweight contraption costs you and I more than £1,000.

The waistcoat is laced up tightly, and then with a jerk even tighter; the helmet that comes next must not be tight, however, merely a perfect fit. It all takes time, it is all done with immense care, as though the operation of the aircraft might depend on a correct connection, as though my life might depend on a proper fit. There are disapproving shakes of the head when I decline the offered gloves, needing my fingers free to work my camera and lenses; all right, I'll take them with me anyway. At least they are not as clumsy as the heavy leather boots that carry my tottering parachuted weight out to the waiting plane.

Boarding the Jaguar is a lengthy business for a tyro, though the professionals can be seen to do it as quickly as practice and training should ensure. I shall be sitting behind Mr Hannam, and about 15 inches higher, beneath my own streamlined canopy. I go up a step ladder, lower myself into the seat, and let the others strap me into place by shoulder, hip and thigh. Blue traps loosely circle my shins: if I have to eject, they will tighten and draw my legs close in to the Martin-Baker ejector seat lest they flail and snap in the violent wind of my projection. To project myself, all I have to do is to pull a ring in front of my crotch; if only getting in could be as quick as getting out – but no, there are oxygen connections to be made (the g-trousers are inflated from the same store of liquid oxygen), electrical connections for the microphone in my breathing mask, tapes for anchoring my spare lenses on a ledge ahead of me, and a two-handed drill to go through for closing and clamping my Plexiglass canopy when, but not until, we are ready for take-off. Satisfied that I am not going to fall out or kick the rudder, Mr Hannam climbs down and reappears moments later in his own cockpit, sinking down out of sight into his seat. I watch the dials fascinated as a tiny Microturbo puffs compressed air into each Adour in turn, and as the engines fire and run up to speed I listen to the radio-telephone drill as the two pilots and the control tower crackle through their clipped essentials.

The Morgan single-seater is to run slightly ahead of us in the take-off, for the benefit of my camera; we line up on the runway, I remember my canopy drill perfectly, and it is time to go. Some planes cannot use their afterburners for extra thrust until they are rolling, otherwise the kick can scrub the rubber off their tyres; but the Jaguar has the refinement of part throttle reheat, so that it can build smoothly up to full thrust without feeling it come in with a frame-wracking wallop. I can see the red glow in the tailpipes of the single-seater and know that our own Adours are building up to their seven and a half tons of thrust.

GO! We are rolling faster and faster. A third of the fuselage and wings is full of fuel, and the drop tanks hold another 528 gallons, so our Jaguar weighs about 11 tons; but with seven and a half tons of colonic fire in its belly it literally runs before the wind, picking up about 15 mph every second. My motorcycle, a Dresda CBX, is one of the fastest things on the road and could hold the Jaguar up to 60 mph or so; but the plane's acceleration seems never to weaken, the push in the back seems never to abate. At 193 mph the nose comes up, and in about 600 yards we are airborne, the wheels come clomping hydraulically up into their retraction bays, and already we are in a climbing turn, making height for a cloud top cruise to Newcastle and beyond, before we drop to sneak into the Cheviots on our bellies.

A hi-lo-hi mission, they call it. Like all aircraft of its kind, the Jaguar flies faster and more economically up where the air is thin. It is no slouch at sea-level, where it can reach Mach 1.1, bettering the speed of sound by ten per cent to notch 840 mph; but at 36,000 feet it can hurdle the 1,000-mph mark to touch the Mach 1.6. The differences in fuel consumption are commensurate: if we were to stay low all the way, our attack radius would be 518 miles, but a hi-lo-hi sequence stretches this by another 300 miles. For today's journey, neither full height nor full speed are called for, and we settle comfily above the clouds with the head-up display showing that we are 14,750 feet up and cruising at a lean-burn 354 knots, or 408 mph. Comfortable is the word. There is an air-conditioning unit behind my head, with its own air intake and exhaust ducts on the roof behind my canopy. Breathing my oxygen is so easy that I hardly know the mask is there. I am warm, but untroubled by the sun streaming in through the Plexiglass. My seat is almost perfect, but I would like it to be a little higher so that my thighs were better supported. At present I am perched on the points of my ischia – baboons of the world unite! You have nothing to lose but your callosities! – but although there is a little lever beneath my left-hand which powers the seat up and down, my helmet touches the roof if I try to get up as high as I would like. That nurse knew a thing or two.

What matter, everything is lovely, with the map unreeling on the lower screen, the plot unfolding on the upper, the engine gauges telling a tale of well-being, and my soul; like that of any romantic would-be high-flier, urging me to reach out and touch the face of God. If I could reach out, I could practically touch the single-seater of Mr Morgan. He is flying closer than a wingman usually does, for my benefit; as he moves around to show my camera the various faces of his faceted cat, I am reminded not to ask whether the Jaguar has good aileron response. The Jaguar has no ailerons: the entire trailing edge of those swept wings is devoted to flaps, working with the leading-edge slats to give it marvellous low-speed stability. For turns and banks there are spoilers which sprout from the wing surfaces, braking the air, breaking the lift. Could I see a slow roll, please? Mr Hannam commands an outward roll, and Mr Morgan oils his Jaguar up and over, to slide down and skim away beneath us. It is beautiful, fluid in line and kaleidoscopic in colour, like a smile won from a warrior angel, a slow wink on the face of heaven. Nine blinks of my shutter at half-second intervals see it all through, a slow roll that took four seconds out of the book of kinetics to interleave them with the pages of my memorabilia.

Kinesthetics now. Mr Hannam calls a change of course and we spoil into a bank that tips the world on its side and runs its edge down my jade reflector. Squeeze: my legs are being squeezed, my belly pressed in an unfamiliar embrace, the G-suit is working. It inflates itself automatically at two G, and if I can get used to the belly-press I shall be glad of it, for there is none of the usual greying of vision and emptying of the head as we bore around the horizon. The downward pressure of head on spine, torso on seat, camera in hands and helmet on head can be felt as strongly as ever, but at least I do not feel the nausea that can easily follow it. That was just a taster, though; the Jaguar is allowed to pull seven-and-a-half G or push minus three G in the RAF, and British Aerospace reckon that its true limit is at least nine G. What would that feel like? I look around for the single-seater, hoping to catch a picture of it climbing the cloudy fringes of the sky but all I get is a feeling of disorientation. That way sickness lies, but the camera is an unforgiving taskmaster, and I comfort myself with the thought that I have never suffered motion sickness since surgeons removed some of my innards along with an ulcer, several years ago.

The Royal Air Force expects its pilots to be tough. They must also be intelligent, responsible, adaptable, young enough for training and old enough for judgment. By the time they have mastered computer programming, weapons technology, instruments and navigation, survival and protocol, law and discipline, mind and body their training will have cost hundreds of thousands of pounds. That investment cannot be squandered in a bout of air sickness; it is not for the pilots that NATO prints its bags. They are desensitised during their training, whirled around on gimballed chairs in darkened rooms, taught to keep their heads still and their muscles tensed when the heavy hand of gravity cramps their movements. I only learned this later.

It is time for us to get down to the ground. We do not merely lose height; neither do we dive. We just seem to fall through the clouds, and we fall quickly. My head begins to feel muzzy, swollen, the usual symptoms of pressure change, no need to worry, just yawn or swallow, but it doesn't seem to be working, we are falling faster than I can even up the pressure inside and outside, suck, blow, it doesn't seem to . . . something explodes above my right eyebrow, my ears were all right but what about my sinuses, sini, to blazes with syntax, my head is bursting, there is a fracture straight down the middle of my forehead, a cranial San Andreas fault with earthquake and volcano, the two edges jagged and splintery where they have been pulled apart, and my helmet is tight on my erupting head.

We are down racing parallel with the geoid, skating in on a thin ice of air between our ventral fins and the green earth, and SLAM we go into a steep turn heading for a gap in the hills SQUASH that ham hand of a G-suit squeezes my guts and my stomach flies up to my throat like the pip from a cherry and I can't summon the strength to tense and resist, not with my head like this, and now we are ground skimming the pregnant heaves of the Cheviots' swelling hills like two porpoises breaking the surface of a green thick sea, two nail sharp fingers running over the belly that would break us if we erred by a scratch. The Jaguars do not err, the ride is incredibly smooth, all the bumps and battering of high-speed low-level contour bashing taken out of our line by the gyro stabiliser via the computer feeding damping corrections to the control surfaces at every rut and hedge; but when the pilot pulls the joystick it is still slam and squeeze and giddy sickly dizzy where-are-we. Wherever we are, there is Mr Morgan alongside, lifting and falling with us and if we are as low as he is then God help the grass beneath us. Up with the land, light over the crest, down again but not quite parallel to the earth, why? That's why, pylons and high-tension cables skimming under the single-seater and under us. THUMP comes the G-suit and we are bending the hills around us, tossing them beneath our shoulders, flipping them level again and stretching forward to shave the next hummock as clean as a toy balloon, lining up for our practice attack, precise and prepared enough to blast the living daylights out of the third sheep on the left between Cushat Law and Bloodybush Edge, Combe Fell, Hedgehope Hill, Scald Hill, we fall and hedgehop between them in a minnowing wriggle of squeeze and bank, slam and gulp, and now we are running side by side along a steep-sided valley that opens into another transverse one, a T-junction gouged in the earth, which ways shall we go BOTH ways ye gods and little fishes, Morgan sliced under us turning hard left to go down the new chasm on his left ear while we tipped right in a vertical bank to go up it but I can't see any more, only the floor of the cockpit between my legs as the G-forces press me down, my back bowed, my head weighed, crushed down by a monstrous multiplication of gravity, crushed in by the massive grip of the G-suit, pulped and useless . . . It went on a while longer, that spirit-shattering sequence of humps overhead and thumps beneath the belt. I was past taking pictures, past taking notice, past doing anything, all my strength being focused on the one vital thing, the one thing I must not do, I could not bear to do I must not be sick in the aircraft. I must not. I must. not. No. No. Can? Ohhhh, no, again? No. So nearly, so often, so help me. The hi-lo-hi trilogy played itself out unnoticed. I must have slept or escaped in some way from my consciousness of that awful physical inadequacy for a war that men like these pilots would have to face on my behalf.

I was gently roused for landing, something that is less dramatic than it looks as the arrow-head Jaguars stream down the runway line, crossing the Coltishall hedge at about 140 mph and rolling to a stop inside half a mile. Mr Hannam told me to stay put, and they would unfasten me and help me out. They were all so gentle, as they loosened all my straps and connections, took all my impedimenta, steadied me as I clambered over the cockpit side and planted one of those grotesque boots on the grateful rung of that steel ladder, so kind and gentle that they might have been lifting the Christ child from a nightmare in the manger. Slowly, methodically, thinking of nothing else, I picked my way down, until at last I felt the ground beneath but I cannot remember anything after that, until I woke up in a warm bed in the station sick quarters, with a medical doctor to acquaint me again, slowly and tenderly, with a world that stood still beneath me, a world into which I could venture again next day, to drive home in another gentler Jaguar, a two-dimensional mover that would never exceed one G unless I drove it into a wall, an easeful, peaceful, different breed of cat.

By LJK Setright, with kind permission of his estate.

GLOSSARY

AAFCE	Allied Air Forces Central Europe
AAM	Air to Air Missile
AAR	Air to Air Refuelling
ACMI	Air Combat Manoeuvring Instrumentation
AEW	Airborne Early Warning
agl	Above Ground Level
AI Radar	Air Intercept Radar
ANG	Air National Guard
AoA	Angle of Attack
APC	Armament Practice Camp
ATC	Air Traffic Control
AWACS	Airborne Warning and Control System
BFBS	British Forces Broadcasting Service
BVR	Beyond Visual Range
CAP	Combat Air Patrol
CBLS	Carrier Bomb Light Stores
CEP	Circular Error Probability
CFI	Chief Flying Instructor
CinC	Commander in Chief
ESG	Electronic Support Group
FAC	Forward Air Control
FSO	Flight Safety Officer
FTS	Flying Training School
GCI	Ground Control Intercepts

GDR	German Democratic Republic
GPI	Ground Position Indicator
HAS	Hardened Aircraft Shelter
HOTAS	Hands on Throttle and Stick
HUD	Head Up Display
IED	Improvised Explosive Device
IFF	Identification Friend or Foe
ILS	Instrument Landing System
INAS	Inertial Nav Attack System
INU	Inertial Navigation Unit
IRE	Instrument Rating Examiner
JTIDS	Joint Tactical Information Display System
LRU	Line Replaceable Unit
M	Mach
MAFL	Manual of Air Force Law
MAWTS	Marine Air Weapons and Tactics
MoDPE	Ministry of Defence Procurement Executive
MPC	Missile Practice Camp
MTBF	Mean Time Between Failure
MOU	Memorandum of Understanding
NAAFI	Navy, Army and Air Force Institute
NAMMA	NATO MRCA Management Agency
NAVWASS	Navigation and Weapon Aiming Sub System
NBC	Nuclear, Biological and Chemical
nm	Nautical Miles
OCU	Operational Conversion Unit
OC	Officer Commanding
PD	Pulse Doppler
POW	Prisoner of War
PR	Photo Reconnaissance
QFI	Qualified Flying Instructor
QRA	Quick Reaction Alert

RHAG	Rotary Hydraulic Arrester Gear
RHS	Right Hand Seat
SAM	Surface to Air Missile
SAR	Search and Rescue
SEAD	Suppression of Enemy Air Defence
SMS	Stores Management System
SOC	Sector Operations Centre
STCAAME	Strike Command Air-to-Air Missile Establishment
TACAN	Tactical Air Navigation (a military VOR/DME)
TACEVAL	Tactical Evaluation
TTTE	Tornado Tripartite Training Establishment
TWU	Tactical Weapons Unit
UAS	University Air Squadron
UKMFTS	UK Military Flight Training System
UXB	Unexploded Bomb

INDEX